KU-497-485

MAD DOGS AND AN ENGLISHWOMAN

Travels with Sled Dogs in Canada's Frozen North

Polly Evans

BANTAM BOOKS

LONDON · TORONTO · SYDNEY · AUCKLAND · JOHANNESBURG

TRANSWORLD PUBLISHERS
61–63 Uxbridge Road, London W5 5SA
A Random House Group Company
www.rbooks.co.uk

**MAD DOGS AND AN ENGLISHWOMAN
A BANTAM BOOK: 9780553819434**

First publication in Great Britain
Bantam edition published 2008

Copyright © Polly Evans 2008

Polly Evans has asserted her right under the Copyright,
Designs and Patents Act 1988 to be identified
as the author of this work.

Every effort has been made to obtain the necessary permissions
with reference to copyright material. We apologize for any omissions
in this respect and will be pleased to make the appropriate
acknowledgements in any future edition.

This book is a work of non-fiction based on the experiences
and recollections of the author. The author has stated to
the publishers that the contents of this book are true.

A CIP catalogue record for this book
is available from the British Library.

This book is sold subject to the condition that it shall not,
by way of trade or otherwise, be lent, resold, hired out,
or otherwise circulated without the publisher's prior
consent in any form of binding or cover other than that
in which it is published and without a similar condition,
including this condition, being imposed on
the subsequent purchaser.

Addresses for Random House Group Ltd companies outside the UK
can be found at: www.randomhouse.co.uk
The Random House Group Ltd Reg. No. 954009

The Random House Group Limited supports The Forest Stewardship
Council (FSC), the leading international forest certification organization.
All our titles that are printed on Greenpeace approved FSC certified
paper carry the FSC logo. Our paper procurement policy can be found at
www.rbooks.co.uk/environment

Typeset in 11/13pt Times by
Kestrel Data, Exeter, Devon.

Printed in the UK by
CPI Cox & Wyman, Reading, RG1 8EX.

2 4 6 8 10 9 7 5 3 1

Mixed Sources
Product group from well-managed
forests and other controlled sources
www.fsc.org   Cert no. TT-COC-2139
© 1996 Forest Stewardship Council

FSC

For Thomas, Jake, Tilly and Gabriella

Acknowledgements

The weather in the Yukon may be chilly in the winter, but the people certainly aren't. I owe thanks first and foremost to Frank Turner and Anne Tayler at Muktuk Kennels (www.muktuk.com) who welcomed me into their home and put up with me for so long. Thanks also to Saul Turner, Fabienne Brülhart, Stefan Wackerhagen, Sebastian Altenberger, Thomas Arnold and Marty Perry for their hospitality and friendship and to Simon Charles for the great food. Thanks also to the officials, vets, volunteers and mushers of the Yukon Quest (www.yukonquest.com); particular thanks are due to Stephen Reynolds who helped me to organize my trip. Thanks, too, to Jewel Bennett for the use of her cabin in Fairbanks. At Yukon Tourism (www.touryukon.com), thanks to Rod Raycroft and Robert Clark. In Dawson John Overell spared me a good chunk of his precious time to explain about veterinary work in the north, so thanks to him and to his assistant Chris. Thanks also to Steve and Tracey at the 5th Avenue Bed & Breakfast (www.5thavebandb.com). Dale Bradley and his uncles at Pelly Farm welcomed us in from the cold, even though they can't have been pleased to see us; thanks to them for providing a soft armchair and hot coffee at the moment I most needed it. Thanks also to Val and Gord Robertson in Inuvik, and to the High Country Inn in Whitehorse, to Francesca Liversidge and Lucie Jordan and everyone at Bantam, and to Jane Gregory, Emma Dunford, Claire Morris, Jemma McDonagh and everyone at Gregory and Co. And, of course, my most heartfelt thanks of all goes to the many dogs who (mostly) uncomplainingly hauled me for miles across the frozen rivers and forests of the Yukon, and still wagged their tails at the end of it.

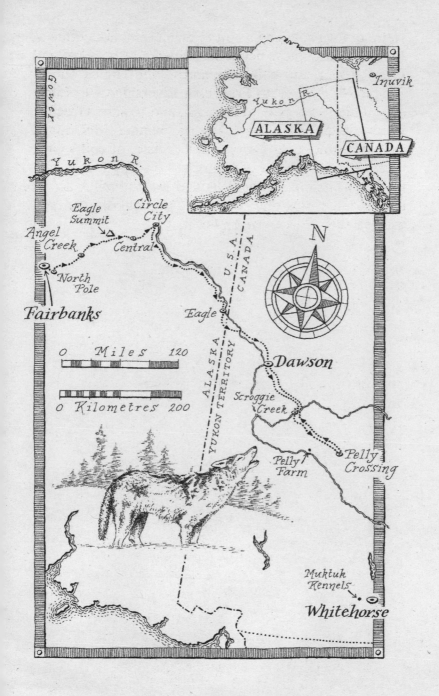

Some say God was tired when He made it;
Some say it's a fine land to shun;
Maybe; but there's some as would trade it
For no land on earth – and I'm one.

Robert Service, from 'The Spell of the Yukon'

1

I flew out on Friday 13 January and returned home on 1 April. The dates had almost selected themselves but they seemed curiously appropriate, for I feared I was embarking on a fool's errand. I was going to spend eleven weeks, in the heart of winter, in one of the most inhospitable climates on earth.

The Yukon is a triangular-shaped territory in the far northwest of Canada. It borders Alaska to the west; at its northern tip lie the icy waters of the Beaufort Sea. Other people travel to the Yukon in the summer when they can enjoy the long, balmy days that blend one into another with little darkness between. In September, though, the tourists pack their bags and leave. The attractions close. The museums' doors are bolted and the buses are laid up until May. Even most Canadian people, who so proudly extol their pitiless winters when basking comfortably in the sun elsewhere, shiver at the thought of coming this far north during the frozen months. The average temperature in the Yukon in January is minus 26 degrees Celsius but the mercury can plunge much lower. Temperatures dip regularly into the minus forties; once, they dived to minus 63.

But there's another side to winter in this harsh land. As the nights grow longer, the milky jade and blood red of the northern lights weave across the skies. The snowshoe rabbits' coats turn spotless white and the Arctic foxes wear plush, dramatic furs. Winter has late blue dawns, and the warm buttery light of the low midday sun. It has the jagged gems of hoar frost, and soft, feathery snow. Winter is the season of solitude and pure, glorious silence. And in winter, the sled dogs run.

It was the dogs that drew me. During my time in the north I'd be based at Muktuk Kennels, the operation of one of Canada's most famous mushers, Frank Turner, and his wife Anne. I'd scoop poop, help with feeding, and learn to drive a sled. From Muktuk, I'd make further trips around the region. I'd follow the Yukon Quest – a 1600-kilometre dogsled race that runs between Fairbanks in Alaska and Whitehorse, the capital of the Yukon Territory. I'd visit Dawson City, the town that sprang up in response to the frenzied Klondike gold rush. I'd fly to the very far north, to the Arctic Ocean itself. And through it all, I'd learn all I could about the howling, capering, tail-wagging world of sled dogs.

A short, stocky man with a salt-and-pepper beard and a well-worn red parka pushed through the swing doors of Whitehorse's airport, a tiny one-gate place where arrivals and departures were not just in the same building; they were in the same room. I recognized his face from his website photographs.

'Frank?' I asked.

'You're Polly?'

At this time, in January 2006, Frank Turner was the only person to have competed in each of the twenty-two

Yukon Quest dogsledding races since the event's inception in 1984. Frank won the race in 1995 and still held the record for the fastest time. This year, Frank – who, in his late fifties, was wondering if he might be getting a little old for that kind of adventure – would not be entering the race, but his 25-year-old son Saul would be running a team.

There was no call for feats of cold-weather endurance on that first night, though: Frank had parked his truck conveniently close to the airport's door and we ventured just a few steps through the cold night air. In any case, the evening was warm by the Yukon's standards, a mere minus thirteen according to the pilot on the plane. I'd been concerned about what I should wear on the journey: would I need my long woollen underwear to walk from the airport door to the car? But might I then overheat on the plane? In the end I'd put on ordinary jeans and trainers, the car was near, and I was fine.

We drove out of town and on to the Alaska Highway towards Muktuk.

'Saul's baby was born on Wednesday,' Frank announced as we sped through the darkness. 'She's called Myla. She's beautiful.'

Conversation moved on to the construction of the road.

'The Alaska Highway was originally built during the Second World War,' Frank explained. Alaska was considered by the US military to be vulnerable to Japanese invasion: the Japanese wanted to control the shipping lanes in the northern Pacific and the attack on Pearl Harbor had crippled the Navy's Pacific fleet. In response to this threat, the Americans set up a defensive line of airfields along the Alaskan coast, and this road, running

2,500 kilometres from British Columbia to Fairbanks, Alaska, was built to supply them.

'The Japanese wanted to bomb the highway as it was a major supply route, so they built it like this.' Frank took one hand from the steering wheel and snaked it into violent meanderings. 'That way they couldn't take out whole sections of the road at once. And then the war ended and they spent the next sixty years and goodness knows how many millions of dollars straightening it out.'

About twenty minutes later, we turned off the main road and wound down a steep, snowy back road that had known little attention beyond the ministry of Frank's snow plough.

'This is all First Nations land.' Frank gestured towards the woods that surrounded us. Frank and Anne's hundred-acre ranch lay just below where we were now, on the banks of the Takhini River. They had bought the plot just six years previously.

'We were really lucky to get this place so close to town,' Frank remarked as we rounded one last bend in the road. And then, seeing a light in an upstairs window of the large log house that stood on the far side of the clearing, 'Oh dear, Anne's still up.' He paused before adding, 'She never sleeps.'

In front of the house a wide, flat yard was dotted with neat rows of small wooden boxes. These were the dogs' houses; it was now past midnight and most of them were asleep in their straw. One sole incumbent stood to attention outside his hut, a dark silhouette in the night. Then, as the headlights picked up his form, we could see him more clearly: a large, dark-coated, tufty-haired husky. He gave three sharp barks in recognition.

'That's Tank,' said Frank. 'All our dogs are friendly.'

We unloaded my bags and carried them up the steps to the main door. A narrow annexe gave on to the main room where Anne greeted us. She was a short, pale-skinned woman in her mid-fifties wearing a baggy sweatshirt and wide-rimmed glasses. Her long, straight, greying hair was tied back into a ponytail. A smallish black and white dog with vivid blue eyes and a slightly waddling gait trotted up alongside her.

'This is Angel,' said Frank. 'She's deaf.' Angel was now an elderly lady, but her ears had been useless since birth. Frank had given her years ago to Anne as a present.

'Talk about bringing coals to Newcastle!' Anne roared with laughter as she told the story. 'Frank's only ever given me two presents. One was the bone from a whale's penis, and the other was a *deaf dog*!'

(I later discovered this wasn't entirely true. There was also a rather beautiful painting by a First Nations artist depicting a spirit grandmother watching over the subsequent generations of her family that hung on the living-room wall.)

Frank's tale about the acquisition of Angel was slightly different: he had gone to a breeder and paid a lot of money for two sled dogs. Worried about how he was going to explain this expenditure to his wife, he found his thoughts settling upon a small deaf puppy with pretty blue eyes that the breeder was giving away. 'Maybe that will calm her down,' he thought.

It later transpired that in her younger days Angel had been a useful lead dog when harnessed next to a reliable partner. The lead dogs are the front pair, and the rest of the team – usually harnessed two by two – follows their example.

17

'If her partner followed the commands, she was great,' Frank said.

Of course if the partner ignored the musher's orders, poor Angel was no help at all.

On the floor of the living room lay a thick-coated, grey and white female. She thumped her tail with arthritic enthusiasm and struggled to rise to her feet.

'This is Louise,' Frank went on. 'She's fifteen.' He walked into the annexe and opened the door so that this benign geriatric could go outside one last time before bed.

'Come on, Louise! Come on, Louise!' he called emphatically.

Louise tried her best but her back legs were weak and her feet slipped on the painted wooden floor. Anne tried to haul her upwards.

'No, she can do it. Let her get up on her own,' Frank insisted until Louise finally dragged herself to her feet and creaked out of the door.

'We keep this closed at night,' said Frank, shutting a child gate between the main room and the annexe once Louise had returned indoors. 'Sometimes Louise has accidents.'

He showed me upstairs to my room.

'We've put you in the house for now,' he explained. The majority of Frank and Anne's tourism operation guests, and their staff, lived in a handful of cabins which lay among the trees to the side of the driveway. I'd move to one a few weeks later, when I'd returned from following the Yukon Quest.

'The washroom's next door,' said Frank. On its door was pinned an A4 sheet of paper instructing users in bold black capitals to keep the door CLOSED. 'We always keep the door shut because the cats might get in,' Frank said, then hesitated a little before adding, 'I'm just afraid they might fall in the toilet and not be able to get out.'

Wisely avoiding the perils of the sewerage system, a cat had taken up residence on my bed. She was an elderly, skinny tortoiseshell – I later learned she had thyroid problems for which medication was administered twice a day. Her name was Kato. She had come to the Turner family many years ago from an animal rescue shelter and she still bore frostbite scars on her nose and ears as testament to her difficult youth. In her more boisterous days she used to ambush Scrapper, Frank and Anne's male Siamese, and so she was named after Inspector Clouseau's martial-arts-crazy manservant. She looked far from violent now.

I pushed Kato out on to the landing and soon fell into an exhausted sleep. It was eight a.m. now in England and I'd left home more than twenty hours before. During the night, I woke to the sound of dogs' howling. It was a strangely beautiful noise, like a plaintive singing. Some voices performed in a clear, treble tone while others took the lower ranges. I was almost certain that, if I listened carefully, I could detect the lusty miaows of Kato trying to join in. Then, suddenly, as though led by a conductor wielding a concert baton, in unison they stopped.

2

Muktuk means 'whale blubber' in Inuit; apparently it tastes like hazelnuts. Fortunately for the jet-lagged urban tourist, however, the kennel's name has no influence on the breakfast menu. 'I just liked the sound of it,' Frank explained.

The time difference had woken me early the following morning and when I'd heard clattering sounds in the kitchen downstairs I'd emerged from my room. Frank was preparing coffee.

'We run a help-yourself system here,' he told me. 'There's fruit and cheese and salami and so on in the fridge.' He yanked open the door of the hulking white refrigerator to display its copious contents crammed precariously into every cranny. 'There are apples and bananas there,' he went on, pointing to a chrome and mesh container that hung above the counter upon which outsized Thermoses dispensed coffee and hot water. In a nearby box teas of all creeds were bundled: alongside the everyday Earl Grey and camomile were green tea with peppermint infusion, ginger peach, and various takes on the theme of chai.

I'd been so tired the night before that I hadn't taken

in much about the house so now I was looking at it as if for the first time. This floor, raised from ground level, was open plan and had a relaxed, lived-in feel. In front of the kitchen counter the dining and sitting area was dominated by a long table covered by a blue cloth. Behind the table a pine staircase led to the first floor and a door gave on to the ground-level garage. The opposite wall of the living room was taken by a long, comfy grey sofa; to one side sat a pink-upholstered rocking chair. Central heating kept the building warm. A bathroom with a shower lay off the living room; outside its door a large pantry cupboard contained bumper boxes of granola bars and oatmeal, enormous tubs of powdered stock, and all manner of other dry ingredients.

The walls were covered with photographs, paintings, drawings and sketches of dogs past and present. Some were portraits in pencil or pastel. Others were huge framed photographs: Frank and his Quest team silhouetted against a spectacular tangerine sunset; the dogs of a Japanese friend who undertook an arduous mushing journey through the Arctic; a smaller photograph of a much younger Frank with a dog and Saul as a very small child. Some paintings were large and painstakingly executed. Others were simple posters in frames recalling Yukon Quests of years gone by. There were wobbly children's drawings of mushers and sled dogs executed in pencil and felt-tip pen. On the fridge door was stuck a cartoon that had been sent via email. A man was holding up a dog, its underside to his face. The caption, in a balloon from his wife's mouth, read, 'Frank! Let him lick his own balls! I swear you spoil that dog rotten!'

Strangely, for a place so governed by the comfort of

its canine inhabitants, the house didn't smell strongly of dogs. Neither did the furnishings appear to be excessively coated in their hair. It was curious: at home in London, I tended to sneeze in houses where dogs resided but here at Muktuk my nose didn't so much as tickle. Maybe it was because here both dogs and humans spent so much time in the healthy outdoor air.

The kitchen window looked out over the dog yard. It was still dark outside; I asked what time it would turn light. At nine o'clock or so, Frank said, then darkness would fall again at four thirty or five. The hours of daylight, then, weren't very different from those in England at that time of year.

We were silent for a few moments. The morning news murmured from a radio on the kitchen counter. From the garage below emanated light thumping noises followed by the sound of spraying water.

'There's Sebastian,' said Frank. 'If you really want to get involved in what we do around here, he's the person you need to talk to.'

He opened the door that led from the living room down a short staircase to the ground-level garage. Sebastian looked up from his task hosing down white, cylindrical buckets. The noise had been their gentle clattering. He was tall and lean. He was wearing bright-red dungarees emblazoned with the logo of an Austrian beer company he had worked for the previous summer and a red-and-grey patterned woollen hat with earflaps.

Frank introduced us. I explained my earnest desire to shovel frozen dog poop at every opportunity; Sebastian didn't think there would be a problem.

The garage was a large, functional room. The corner where Sebastian was hosing his buckets was taken up by a concrete-rimmed, rectangular drainage area with taps on the wall above, like a very large, grey, floor-level sink. Beside it, a small porcelain basin was installed, with a bar of soap and a towel for the washing of hands.

ABSOLUTELY NO
SOLID ANYTHING
(DOG FOOD, STRAW ETC.)
SHOULD EVER
BE PUT
IN THIS SINK!

pronounced a laminated pink sheet above the taps. After the 'EVER' some enraged soul had added in black felt tip 'EVER, EV' but then the paper had run out, leaving the pen and its infuriated wielder impotent to scrawl any more.

On closer inspection, I found there were notices everywhere in this garage. Whiteboards listed jobs to be done, feeding routines, and details of medication to be administered to ailing animals. More general notices advised the incumbents of the garage on how to live a harmonious and stress-free life, Muktuk-style.

'Path to Happiness' declared one whiteboard before going on to detail in blue marker pen:

1 Do not leave a mess for someone else to clean up.
2 Always return everything to its proper place.
3 If you have a better way to organize things [there followed some blotchy rubbings out before the instruction finished clearly with] just do it!
4 All work areas need to be kept clean and organized. Don't wait for someone else to do it.

And then the final point: 'Always remember to say, "Good morning, boss! Have a nice day!"'

Across the floor to the left of the stairs, a door gave on to the dog yard. On one side of the door, by the sinks, a large cabinet contained every conceivable canine medicine. Frank was one of the first mushers to use homoeopathic remedies on his dogs, and the cupboard stored arnica rub and a paw cream made from poplar buds, yarrow and chickweed (a miracle cure for human chapped lips as well, it turned out) alongside more conventional balms and bandages.

On the other side of the door, bunches of harnesses hung from hooks, each harness marked in black pen with the name of a dog. The middle of the room was taken up by a large wooden table; on its other side were rails of parkas and snow pants, boxes of hats, mitts and neck warmers, and racks of great, bulbous, white rubber boots that looked as though they'd come from the pen of a cartoonist. These were bunny boots, the extreme cold weather footwear created for the US military in the 1950s and still favoured by Arctic enthusiasts today. Apparently they are not so called because they make you look like a nimble-toed bunny (on the contrary, they make you look like a lumbering Godzilla) but named after the snowshoe rabbit whose fur is white in winter.

'When you're in a room of ten people, are you among the five who find the room too warm, or among the five who think it's cold?' Frank asked me an hour or so later.

We were back among the clothing racks in the garage because on this first morning we were getting straight down to business. A journalist named Bob had stayed at the kennels last night; he was writing a story for the *New York Times* about how to spend thirty-six hours in Whitehorse. A very quick mushing adventure had been squeezed into his tight schedule and Frank had invited me to come along too. Bob was in a rush – he had only a few hours in which to conquer the Takhini; drill through the ice to indulge in a spot of ice fishing; educate himself in the museums in town; check out the leisure centre; eat, drink and be hurried.

I told Frank I was firmly among the five that think the room's too cold. I didn't like to add that, where nine of those people were politely perspiring and commenting that it was humid for the time of year, I'd be the one who was blue and shivering and wishing I'd brought an extra sweater. Had I told him the whole truth, I feared, his eyes might have gaped behind his round, metal-rimmed glasses and he'd have asked me with horrified incredulity what in heaven's name I was doing there.

'The most important thing is that you're not too hot,' Frank went on. He seemed in no way perturbed by my confession about feeling the cold. 'The perfect way to feel is a little bit cool. If you get hot, you sweat – and then when you cool down you freeze. You should never sweat!'

Then he handed me thick bibbed pants, a down parka, a pair of mitts, and a pair of gloriously inelegant white rubber boots. He told me to put on long underwear – on Anne's instructions I'd bought merino wool long johns before leaving home – and an extra fleece on top of the two woollen jumpers and thin fleece I was already wearing. And instructing me that, come what may, I was not to wet my socks – and thereby risk freezing my feet – by treading in wet patches on the floor, he handed me two carbon hand warmers to put inside my mitts.

In any case it was warm today, Frank declared a few minutes later when, appropriately clad, we marched through the garage door and out into the terrifying, sub-zero world beyond. A large, circular, black and white thermometer hung from a pillar just outside the garage door. It recorded a balmy minus fifteen.

'Bob doesn't have much time,' said Frank, 'so I'll just tell you the basics quickly. I'll explain everything else another time.' He hauled a sled from the shed that ran to the side of the house. Surprisingly, the cold didn't feel too biting. In fact, beneath all that clothing and my fleece hat, I felt so unexpectedly comfortable that I didn't yet need to put on my parka.

'Never put your clothing on the ground!' Frank told me as I dumped it on the snow. 'If you need to put it down, you should put it in the sled to keep it dry. And never leave your mitts with the opening facing upwards. If snow gets in them and they get wet, they'll freeze – and then your hands will be in big trouble.'

Clothing safely stowed, Frank introduced me to the sled. It was around two metres long, its wooden frame based upon two flat runners about hip-width apart that curved up at the front like skis. Towards the back of the runners, two vertical posts were topped with a horizontal handlebar at about waist height. The runners stuck out half a metre or so behind the handlebar: this was where the musher stood. Strapped to the handlebar posts and the long base of the frame was a canvas sled bag in the shape of a three-dimensional right-angled triangle, which was used to carry supplies for longer trips.

Frank showed me the sled's braking system. From

my position standing on the runners, I could unhook a black rubber pad with eight bolts through its bottom and stand on it, thereby using some or all of my weight to slow or stop the sled. Secondly, I could press my foot on a metal bar held in position by elastic cord from which two, more ferocious, spikes descended. When leaving the yard, Frank said, the dogs would be very excited and I should stand fully on the black pad.

The gangline, the central rope that connected all the dogs to the front tip of the sled, should always be taut. If the line was not tight but loosely flapping around the dogs' feet, they could easily become tangled. If I needed to leave the sled to disentangle them, I should tip it over on to its side as the dogs could pull it less easily when it wasn't upright on its runners.

'This is not bungee jumping,' Frank pronounced gravely. 'It's all about control.'

I nodded nervously. Control sounded quite lovely, but I wasn't confident that I would be able to achieve it. Even these basic instructions seemed a lot to remember for the uninitiated. And the dogs, now that they had seen that an outing was on the agenda, were whipping themselves into a frenzy of joyful excitement that tied my stomach in knots.

Frank, on the other hand, didn't look remotely concerned. He had done this thousands of times before. He tied two sleds – one for Bob and one for me – to two posts in the yard, parked a skidoo (a snow machine like a motorbike on skis) for himself out front, and hooked up two four-dog teams. Bob and I put on our parkas and mitts, which kept one's hands warm on the sled where one didn't have much need for individual fingers. Frank climbed on to the skidoo and gave a thumbs-up signal from in front. We raised our own thumbs to indicate that we were as ready as we ever would be. And with that we tugged free our ropes from the posts – and we were off.

Most people remember clearly the first time they leave the Muktuk dog yard. It's the kind of experience that recurs in the night-time subconscious of those professional types who are disconcertingly competent in all other areas of life: the cacophony of crazed barking as the dogs, seeing the sleds being prepared, run round in frantic circles at the ends of their chains, then jump on to their houses and leap back down again; the crescendo of excitement as the chosen few are harnessed and hooked up; the ebullient yapping, leaping and tugging as the desperately eager team tries to pull the anchored sled from its post – and then, as the rope is pulled, the silence . . . and the horrible realization that all semblance of control has plummeted into a bottomless abyss.

It shouldn't be like that, of course. As Frank had explained, dogsledding isn't supposed to give you an adrenalin rush. Many weeks later, when my abilities had been honed, I couldn't understand how I'd ever been so hopeless. Once I'd come to know and love the individual dogs, once I'd fed them goodness knows how many kilograms of kibble and shovelled away the corresponding weight in poop, I couldn't see how there might have been a problem. But this was day one, the dogs were huge and noisy and foreign, and I was scared.

Frank went first on his skidoo. He doesn't much like riding motorized snow machines – they're noisy and smelly and they don't have paws – but the vehicle gives him the chance to respond to the crises of beginners more quickly than he could if he drove a dog team of his own. Then Bob took off, and I followed in the rear.

For the first few seconds all was well. The dogs attempted to rocket out of the yard, I stood on my mat as instructed, and we chugged in a not-too-terrifying manner towards the river. And then we came to a pile-up of confusion.

The problem was that there's a ninety-degree bend between the Muktuk dog yard and the river. The trail has been laid so that the novice musher can take it in an easy, gentle curve. Instead of turning sharp left, the dogs should veer first to the right, then take a soft swoop to the left so that they travel in the shape of a question mark. Barriers of sticks have been set up across the shorter route to encourage the dogs and drivers to steer correctly. Even without the musher's commands, though, the dogs know the way. They have been there hundreds of times before.

But the dogs can scent a novice at a thousand paces. Perhaps it's the death grip on the handlebar. Maybe it's the putrid stench of terrified perspiration as beginners, despite their best efforts, break the no-sweating rule. It could be the exaggerated breathing and wobbly commands. Whatever the dogs' powers of perception, when they know they have a rookie in tow, they like to play. And on this first day they were like a small class of hyperactive children with a brand new, fabulously incompetent teacher.

Unable to convince his dogs to take the correct path, Bob had stopped just to the side of the stick barrier. Frank had turned round to help him.

I attempted to brake so as not to run into them, but to no effect. The snow was too shallow for the bolts to anchor, and the dogs were fresh, wildly excited and determined to join in the fun. From the front Frank shouted, 'Whoa! Whoa!' but the dogs took no notice of him, either. I had about a second to take some form of action. Frank had said in his very brief briefing that, in order to stop the dogs taking off, one could turn the sled on its side. So, not realizing that this was only an option if the sled was at a standstill, I made the instant but very poor decision to give it a go. I jumped off the runners, threw the sled on its side, and watched in horror as the dogs galloped off regardless.

'*Never* let go of the sled!' Frank shrieked as he grabbed the leaders of my team and disentangled my dogs from Bob's. The calm demeanour I'd seen in Frank as he'd helped me with my clothing and shown me around the sled seemed to be vanishing fast. His face now echoed the red of his parka, his eyes were wide and exasperated. There were no two ways about it: Bob and I were not making a good show of things.

Frank, on his knees now, bit the ear of Jojo, one of my leaders, to discipline her. Jojo yelped. I winced, feeling embarrassed by my own uselessness and guilty that Jojo should take the blame. I suspected that, in a fair and just world, my ear should have been the one to be nipped. And then, the teams gratifyingly separate once more, we continued on our way to the river.

It had snowed a little overnight and the river's icy surface was covered by a layer of virgin white that cut through the cliffs of butterscotch clay. Soon the dogs settled to a steady trot. Above the white of the river, the sky gleamed a pale oyster grey. Tiny specks of snow floated down. They were hardly flakes; they were more like a light flurry of whiter-than-white laundry detergent that spattered from the sky as some cleanliness-obsessed deity emptied the dregs from the celestial washing-powder box. The trees sparkled with hoar frost which defined each branch and twig with glittering clarity.

Whenever we stopped, the dogs rolled on their backs or lay on their tummies with their legs splayed as they licked and ate the cold, fluffy snow. Their thirst satisfied, my leaders doubled back to cavort with the two behind. Such social behaviour was strictly forbidden: the line was meant to stay tight at all times. Two months later, the dogs would rarely even try such a trick with me; they'd just take a roll in the snow, grab a refreshing mouthful, wag their tails, bark a little and look back to say, 'Come on! Get your foot off that brake! We want to run!' But this was still day one and Frank had to come and disentangle them. As he did so, he stopped and gave an extra petting to Jojo.

'You didn't do as you were told back there,' he purred affectionately as he ruffled her fur. Jojo lovingly wagged her tail and we trotted off once more.

From the back of the sled I watched as the steam billowed from the dogs' mouths and their ears bobbed up and down. Each animal's ears, I noticed, were different: Jojo had velvety little triangles that rippled and undulated as she ran, while Terror's ears pointed pertly and scarcely moved at all. Duchess had one ear that bobbed up and down while the other stayed pricked and straight – and every time I put my foot on the brake, she turned round and gave me a reproachful stare.

The snowy wilderness of North America has long been imprinted by canine paws: it's reckoned that Arctic peoples have been hitching dogs to sleds for many hundreds of years, and they've named their land's features accordingly. In the Yukon there's a Husky River; over the border in Alaska there are settlements called Howling Dog and Burnt Paw.

As early as the thirteenth century, Marco Polo recorded the practice of harnessing dogs to sleds in Siberia.

'There is a stretch of country where no horses can go, because of the ice and mud . . . Accordingly they have made sledges with no wheels, so constructed as to glide over ice or mud or mire without getting too deeply embedded. The sledge is then pulled by a team of six dogs,' he wrote.

From the sixteenth century, Europeans began to trade in Canadian furs. The French colonized Quebec in 1608; the new settlement subsisted primarily from the fur trade. The English countered in 1670 with the founding of the Hudson's Bay Company, whose representatives bartered furs from native trappers in exchange for manufactured goods such as knives, kettles, beads, needles, and blankets. As the years progressed and the European fur traders ventured further afield, they learnt to use dog teams on their journeys of trade and exploration through the frozen winter months; it is from the French 'marche', meaning 'walk' or 'move', that the word 'mush' is supposed to have derived.

Following the end of the Napoleonic wars in 1815, the British Navy found itself drawn to the north, too. After many years of fighting it was suffering from a surfeit of officers. Most of them had nothing to do. They were languishing on half pay and desperate for action but, inconveniently, the French had been quelled. There was no war to occupy these men ardent for adventure and so, in a bid to justify its existence and expenditure, the Navy entered into a series of voyages of exploration.

While some of those upright naval officers considered it beneath their dignity to mimic the ways of the natives, others saw that the Inuit dogsleds could help them on their overland journeys. In 1829 John Ross made a second voyage to the Arctic, accompanied by his nephew James. With their men, they overwintered in Felix harbour at the bottom of the Boothia peninsula in current-day Nunavut. Fergus Fleming related in his book *Barrow's Boys*:

The sledges were a source of wonder to the Europeans. The standard model comprised two lengths of frozen salmon, wrapped in hides and joined by cross-pieces of bone. (When times were hard it could be thawed and eaten.) Alternatively they could be made out of ice, carved elaborately into a recognizable sledge-shape, or simply scooped from the ground to form a bowl that slid happily over the snow.

Handling the sledges was a matter of some difficulty. James Ross picked it up quickly enough, although his team frequently ran wild, depositing him in the snow and being retrieved only after a chase of several miles when they would be found, exhausted and with the sledge jammed between outcrops of ice. His uncle had less success. On his first attempt the dogs ran in opposite directions so that he went nowhere; on his second they ran in circles.

In the decades that followed missionaries came north, too, and learnt to handle teams of dogs in order to travel between native encampments preaching the word of God. Others began to trickle to the Canadian northwest from the 1870s searching for gold. These prospectors, too, relied on their dogs for companionship, transportation, hunting and trapping, and for the delivery of mail during the winter months. In 1894 a small force of the North-West Mounted Police appeared in the Yukon having correctly forecast the Klondike gold rush, which erupted in earnest a few years later. The police too travelled between remote outposts by sled.

In the twenty-first century there are few people who depend on dogs for survival. While a handful of hunters and trappers – people who make a living by trapping animals for their fur – continue to employ dog teams for their stealth and sense of smell, a greater number prefer the convenient thrum of a snow machine. But dogs still embody the spirit of the north. A snow machine, after all, is never delighted to see you. It doesn't run round in wildly excited circles the moment it sees a harness in your hand. It doesn't lick your face while you're trying to rub paw cream into its feet.

Back at the kennels, the dogs had exploded into a commotion of delighted barking: it was lunchtime, and Sebastian and Thomas, Saul's dog-handler, were preparing to feed them their midday snack of water and horsemeat. Aged just twenty-one, Sebastian seemed to be one of those people blessed with a perpetually patient, sunny personality. He had worked at Muktuk the previous spring, then spent the summer months in his native Austria before returning to Canada in October for the winter season.

Thomas was from Switzerland but he too had been at Muktuk for several months; as Saul's handler he was helping him to train for the upcoming Yukon Quest. Originally, Saul had intended that his girlfriend, Fabienne, should be his handler. Fabienne had previously worked as a mushing guide at Muktuk – it was there that the pair had met – and they were keen to make the race a joint enterprise. But her pregnancy had forced a change of plan and Saul had asked Thomas to help him.

As well as assisting with training, Thomas would be Saul's right-hand man during the race itself. He wouldn't go out on the race trail, but he'd drive the dog truck from checkpoint to checkpoint, collect any animals that needed to be dropped from the team through injury, and look after the dogs at the race's halfway point at Dawson where each team was required to rest for thirty-six hours. Staying at Muktuk with Thomas was his devoted German shepherd, Ira, whose enthusiasm for following Thomas everywhere was such that, when he went on a training run, she had to be tied up or confined to the house so that she didn't gallop out of the yard in loyal pursuit.

Thomas had very long, lustrous, dark-brown hair that would have reached some way down his back had he let it hang loose, but he always wore it in a ponytail tucked up inside his hat. The other striking thing about Thomas was the way his body generated heat: he was always warm. When everyone else was wrapped in wool and down, Thomas would be dressed in a single fleece. When others stripped down to two or three layers, Thomas would wear a T-shirt. And this wasn't testosterone-induced bravado. He was a gentle soul and he was just hot.

As well as training with Saul and looking after the Quest dogs, Thomas assisted with more general tasks. A carpenter by profession, he had built six new sleds for Frank; Frank was pleased with them and was eager for more. Thomas also helped with feeding, poop-scooping, and any of the other myriad odd jobs that presented themselves with exhausting regularity. As Saul had become a father just three days previously and was deluged with the newfound mysteries of nappies in the home he and Fabienne shared halfway between Muktuk and Whitehorse, Thomas too had a few days off from training and was helping out around the yard instead.

In the garage, Sebastian and Thomas dumped chunks of frozen horseflesh into large, white-plastic buckets, which they filled with warm water. As the meat thawed, they broke it up with their hands until the mixture resembled very sloppy road kill – bright-scarlet water littered with unidentifiable chunks of mangled flesh. I then toured the yard with them, putting one large ladleful of this concoction into each dog's bowl, or into a can attached to the post outside its house. The warm flesh mixture smelt bloody, but the dog houses themselves were odour-free in that cold air.

One dog didn't have a bowl so I missed her out and made a mental note to return when I'd found a container. She ran round on the end of her chain, with a desperate expression in her eyes that clearly squealed, 'You've forgotten me! You've forgotten me!'

'After we feed them, they usually sit on their houses

and howl,' said Sebastian. 'If you miss one out, they don't howl. Then you know you've forgotten one.'

The dogs weren't the only creatures interested in their food bowls. The yard was also home to a number of huge black ravens who pecked continually at the aluminium dishes so that the yard resounded perpetually with tinny ting-ting-tings. With their tarry feathers fluffed up in the cold, these ravens appeared to be almost the size of cats. They didn't caw like the birds back home. These had a much sweeter song, and made an extraordinarily dulcet glugging sound, like water tinkling through a pipe.

Ravens are revered by the First Nations people of the north, who incorporate the bird into their stories of creation. The First Nations people call the birds 'grandfather'. Frank said that sometimes, during mentally tough sections of the Quest trail, he would chat to a raven flying overhead. He would call it 'grandfather' as had the people who had travelled across this land centuries before, and he'd find these conversations gave him an emotional lift.

Most of the dogs lived in the yard in their individual wooden houses. They were each tethered by a chain that ran from the post outside their house: the length of the chains and the distance between the houses was carefully calculated so that each dog could socialize and play with its neighbours, but they could not fight as a pack. The dogs were intentionally housed next to those with whom they were most friendly: dogs, like humans, get on with some better than others. And so they spent their days when they weren't running chatting to their friends, or snoozing inside on their straw, or simply sitting on top of their houses and surveying the scene.

'How long did it take you to learn the names of all the

dogs?' I asked Thomas as we made our way back to the garage with our empty buckets.

'About three weeks,' he said.

This struck me as impressive. There were 108 dogs in the kennels – give or take a few. Nobody seemed sure of the exact number. They appeared to have given up keeping count. Puppies came, veterans went.

A handful of geriatrics roamed loose: Frank and Anne refused to cull their retired dogs but kept them through their old age. As a result, the house and yard were well populated with elderly animals living out their days at leisure.

The old men – Streaker, Bozo and Murphy – spent their nights downstairs in the garage, and during the day they roamed as they pleased. Streaker and Bozo had both become skinny in their dotage and, on colder days, Sebastian would try to convince them to stay in the garage to conserve what little fat they had. But these old boys were unconvinced of the delights of central heating. They preferred to hobble around outside and to sit wistfully by the pens where the females in heat were kept, dreaming, perhaps, of more active times.

'Those old males are our heat detectors,' Sebastian told me. He waved over towards Murphy and Bozo who were loitering outside the door to the garage. 'When we see them sniffing around one female, we know she's in heat.'

Bozo had once been one of Frank's most long-standing Quest dogs: Frank reckoned he'd clocked around forty thousand kilometres in his lifetime. That's the equivalent of having run all the way round the equator.

In the main house lived three old ladies who lounged

on the furniture like the inhabitants of a retirement home; only the television chat shows were missing. Louise and Angel, whom I'd met when I first arrived, were joined in the daytime by Rocky. Rocky had cancer. A rapidly swelling tumour protruded from her tummy, but she appeared not yet to have realized that the end was nigh. With her outsized ears, grinning mouth and gregarious personality, Rocky was a big favourite among family, guests and staff. Her illness had turned her breath smelly, but she was so well loved that nobody cared, for sitting in the same room as Rocky was a sociable affair. Every few minutes her head would appear in a lap beneath the table, or she'd tap a leg with her paw in an invitation to say hello. She'd not been in the house when I'd arrived at midnight because Sebastian took her every evening to spend the night in the comfort of the staff cabin where she was generously fed and generally pampered.

Then there was Molly – a black and white dog who spent her days in the garage and the yard, and her nights in the cabin with Sebastian, Rocky, Thomas, Ira and the rest. And lastly, two of the matronly females preferred not to venture indoors at all: Maud, a stout black dog with white paws – since her hysterectomy, Sebastian told me, she'd been putting on weight – and Fox, who was equally plump with luxuriantly soft black and brown fur, lived in a little straw-filled hut in front of the garage.

There were puppies, too, who lived in enclosed pens to one side of the main yard. During my stay the puppy pens housed ten creatures of varying degrees of small- ness from three different litters.

'Is there a breeding programme here, or are the

puppies mistakes?' I asked Sebastian. He replied that the breeding was for the most part predetermined, but accidents sometimes happened.

'Those puppies were a mistake,' he said, pointing to the pen where the four smallest gambolled. 'And Mozart – ' he indicated the scrappiest dog in one of the larger puppies' pens ' – he was definitely a mistake. His parents were brother and sister. There were actually three puppies in the litter, but the other two died.'

Mozart was a robust little thing. His colouring was pale except for a dark ring around his right eye that gave him the perpetual appearance of having been in a fight. To save him from loneliness, Frank had housed him in a pen with the male puppies of a litter a month or so older than he. Perhaps it was the constant struggle to compete with dogs bigger and brasher that made him hustle for every morsel of food.

The dogs were a blend of breeds, as are most modern sled dogs. The traditional Siberian husky is usually considered too slow and insufficiently athletic for contemporary dogsled racing. These were Alaskan husky combined with a bit of Siberian from way back when, mixed with Labrador retriever, Indian village dog and collie.

They were all colours, too: biscuit, brown, sandy, black, patchy and speckled, some the dark shade of liquorice, others caramel and butterscotch. Keeper was the colour of pale straw, with eyes of clear lilac. Aida was black with a white belly and chest, and pale cheeks, muzzle and eyebrows. As with Keeper, her most striking feature was her eyes: one was a coppery brown, the other cornflower blue. Elsa, too – a small, pale-coloured female in Saul's Quest team – had eyes of different colours.

Panda, predictably enough, had black and white patches while Glacier was pure, glorious white. Today she was in heat but she had managed to break out of her pen. Free and fabulously fertile, she bolted round the yard while the elderly male dogs limped wishfully in her wake.

3

In the heart of the primeval forest men of the United States Army Engineering Corps ... lived up magnificently to their frontier traditions. Bridging unpredictable glacial streams, scaling white-capped peaks, wrestling with quaking bog and muskeg; fighting mosquitoes and bulldog flies in summer, and stinging, searing winter cold that froze the very marrow in their bones – through tropical heat and Arctic cold they ploughed ahead. And, in seven short months, the pioneer Hudson's Bay fur trail ... was converted into a 1,600-mile military highway.

So wrote Philip H. Godsell, a former Hudson's Bay Company inspector, in his book *Alaska Highway*, first published in 1944 when the horrors of war still pervaded and patriotism ran high.

The Alaska Highway transformed the Yukon. In 1941, there were around four hundred people living in Whitehorse. Work started on the road in March 1942; it opened officially on 20 November that same year. By that time, Whitehorse – a strategic base for US servicemen and civilian contractors due to its position roughly in the middle of the highway's proposed route and its railway link to the Pacific port at Skagway – had a population of twenty thousand.

The road wasn't the only major construction project that came to the Yukon as a result of the Japanese threat. In the early months of 1942, the Japanese were sinking American tankers at an average rate of one every three days, and fuel was growing scarce. And so, in order to fill the trucks that were to supply Alaska, the US military urged the piping of oil overland to Whitehorse from Norman Wells in Canada's Northwest Territories. The contract for the Canol pipeline, as it became known, was awarded to Bechtel-Price-Callahan, a partnership of construction companies. The company's recruitment poster did its best to deter applicants:

THIS IS NO PICNIC
Working and living conditions on this job are as difficult as those encountered on any construction job ever done in the United States or foreign territory. Men hired for this job will be required to work and live under the most extreme conditions imaginable. Temperature will range from 90° above zero to 70° below zero. Men will have to fight swamps, rivers, ice and cold. Mosquitoes, flies, and gnats will not only be annoying but will cause bodily harm. If you are not prepared to work under these and similar conditions DO NOT APPLY.

During the construction of the road, the military built greenhouses at the Takhini hot springs, whose waters surface thirty kilometres outside Whitehorse. The soldiers channelled the thermal water to heat these glass constructions, which they used for growing fresh vegetables.

The greenhouses are no more, but now the site has been developed to include two man-made pools, changing rooms, and even a licensed café. The source of the water is something of a mystery. Scientists are unsure whether it is heated by nearby volcanic activity, or whether it simply circulates downwards through fault lines until the heat at the earth's core raises its temperature sufficiently to force it back up. Either way, the water surfaces here at a rate of about 340 litres per minute – that's about the same as the output of thirty bathroom showers, and a modest flow by hot springs' standards.

I headed out along the highway that had been built with so much hardship and hurried towards the hot springs the following evening. In the truck with me were two visitors from New Zealand, Tina and Margaret, and Marty, one of Muktuk's guides. Marty was a French Canadian from Montreal. He'd only been at Muktuk for three weeks but Tina and Margaret had known the place for longer. They were repeat visitors, as were many of the Turners' guests. The people that came on holiday were of all ages, shapes and sizes, and they ran the gamut of experience. Some had never stepped foot on a dogsled before; others were keen mushers with their own dogs at home. Some had no outdoor gear and borrowed what they needed from Frank and Anne while others arrived fully kitted out. Some were seeking hard-core adventure with multi-day camping trips. Others preferred to make short day trips and half-day outings from the comforts of the kennels. All of them, however, shared a love of dogs and a passion for the outdoors, and most enjoyed a soak in these thermal waters.

'What should I wear at the hot springs?' I'd asked earlier as I'd stood in the kitchen at Muktuk with Sebastian and Anne.

'Oh, you don't need to wear anything,' Sebastian said airily. 'Everyone just goes in naked.'

'Don't listen to him!' retorted Anne. 'Never believe anything either Sebastian or Frank tells you. They just love to have people on.'

Thanks to Anne's intervention, I had armed myself with a swimming costume. Margaret, Tina and I went to the ladies' changing area, then ran semi-clad along the fearfully cold concrete corridor that led to the pools before plunging into the warm, rust-red water. Its colour came from the iron that infused it along with calcium and magnesium. Gratifyingly, though, the water didn't smell. There was no sulphur in these springs.

The outside air temperature had dropped to minus twenty-two degrees that Sunday evening but the water was a radiant plus thirty-five. A few teenage girls sat in their bikinis on the underwater bench that lined the pool so that the water came to their necks; a father and son scudded an inflatable ball through the steamy mist. The water was comfortable but above its surface my hair froze in white, streaky highlights. It was as though I'd suffered a severe fright that had turned my locks silver. I wasn't alone. The teenagers looked as though the rigours of an evening's soak had aged them by fifty years. The wall around the pool was encased in snow and ice that dribbled down like the melting wax from a huge ecclesiastical candle.

'I feel like a snake that's shed its skin,' Marty pronounced as we drove home an hour or so later. The sun had already set. I too felt invigorated. Perhaps it was the minerals, I don't know, but I felt energized and renewed. The mountains in front of us turned candyfloss pink as the unseen sun's rays reflected from the snow that covered their contours. A full moon, reddish-gold like the iron-infused water we'd bathed in, hung low in the sky.

'I'm boiling here,' boomed Rob, a rotund guest from Texas, as he piled on the gear Frank had lent him.

'Whatever you do, don't sweat!' hollered Frank from the other side of the garage.

It was Monday morning and they were preparing for a two-night camping trip leaving from Fish Lake, a short drive from Muktuk. Fraser, a guest from Halifax, would be going camping too. Marty, Margaret and Tina were going to Fish Lake with them but theirs would be a day trip: they'd return to Muktuk that evening.

'The northern lights this morning were amazing,' Margaret said. 'At about six o'clock, they were right across the sky. We even saw the arc. It was incredible.'

I had been asleep, of course. That was the problem with the northern lights: they only ever put on a display when I was happily dreaming. I couldn't set an alarm to wake myself up because the lights weren't good time-keepers. Frank said that between midnight and one a.m. was a good bet but last night, according to Tina who had been awake with the pain from an injured nerve in her wrist, there had been nothing at midnight and they'd chosen to appear at six. One could, in a state of real desperation, stay up all night – but then they might not appear at all. Obviously they wouldn't be visible on a cloudy night but even on a clear one a sighting was far from certain.

Last night had been cloudless and the temperature had dropped. Now the thermometer recorded minus thirty. The dogs, who usually stood outside their houses or on top of them, hunkered inside wrapped warmly in their straw.

Personally, I was nervous even to leave the garage. I had never been in this kind of cold before. I had no idea what it would feel like. I had assumed that the cold would hit me physically, like the wall of warmth you feel when leaving the airport in hot and humid countries. I had thought the cold would instantly envelop me, as the tepid air wraps the body in sultry climates. So I was surprised to find that when I ventured outdoors I felt very little. Wrapped up in all those clothes, I felt a tiny bit chilly, but not as cold as I'd frequently felt standing at a wintry London bus stop. I had heard stories of the cold entering the lungs like razor blades or burning like fire but my breathing was perfectly comfortable.

It was snowing lightly still. Tiny spots of flakes drifted from the sky. As they settled on my clothing, I saw that these were flawless, single snow crystals. Just a few millimetres in diameter, they were breathtakingly perfect in their formation. Each had six tiny, glistening, intricate prongs, which forked out into smaller spikes to form complex symmetrical arrangements of ice. The remarkable thing was that almost every one of them seemed to be immaculately composed: at the same time as being fantastically delicate, these crystals were so robust that their tiny cusps had remained unbroken during the flakes' tumultuous journeys through the buffeting clouds, along the rambunctious air currents, and finally down on to the surface of my fleece. Yet they were so light that, when they settled together, they seemed almost to hover one on top of another forming airy, fluffy little mounds of still-unblemished lace.

We waved off Frank, Fraser and Rob, Marty, Tina and Margaret. With sleds, skidoos, tents and supplies loaded, and the dogs safely stowed in the customized dog truck, they went on their way and Sebastian and I retreated inside for lunch. And then, after we'd fuelled ourselves for the afternoon ahead, I was inducted to the world of 'scooping poop'.

To the untrained eye, it may look like a simple case of shovelling shit. To a musher, though, this is one of the most important jobs in the yard. On one level, it is vital to keep the yard clean: viruses can spread through a kennel littered with excrement. But equally important, the dog's stool reveals secrets about its health that the animal itself can never tell you.

Sebastian gave me a wheelbarrow, a shovel, and a long-handled aluminium pan. I was to scoop the poop into the pan, then dump it in the wheelbarrow.

'You need to pick up everything – even the tiny bits,' he told me. 'And if there is any diarrhoea, try to remember which dog's house it is by, and tell me.'

I made my way to the back of the yard while Sebastian started with the puppy pens. The rearmost two rows housed the male dogs: Oreo, Toby, Alex, Brody, Cody ... I talked to each of them and tried to memorize their names. Oreo was black and fluffy; his long, dark hair was hoary with frost that echoed the white wisps around his chin, making him look old beyond his years. Toby was black with one white paw. Alex was a large dog with the look of a traditional husky: speckled brown and black with a pale face and belly. Brody and Cody were almost-identical brothers. With their short hair, sandy colouring and little floppy ears they looked as though they carried a lot of Labrador in their genes. Firm friends, they preferred always to run in the same team.

Gratifyingly, their offerings were mostly frozen and odourless. Occasionally, a particularly generous dog would produce a fresh, sticky stool, but generally poop-scooping was a pleasant, relaxing way to spend half an hour or so. At feeding time it wasn't possible to stop and talk to the dogs individually as the next one in line would be desperate for its delicious portion of bloody water with scraggy horseflesh, but during the poop-scooping session I could loiter as long as I pleased. It seemed curious that I should take pleasure in shovelling frozen dog shit, but the dogs were friendly, the air was invigorating, and the view of the snow-covered hills beyond the yard was spectacular. Fat, jagged icicles clung to the spruce twigs, glittering like gaudy faux gems. It was a world away from my computer-laden desk back at home.

I worked my way down the rows. Panda had diarrhoea. I later discovered that this was an almost perpetual problem for him: he was a hyperactive creature and his personality seemed to have infiltrated his bowel. The problem was that he was already skinny and his digestive troubles only made matters worse. Rimsky was entranced by the wheelbarrow with its tempting smells and jumped up, tipping it over so that its contents rolled across the snow.

In the next row, where the females resided, Blizzard, pure white as her name implied, bounded about in joyful anticipation of petting. She was lively in the kennels but, I would later learn, in the harness she became frightened and refused to pull. Diesel, a shy black and white dog, shot into the safety of her house as soon as I came near while Natasha, a smaller black female with white eyebrows, danced around the wheelbarrow and butted her nose into all her neighbours' business. A kind of kennels' busybody, she was thrilled by any activity and poked her face so close to the shovel that I worried I might scoop her nose.

Saul returned from paternity leave that afternoon. His break had only lasted five days: he may have just become a father but the Quest wouldn't wait for him. In less than four weeks he'd be at the start line of the toughest dogsled race in the world and, baby or no baby, his team's training had to continue.

At this point, Saul had eighteen dogs in his squad and he and Thomas were going out with nine dogs each. (When the race started, he'd have whittled the final team down to fourteen.) They harnessed and hooked up their dogs. The rest of the yard barked and caterwauled with deafening enthusiasm. And then, when the chosen few and their drivers raced out of sight, those left behind sat on their houses and howled.

It was interesting to watch these dogs, and to see how they longed to run.

'They are instinctively sociable. They are natural team players,' Frank explained to his guests time and again.

'Dogs are not wolves. Dogs are not running as a pack. A pack is about chasing something. Sled dogs are running because other dogs are running. They are motivated by something the animal behaviorists call social facilitation,' Raymond Coppinger wrote in his book *Dogs*. Coppinger is a professor of biology at

Hampshire College in the US and a former sled dog racer. He went on to write of his racing days: 'I had standing orders from my family not to leave any dog at home on race weekends. The left-behind dogs would howl, bark, and cry all the time I was gone. The first time I ever did it, I left Rena, who had sore feet, to give her the weekend off to rest and heal. I never did that again. When I got back Sunday night, she was hoarse.'

At Muktuk, the story seemed to be similar.

That day, though, the Quest dogs didn't have the run they might have hoped for. After an hour, Saul and Thomas were back in the yard.

'We couldn't brake,' Thomas explained. 'There wasn't enough snow.' Until now, Saul and Thomas had been travelling to train in snowier areas. This was the first time they'd tried to run straight from the yard and on to the Takhini; Saul had hoped that the light snowfall of the last few days would have given sufficient covering. But teams of nine athletic dogs had proved too strong for the conditions and the drivers hadn't been able to control their speed. For safety's sake they had come back and tomorrow would truck the dogs to snowier parts.

The lack of snow this season was provoking discussion around the region. Nobody could remember a winter with so little. On the radio just that morning an official from the Yukon Quest had been talking about his concerns for the state of the race trail. Parts of it were very bare. But there was still plenty of time, he said. If temperatures fell to minus forty for just a few days, conditions could improve dramatically.

It was hardly breaking news that the weather in

the Arctic – and here in the sub-Arctic – was being dramatically affected by global warming. While the climate across the globe was changing, it was at the earth's polar extremes that the effects could be seen most dramatically. The Arctic had been likened to the canary in the coal mine: temperatures were rising considerably faster here than in other regions.

Environmentalists had been drawing attention to the melting polar ice cap for some years. Newspapers, magazines, television documentaries – and even, latterly, politicians – had voiced their concerns. In September 2005, four months prior to my arrival in the Yukon, the United States' National Snow and Ice Data Center (NSIDC) announced that the Arctic ice cap had diminished over the summer to its smallest size ever. The decline in sea ice since records began in 1978 amounted to approximately 1.3 million square kilometres – that's to say, the ice had shrunk by an area twice the size of Texas, or more than five times the size of the UK. In turn, it was not recovering in winter to the extent that it used to. It was covering a smaller area, was thinner, and was melting earlier in the spring.

While pale-coloured sea ice reflects the sun's energy back into space, dark ocean water actually absorbs the sun's radiation, NSIDC explained. The increased absorption of energy warms the planet and further prevents the formation of ice. With this destructive loop spinning ever more heatedly, the trend looks set to continue: NSIDC predicted that by the end of the twenty-first century, the Arctic could be completely free from ice in the summertime. With the northernmost coast of the Yukon stretching to just a couple of hundred kilometres from the 'permanent' ice cap, the territory too was feeling severely the effects of climate change.

I helped with the evening feed a couple of days later. The dogs' supper time was around six p.m., and night had fallen. We carried buckets of kibble soaked in water from the garage into the yard, our way lit by headlamps strapped to our foreheads. In the lamps' beams, the dogs' eyes reflected a dazzling array of colours. Some shone green, others turquoise or deep scarlet. Like kaleidoscopes, they flickered through the blackness.

Dooley and Panda were on special rations as they had diarrhoea. When I passed over their bowls with the bucket of regular feed, they rushed around in frantic circles clearly crying, 'What about me?'

In the pens, the puppies were given dry food. They were lively, sociable creatures: Frank always handled his puppies when they were just a couple of days old, before they opened their eyes, as he wanted them to get used to people, to have a sense that there was a benevolent presence beyond their mother. They certainly seemed pleased to see me with my bucket and they stormed their bowls as soon as the first kibbles clattered in.

In the garage, the old dogs were less enthusiastic. Bozo barely glanced at his supper.

'Don't worry,' Sebastian told me. 'He'll eat it when we've gone.'

As we ate our own dinner an hour or so later – roast turkey with potatoes, beans, broccoli, tomato salad and a cranberry sauce with a sharp citrus twang – Frank, back from his camping trip with Fraser and Rob, told us that a neighbour had phoned him that morning to say he'd seen three large wolves in the area.

'Is that a problem?' I asked.

'It is if they're hungry and they come round here.'

'Might they try to kill the dogs?'

'They won't *try*. They don't survive by *trying*.'

'Because we have such a large number of dogs, and because the yard has open land around it, it's not the first choice for a wolf,' Anne explained. 'That's part of the reason we've built the yard this way. But if a wolf comes into the yard, the dogs won't bark. They just lie down and submit. The wolf can just come in, snatch a dog in its jaws, drag it out of its collar, and take it away. When you go out in the morning, there's nothing but an empty collar on the end of its chain.'

There was a short lull as we contemplated the horrible prospect. Then Stefan, the other of Muktuk's two guides, broke the silence.

'I saw a wolverine today,' he said.

Stefan had been away on a camping trip with two American guests during my first couple of days at the kennels but had now returned, and those guests had reluctantly made their way back to their choked cities and crowded offices. Stefan was twenty-eight-years-old and German. He had very short, crew-cut blond-grey hair and clear blue eyes.

'It's OK as long as you see the back end of a wolverine. You just don't want to be seeing its front,' declared Anne.

Wolverines are elusive animals and rarely sighted. The largest members of the weasel family, they look a bit like small bears. They're known for their independence and ferocity – they generally live by scavenging and can drive animals far larger than themselves from a sought-after carcass. Indeed, they have been known to attack nearly every local animal other than humans, who are their principal predator: wolverine pelts are popular both for their rarity and because the hair does not hold moisture and therefore makes an effective frost-proof trim for parkas.

'But the worst animal you can meet on the trail is a moose,' Anne continued. 'If you come face to face with a moose, the moose can just charge straight into your team. Sometimes dogs are killed that way. If you ever see a moose running from behind, you'll see that its legs just fly everywhere. It's not an orderly lope. When you see how a moose's legs go, you can understand how they can inflict so much damage.'

Over breakfast the following morning Marty seemed worryingly eager to continue the conversational theme of death and destruction. Perhaps he'd been mulling on gory subjects overnight.

'There were huge cracks in the ice on Fish Lake when we went there the other day,' he pronounced.

'Don't worry. The ice there is thick,' Stefan replied, munching through a great basin of muesli and fruit. It was remarkable to see the quantities these people ate while never gathering a gram of fat.

Marty wasn't going to be dissuaded by the calm voice of reason, though.

'You know, if you fall through the ice, you should always submerge your arms,' he went on. 'People lift their arms out like this.' He made frantic scrabbling motions. 'What you should do is put your arms in the water, then put them on the ice – and the water will freeze so they'll stick. Then you can try to lift yourself out.'

'But the temperature has to be right,' said Stefan. 'It's no good if it's too warm because the water won't freeze.'

I later read up on the work of Dr Gordon Giesbrecht, a professor at the University of Manitoba, who studies the body's response to extreme environments. Nicknamed Professor Popsicle and billed by *Outside Magazine* as 'the world's leading authority on freezing to death', Giesbrecht has conducted experiments in which he has submerged himself in frigid waters and observed his own body's reactions. His subsequent tips for survival stretch further than merely suggesting that you slap your wet arms on the ice and pray hard that they freeze.

Giesbrecht points out that most people who die from falling through thin ice don't die from hypothermia. They drown.

'People are often surprised when I tell them that you could live for an hour or two in ice water if you do everything right,' he explains in a video he made for Discovery Channel Canada. He cites survivors' experiences from the sinking of the *Titanic*: the lucky ones in the lifeboats heard screams from the water for a full hour or two. Those screaming were wearing life jackets, so they didn't drown – and it took them an encouragingly long time to die from hypothermia.

When the body is first plunged into very cold water, the body triggers the cold shock response, Giesbrecht explains.

'You first start gasping and hyperventilating and breathing way more than you need to. And that's really bad if your head goes under the water when you gasp the first time – then you drown immediately.'

In the video, he has simulated a cross-country skiing accident. He is speaking for the camera in breathless spurts from a watery hole that's been cut into the ice and that he has purposely – perhaps insanely – just skied into. Depending on the person, he says, the cold shock will last between one and three minutes. 'The main thing you need to think about for the first minute is just not drowning.'

After that first minute, he goes on (still gulping air from his frigid hole) he has a window of between two and five minutes in which to get himself out of there. To increase his chances, he doesn't attempt to lift himself straight up but lies on his front, kicks with his legs, and pulls with his arms. You should exit by the same place you fell in, says Giesbrecht – after all, the ice was strong enough to hold you until you fell. And once out, you should roll away from the hole, then crawl, because if you stand on thin ice you risk breaking through again.

After that window of opportunity, though, the body will be so weakened by cold that the chances of surviving without outside help diminish.

'If I haven't gotten out of here within five to ten minutes, I'm not going to get out,' Giesbrecht gasps. By this stage of the film he's starting to look a bit peaky. Unless he is rescued, he explains in laboured but matter-of-fact tones, he will eventually lose consciousness and drown. 'So if I just thrash around I'm going to lose more heat, and I'm going to get exhausted, and I'll drown even quicker.'

To give Marty credit, Giesbrecht does now alight on the subject of allowing one's arms to freeze to the ice. He demonstrates how one should place one's arms so that as much of the body is lifted out of the heat-sapping water as possible.

'So at this point, I'm just going to get my arms on the ice, and I'm going to keep them here and not move them. It might sound a little silly but, if I'm lucky, my arms will freeze to the ice before I become unconscious. If I become unconscious and I just slip down here, I'll drown. But if I become unconscious and my arms are frozen to the ice, I'll at least be here for a little bit longer.'

In a subsequent interview recorded on safe, solid snow, Giesbrecht expands: 'There have actually been a number of cases when people have become so cold they've become unconscious, but they were frozen to the ice and they were rescued, and they survived because either their arms, or their beard for instance, was frozen to the ice.'

There were no such dangers in store for me that morning. The greatest perils that day lay in the not-too-terrifying hazards of being ambushed by puppies. I had volunteered my services as trainee poop-scooper again. It was Sebastian's day off so this time Marty was in charge of cleaning the yard. He started in the far back corner with the males – Oreo, Toby, Alex and so on – while I took the pens, which meant trying to work while being leapt upon by over-excited puppies.

Glacier – who was in her own pen as she was in heat – was determined to join in the fun. After all, there are only so many opportunities for mischief when you're in solitary confinement and, hormones rampaging, she was eager to seize every possible chance for merriment. As I entered her pen, she galloped towards the gate to greet me, then nipped the mitt from my hand. She did so very gracefully, gently whipping away the glove without so much as a tap of her teeth to my fingers; if I were a suspicious soul, I might even imagine she'd had some practice at this kind of disrobing. Joyfully, she placed my mitt on the ground, goading me to collect it. I bent down and – zap! – she grabbed it between her jaws again. She then danced around the pen for some seconds, tail wagging exuberantly.

'Glacier!' I said, trying to sound commanding. 'Give me back my mitt!'

Glacier dived into her house, waggled her bottom, and emerged again empty-mouthed. She gave me an exuberant grin. I reached in to take it – but, no! Glacier was faster and, mitt safely secured between her teeth, she tore off round the pen in a series of victory laps.

This went on for some time. By the time I had regained possession of my clothing, poor Marty had cleaned the rest of the yard.

4

As I sailed through the air, vaguely aware of my dog team trotting driverless beneath me, Frank's admonition of a few days earlier rang clearly through my mind: '*Never* let go of the sled!'

I had just embarked on my second dogsledding escapade and things weren't running any more smoothly than they had on the first. I was out this time with Stefan and Fraser. We had each taken a sled with six dogs. Given that he had only two people to mind, and that Fraser had some mushing experience, Stefan had decided that he too would travel by dog team rather than by the noisy skidoo. It was an error he wouldn't repeat for the rest of the season.

'Be nice to Rimsky,' Sebastian had instructed me as we hooked the dogs up to the sled. 'He's only young. You should pet him and tell him he's doing well.'

I would have rejoiced at the opportunity.

With irrepressible enthusiasm, my team had burst out of the yard. I had two females, Brandy and DeeDee, in the lead then the young and frisky Rimsky and the hyperactive Marley in swing, or the middle. At wheel, or the rear, were Percy – a female despite her name

– and Tucker, a large, affectionate male. I was to take all of these dogs out again over the course of my stay at Muktuk and later found them to be responsive and sometimes even obedient. But at this stage I was still a fearfully incompetent novice and upset number one occurred within seconds.

We approached the bend in the trail that led to the river – that same bend that had caused trouble when I'd been with Frank and Bob. Stefan's team behaved perfectly. They trotted neatly to the right, taking the turn in the prescribed gentle curve. My dogs had other ideas. Refusing to heed my bellows of 'Gee!', the dogsledding command to turn right (left is 'haw' and stop is 'whoa'), they galloped straight ahead, veering round the inside of the stick barrier so that the sled avoided collision by about a centimetre. I muttered thanks to the gods for delivering me from a twig-punctured demise, and dogs and sled hurtled on. We were now heading for the shortest, sharpest angle round the corner – and as we shot towards it, I saw that a log about the size of my leg lay across the path. The dogs darted round it through a painfully narrow channel (there appeared to be exactly a sled's width between the end of the log and a particularly prickly bush); miraculously, the sled followed unscathed. I hung on with a fearful lack of control and the sled swung bumpily round the bend. As I came through the corner I almost whooped: amazingly, I was still on the runners. The adrenalin rush of bungee jumping had nothing on the giddy thrill I felt at having survived so far.

We juddered along the last part of the path before the river – and then my team decided to cut one last corner. Instead of taking the simple, perpendicular slope down the river bank and on to the ice, they descended at an angle, dragging the sled over a clump of foliage. It was one mishap too many. The sled jumped. I flew from the back. As I soared through the air, my team merrily ran on beneath me. They were relieved, no doubt, to be rid of my cumbersome, wailing presence behind them.

Fortunately, hearing my shrieked expletives, Stefan had stopped just a couple of metres ahead. He stood and watched, bemused no doubt, as I hit the snow and then, determined at all costs to catch the dogs, leapt straight back to my feet and started at a lumbering lope in my hefty boots after the sled. The dogs, in any case, had drawn to a halt. Stefan was stationed in front of them and they'd had their fun, for the moment at least.

I was lucky. The reason that one should never let go of the sled is simple: the dogs, eager to run, may well not wait for their driver and, quite apart from the fact that a musher might have to go to immense trouble to find the animals again, loose dog teams are a danger to themselves. Dogs can become tangled in the lines and, unsupervised, they may then sustain injuries or fight.

Frank and Anne used to operate moonlight dog-sledding outings until, on one unfortunate occasion, a guest lost her team and Frank was obliged to stay out into the early hours of the morning searching for his escaped dogs. But even Frank, a dogsledding veteran, has had his terrifying moments. He sometimes told the story of one particularly awful descent down Eagle Summit, the steepest point of the Yukon Quest trail. Having fallen from his sled in bad weather, he lost his team. Horrified at what might happen to them, he had no choice but to start to walk down the mountain on foot. Fortunately for him, there was another competitor shortly ahead of him, and she managed to hold his dogs until he reached her.

I brushed the snow from my face and clambered back on to my runners, and Stefan, Fraser and I continued on our way along the easy, flat river trail. There was no danger here that we might have to practise our cold-water survival skills: the ice, according to Frank, was more than half a metre thick.

'It's thick enough to drive a truck over,' he'd assured one anxious guest a night or two earlier. Frank was always the first person to test the ice of the Takhini each autumn. When he judged that it was safe, he'd go out on a skidoo and mark the trail that his dog teams, guides and guests would use for the winter season. So far, his judgement had always been sound.

While there were no problems with the ice, something else seemed to be troubling Fraser. He was dropping behind. Finally, Stefan decided to park his team and go to investigate. There wasn't enough snow on the river to embed a snow hook, which is attached by rope to the sled and acts as an anchor, so he hacked a hole in the ice with his axe, planted the snow hook in the indentation and, to prevent me from getting into trouble when I was left there alone, he tethered my leaders to his handle-bar. Then he turned back and ran on foot to find out what was wrong with Fraser.

His plan would have worked had his loyal team not decided to follow him. The angle of the snow hook, set as it was in the ice, prevented the dogs from moving forward but, if they executed a sufficiently deft U-turn, they could release the hook from behind. There was, after all, little snow to hold it. Being ingenious dogs, it took them just a couple of minutes to free the hook and, greatly pleased by their own cleverness, they trotted off in Stefan's wake. My leaders, of course, were tied to the back of Stefan's sled so when his team moved, mine went cheerily with them. In vain I stamped down on the black rubber mat, and on the metal brake as well. Desperately, plaintively, furiously, I yelled, 'Whoa!' And still we skipped on, twelve dogs, two sleds and one very worried learner driver.

I changed my tactics. I revised my shrieks. I stopped shouting 'Whoa!' and instead bellowed, '*Stefan!*'

He was some distance ahead but still within sight. Hearing my faint, hysterical yells echoing across the ice, he turned round to see the little caravan of very contented dogs and wildly out-of-control novice chugging gently towards him. He too executed an about turn and, instead of heading for Fraser, now sprinted towards me as fast as his heavy boots would allow. Later, when we were home and safe and the dogs were secure in their houses, I commented that it had been a good day for his fitness training.

'It is normal for me. Sometimes I go out with the Japanese,' Stefan shrugged, the tiniest of wry smiles breaking through his dry Teutonic exterior. The Japanese tourists, who tended not to stay at Muktuk but were regularly trucked in by their tour operator for short half-day trips, were notorious for their limited control and non-existent English.

It turned out that one of Fraser's dogs, Toby, was limping. Having firmly reset his own snow hook to hold his team, Stefan helped Fraser unhitch Toby and they loaded him into the sled bag to prevent further damage.

Finally, we were ready to go once more. For a few

minutes, we enjoyed a kind of peace, disturbed only by Toby's frustrated barking: the injured dog wasn't remotely grateful for his ride and he showed his displeasure by yelping, jumping and making repeated bids for freedom. On one attempt he even succeeded in leaping from the bag even though he was tethered by short necklines to the handlebar of the sled. Still, despite Toby's protests, there was sufficient lull in the action for Stefan to point out a huge elk belonging to a local farm that stood on a hill above the right bank of the river and stared down at the small, chaotic creatures who were making such a mess of things below.

But this halcyon respite wasn't to last. We were scarcely out of sight of the elk when Fraser's team, for no apparent reason, veered left from the trail and started to head for home. Maybe they'd had enough of Toby's moaning. As Fraser and his team disappeared into the distance, ever-diminishing cries drifted over the ice of the once-tranquil river: '*Whoa!* WHOA! Gee! Gee!' and finally the airiest of faraway laments: '*God darn it, you stupid dogs!*'

Eventually, Fraser managed to return to us and once more we attempted to continue. But the covering of snow on the river's surface was so thin that neither Fraser nor I were able to check the progress of our energetic dogs. We could brake and shout 'Whoa!' all we liked but the dogs had their own agenda, and that was to run.

Once, I did manage to stop my team. Percy seemed to be tangled. In fact, she had merely straddled the line and I would later discover that a dog can perfectly easily sort this situation out for itself, however uncomfortable its hopping may appear. But on this second outing of my dogsledding career I didn't know that. I successfully drew my dogs to a halt. Gingerly, I nipped off the sled and, holding on to some part of the sled at all times, ran to the dogs, grabbed the line – and they took off, dragging me on my knees for maybe a minute before my anguished cries of 'Whoa!' and useless tugging on the line inspired sufficient sympathy to persuade them to slow enough for me to hop back on the runners. Percy's tangle, I decided, could wait.

No sooner had I regained my position on the back of the sled, however, than I saw another drama playing out. Fraser was ahead of me now, with Stefan leading from the front. Stefan had anchored his team to help Fraser with some problem and, again, his team had broken free. Now both Stefan and Fraser were on the back of the second sled. Each had his inside foot on a runner while the other foot pedalled wildly as they tried to increase their speed and come up with the loose team in front. They were gaining on them slowly – Stefan had put his sled on its side so the dogs didn't have the benefit of the smooth runners – and after about five minutes they caught them.

We stopped for lunch. We gave the dogs snacks of frozen Arctic charr, then broke branches to make a fire – the dry cold made the wood rewardingly easy to snap – before sitting round the blaze to eat our own cheese and salami sandwiches and cookies. We'd transported the food in a coolbox, though here the insulated container was used not to keep our lunch cool but to prevent it from freezing.

As I sipped my second cup of steaming hot chocolate, I finally worked up the courage to voice the question that had been bothering me for the last hour or so. Tentatively, I asked, 'So . . . is this normal?'

It had seemed to me to be a rather chaotic morning, but perhaps that was the nature of dogsledding.

There was a brief, surprised silence, then Fraser roared with laughter and even Stefan gave a sheepish smile. 'Normal?' they echoed. 'No!'

'Usually you just go down the river, turn round, and head back home,' Fraser said.

On the way back the dogs were mercifully calm. As we neared the sanctuary of Muktuk, Stefan gestured from in front that I should turn round and look. There behind us the sun's last rays illuminated the mountains a soft pink. On the towering cliffs of the river bank, a line of snow-covered trees stood in stark silhouette against the coral of the evening sky.

5

'What happens if a musher loses control of the sled?' some rookie clients once asked Frank. He told us how he'd replied as we ate breakfast the following morning.

'I told them, "Well, I had this one couple, and their dogs just took off and they couldn't stop them. The problem was, my skidoo wouldn't start. I was trying and trying to start it but by the time I got it going they were out of sight. I tried to follow them but, after I while, I couldn't even find the tracks from their sleds. I spent hours looking for them out there, but I just couldn't find them. I never did discover what happened to those two."'

An hour or so later, as Sebastian and I gathered wheelbarrows and shovels for that day's poop-scooping stint, Sebastian told me another tale.

'A few weeks ago we had two Americans here, a mother and her son. Frank was getting ready to take them out and he said to me in a loud whisper so that they could hear, "I really hope it works out that I bring them both back this time."'

Maybe it was from Frank that some of these dogs had learnt their sense of mischief, I thought to myself that morning as the ever-excitable Panda ran round and round my legs in tight circles, tethering my ankles together with his chain so that I was rooted to the spot outside his house.

I freed myself and made my way down the lines – Sebastian had chivalrously volunteered himself for assault-by-puppies in the pens – and eventually arrived at the Quest dogs. The dogs in Saul's race squad were kept together and, as high-tier athletes in training, they were fed a different diet from the rest of the kennel. The disparity was reflected in the quantity of their excrement: one day's ordure from a single dog in these rows could fill an entire pan. As I laboriously worked my way down the line, a dog whose area I had just cleaned produced a prodigious, steaming pile. My sense of diligence deserted me. I had already passed that house; I needn't have seen. It was minus twenty-eight degrees: this latest offering would be frozen within minutes but for now it was fresh and glisteningly wet.

'That one will just have to wait till tomorrow,' I concluded as I quietly continued to the next dog, which had moved its bowels rather less recently.

I'd been at Muktuk for almost a week now, and my trip was far surpassing expectation. Best of all, I was surprised to find that already I was starting to know the names and personalities of many of the dogs. I had never imagined that, in a yard of this size, each animal could be individually known and loved to the extent that they were here, still less that I would come to recognize them myself.

Poor Toby was now easy to identify: he was tethered by a leash inside the garage where the warmer temperatures would better promote the healing of his injury. Frank hoped his problem was not too serious: he thought it was a wrist sprain, which should sort itself out in a few days. But until Toby showed signs of improvement he would stay in the heated garage. Toby didn't think much of his new quarters and yelped and cried whenever a potential saviour came near.

Vanek was blond, beautiful and shy. His face was almost wolfish in shape; his long, angular muzzle ended in a nose that was liverish pink. He had dark-brown, almond-shaped eyes that looked nervously at the newcomer approaching his house, then he sank to the ground in submission. Once in the harness, though, his confidence grew. At just a year old, Vanek was a promising sled dog. He had been named after Jerry Vanek, a long-time vet on the Yukon Quest race whom Frank liked and admired. No longer working for the Quest, Jerry would this year be joining the Muktuk support crew and lending his expertise to Saul.

Stanley and Livingstone were brothers. They were both pure white. To distinguish between them, one had to look at their ears; Livingstone's two ears were floppy, but Stanley had a right ear whose tip fell forward while the left one pointed straight to the sky. They may have looked almost identical but their personalities could scarcely have been more different. Stanley was an exuberant extrovert while Livingstone was sensible and serious.

While some of the dogs were named after people, many of their names ran in themes. There was a Terror, a Rascal, and a Mischief; there was a Duchess and a Lady; a Log and a Kindling. Some had human names: Albert, Alex and Andy, Sammy and Percy, Heidi, Natasha and

Sue. There were dogs with coffee appellations – Decaf, Java and Kahlua – and those with a musical motif: Beethoven, Schubert and Mozart. Jazz (now deceased) had given birth to an upbeat litter named Ella, Tango, T-Bone and Cooder. Others were named for local towns and lakes: Dawson, Pelly, Tok, Kusawa, Klukshu and Minto.

'You know Minto?' Frank laughed later over dinner. We were talking about the dogs' names that I had memorized so far. Minto, for some reason, had established herself early in my mind. She was a grey and white female of middling size with no outstanding physical characteristics but somehow her benign, friendly nature had imprinted itself in my brain. 'Who else do you know?'

I ran through a small list of names, ending with Albert. Albert was a huge dog with a teddy-bear face, black with tan patches over his eyes, and soft, stubby little ears.

'Ah, Albert.' Frank smiled fondly. 'The lights are on, but we're not quite sure if anyone's home.'

That evening, a friend of Frank and Anne's, Gina, had stopped by and had joined us for supper. She used to live locally but had moved away to warmer climes. She and her husband still kept a cabin in the Yukon, though, and they visited from time to time.

'I've decided,' she announced emphatically as we tucked into our food, 'I've got to get a toilet. Sitting in the outhouse this morning at twenty-eight below, I just decided – we're installing a toilet indoors.'

It wasn't just the call of nature that had forced Gina from her bed during the night. At one o'clock in the morning, she explained, she'd been so worried that her car might not start in the morning that she'd gone out to turn over the engine.

'Who would come and find me if I couldn't start the car?' she lamented. 'Nobody would know I was stuck there.' Her husband was out of the country at the time, doing community work in the rather warmer Ethiopia, and mobile phone receptors didn't stretch beyond the city limits of Whitehorse.

People lived differently here, I was learning. The simple task of driving into town was complicated by the need to warm up the car's engine before it would start. All vehicles in the far north came equipped with engine block heaters that plugged into an electrical source via a retractable cable that extended from beneath the bonnet. The heater warmed the oil, battery and other parts; without it, a car that had sat outdoors overnight would not start if the temperatures dropped really low. The problem was, the engine needed to be plugged in for a couple of hours before the car could be driven; at Muktuk, where the electricity came from a generator, the generator had to be warmed up for an hour before it could be turned on, so a short spin to the shops could involve half a day of forethought.

'Electricity is our greatest challenge out here,' Frank explained. The house was fitted with solar panels but still, keeping the generator batteries charged without pumping in more energy than they needed – which was both expensive and unnecessarily polluting to the atmosphere – was for him not just a daily, but almost an hourly concern.

'They don't turn the really large trucks off at all,' Frank told me. The bigger the engine, the longer it took to warm. 'They keep them running for two weeks at a time. They just keep filling them with gas and oil, but they never turn off the engine. If they do, they may never get it going again.'

'And we never fill our tyres to the recommended level here,' added Anne. 'The rubber gets so hard that, if the tyre was pumped really full, it would burst the first time you hit a rut on the road. We get what we call "square tyres" – in the morning, it takes a while for the flat bit that's been on the ground overnight to warm up.'

It wasn't until a couple of days later, though, that it became emphatically clear to me that while I was in the Yukon I should stick to the passenger seat. A journalist had come to Muktuk to interview Saul about the upcoming Quest. When she'd left, she'd had trouble negotiating her way up the steep, snowy driveway from the house to the main road.

'She just turned the key, put her foot on the gas, and expected it to go!' Fabienne exclaimed in astonishment while everyone around guffawed derisively.

6

Then the thermometer soared to two degrees above zero. What little snow there was began to melt and water cascaded from the higher pitch of the house's metal roof on to its lower level in heavy drops that resounded in chromatic tones like the hammering of a steel drum. The change in temperature from one day to the next seemed incredible: the mercury had leapt a full twenty-five degrees overnight. And now that my body had adjusted to the Yukon climate, two degrees felt like summer. I was surprised to find myself comfortable in the yard in just a couple of sweaters, with no hat or gloves.

The heat wave continued the following day. By afternoon the hoar frost and snow had melted entirely from the branches of the spruce that surrounded the yard, and I took the bigger puppies for a walk along the Takhini. There were six of them in two pens, divided by gender. In the boys' compartment were Justin, David, Sash and the younger Mozart; the girls were Katrina (named after the hurricane) and Shelby. In these two pens, Frank had constructed giant wooden circular contraptions like outsized hamster wheels in which the puppies could exercise when they weren't bombing across the Takhini.

The dogs raced off down the river. After about half an hour, I decided it was time to turn for home. I called the puppies and gave them each half a biscuit to encourage them to follow my change of direction. But when I had finished doling out snacks, I realized my right glove was missing. I'd taken it off before putting my hand in the biscuit bag, so had I dropped it? In which case, why wasn't it lying on the snow?

I retraced my steps, searching for my glove. The puppies bounded around me, bemused by my pacing up and down, and wondering if my strange behaviour might mean more biscuits for them. Then, just as I'd given up hope of ever seeing it again, David appeared from a bush high on the bank, glove in mouth, tail pumping. I clambered up the bank; David shot back into the bushes, then darted out again, skipping round in circles, always out of reach.

I stumbled after him. I blundered through some shrubs; I tripped and fell in the snow. My attempts to chase him were clearly failing – now I was out of breath, covered in bits of twig, and dripping with melting snow to boot. So I changed my tactics. I fixed David with my most displeased gaze and told him sternly, 'You are a very bad puppy.'

David looked crestfallen. Downcast, he dropped the glove at my feet just long enough for me to scoop it up. It was drenched in puppy drool and caked in half-chewed biscuit, but it was mine once more and for that I felt triumphant.

*   *   *

It wasn't just my authority over the puppies that was improving. As the days went by my other skills began to develop too. My first attempt at fitting a harness was shambolic: poor Sue stood outside her house with her legs through the wrong holes and the harness a convoluted tangle round her neck. But she was a patient creature and didn't stoop to so much as a doleful stare as we waited for Marty to come and sort out the mess. And then I harnessed Dawson and Tulina – both glorious fluffy white dogs – without a problem.

In preparation for an outing, the sleds would be secured by ropes to posts positioned along corridors in the yard. We'd harness the appointed dogs and, on colder days, fit booties on their feet. In lower temperatures, the snow was harder and ice would ball up in the dogs' paws, causing tiny cuts; to prevent these splits the dogs wore rectangular nylon pockets that slipped over their paws and were fastened around their wrists with Velcro straps.

We'd then walk each dog from its house to the sled, holding its collar in one hand. Usually this meant that the dogs hopped along on their back feet. Even on two legs, though, they were fantastically strong and would charge towards the sled in a sprightly waddle, or bound like kangaroos on speed, straining, forcing, rushing forward. Once hooked to the gangline – the neckline clipped to their collar and a rear tugline attached to the end of the harness – the dogs were meant to keep the line tight. They didn't want to, of course. They preferred to double back and sniff their teammates, or trot across to greet the dogs in the houses next to the sled.

'Tight!' we'd yell at them, to little avail. Usually,

therefore, one person would hold the leaders in place while another would fetch the remaining dogs.

The hooked-up dogs would be desperate to start running. Impatiently, they'd skip up and down on their back legs. They'd clamour rumbustiously because the rope anchored to the post stopped them from leaving. The other dogs – those who weren't going out on that particular run – would by now be quite delirious as well, and would add their own frantic voices to the uproar. Amid the racket, there was a sense of urgency: the hooking up and exit from the yard were the most risky part of any run because the dogs became so tremendously excited. Left too long in this volatile state, they might start to fight.

The emotional impact of a hundred-odd dogs all working themselves into a frenzy was striking. Even after some weeks, when I'd hooked up many teams, I found it difficult to keep my own reaction apart. While I tried to remain outwardly calm I'd find that, inside, I'd become wound up and anxious as the terrific noise and tension engulfed me.

Finally, the teams would be ready. The mushers would be standing on the brake mat on the back of each sled. The guide, out front on a skidoo, would give a thumbs up. Each of those behind would reply with a thumbs up of their own to signal that they were ready. The skidoo would chug down the first stretch of the trail, the first musher in line would pull his tether free and his wildly barking dogs would suddenly fall silent as they attempted to charge out of the yard, their speed checked – hopefully – by the musher on the brake. Then the second musher would pull his rope; then the third. One by one their teams would fall silent. As the last sled headed towards the trail, we'd enjoy a few seconds of blissful, blessed peace. And then the dogs left behind would begin plaintively to howl.

Sometimes I joined the clients on their dogsledding escapades.

I went out with Stefan again, and a father and daughter from Maine. Emmie, the daughter, was only thirteen years old so I doubled up with her on one sled for her first outing. I started out on the runners while she took a ride inside the sled bag; after a while we swapped places.

'Be careful – I'm entrusting you with my daughter's welfare,' said the father, Jeff, as we prepared to leave.

'It's probably not a great idea,' I told him. 'I haven't yet managed to leave the yard without an upset.'

Yet again, I failed to follow the trail properly, but we none the less made it to the river intact. One of the dogs on our team, Sooner, didn't seem to much enjoy her outing, though. When finally we arrived back at the yard and I took off her booties, I noticed that her rear haunch was trembling and her tail stayed tucked between her legs. I pointed out to Stefan that she seemed miserable. I was worried that I might have done something to upset her.

'It's OK, she's always like that,' he said. 'She doesn't really like it. We are thinking of retiring her.'

A few days later, two more guests arrived: Bettina, a chemist from Germany in her early thirties, and Bruce, a 63-year-old cattle farmer from Australia. Together we mushed through the bush trails that wound through the woods above the house. Poplar trees grew among the spruce. With their branches bare of leaves, their trunks glimmered silver beneath the sun like spray-painted ornaments. This route only lasted an hour or so but it was a much more energetic outing than a jog down the flat river. We had to jump off the runners and run behind the sled up the hills. We had to steer round the swooping bends and tight corners by transferring our weight to the outer runner. Sometimes, to keep up the sled's momentum on a turn, we had to hop off and run, pushing the sled round the curve. And then, on the downhills, we needed to brake so that the line was kept tight and the sled didn't threaten to crash into the dogs.

The dogs seemed to enjoy themselves, too. That day I had just four: Dickens and DeeDee in the lead, then Dawson and Diesel. Dickens was a docile black male – a brother of Toby (who was still whimpering in the garage), Molly and the portly Maud. DeeDee had been in my team that chaotic day on the river but she didn't seem to hold it against me. She was an energetic grey, brown and white female who barked and whined with frustration each time we stopped. She had soft, floppy ears that lay almost flat on her head when she ran. Dawson's pure-white ears were the opposite: they were strong and pert. Diesel was a shy black and white female. Her antics at feeding time always made me laugh. She'd stand outside her house as I approached with the bucket, barking and growing increasingly excited as I drew closer. Then, as I arrived at her bowl, her nerve would desert her. She'd bolt into her house and hunker down. Sometimes I'd reach in to pet her and then, when I moved on, she'd poke her head out and look at me as if to say, 'Hmm, well, that wasn't too bad. You could keep it up if you liked.' Today, in the harness, though, her reticence seemed to have left her.

A few days later, however, Diesel did not perform so

well. I was out on the bush trails again with Sebastian. Sebastian went first, with Diesel in his team – but she just wouldn't run. Instead she repeatedly lay down in the snow and refused to move. Several times Sebastian stopped to pet and coax her, but to no avail. In my team were DeeDee and Dickens again, and this time I had Glacier and Percy at wheel. In the end, Sebastian decided to switch Diesel with Glacier and, now following Sebastian's sled, Diesel ran fine.

'She's done that to me lots of times,' Stefan agreed when Sebastian talked to him about it later. 'In the end I've just decided she doesn't like to be in the front team. She's a shy dog, and she prefers just to trot along at the back.'

Frank frequently explained that running dogs was about teamwork.

'These are highly social animals. They want to run in a team. Our job is to organize that team so that each dog performs as well as it can,' he explained to his clients week after week.

Some dogs like to lead, some prefer to run on the left or on the right. One dog might lead brilliantly in stormy weather, but be better in the middle of the pack when going up a hill.

'To get a great dog team, you have to experiment with different combinations in order to figure out the perfect mix,' Frank said. 'If they want to work for you, they're hugely powerful. If they don't, there's not a lot you can do.'

I soon took to the bush trails with Sebastian once more. He wanted to run some dogs who hadn't been out for a while: Kola who had an eye problem, Casper who had been in heat and Sammy who was bad-tempered towards the other dogs and so didn't go out with clients. I had Lady and DeeDee, Tucker and Trooper. As we left the yard Lady made for the river.

'Lady! Haw!' I shouted and she veered perfectly to the left. Seconds later, the whole team looked as if it were going to follow the drive round to that side.

'Gee,' I shouted, and they turned correctly.

Just for a moment, I felt that I was getting something right.

A couple of days later I took an extended route around the bush trails with Stefan. He proposed we took six dogs each.

'Wouldn't five be enough?' I asked in a voice full of cowardice.

'Why, how many did you take before?' he asked.

'Well, Sebastian and I took four each.'

Stefan paused thoughtfully before replying, 'Wouldn't that be a little bit boring?'

On the first few bends I mounted the banks and ran into trees.

'You're going too slow,' Stefan told me. 'You have to speed up as you go round a corner.'

I tried it and the momentum kept the sled in a perfect wide arc. Now, with a little tuition and the power of six dogs to pull me, I was flying along fabulously.

One afternoon, I went out with Frank and a group of Japanese who were taking the two-hour 'Takhini Express' trip down the river and back again. On these shorter trips, two people doubled up so that one person drove the dogs and a second rode in the sled basket.

I started off on the runners while a Japanese woman rode in the sled. I was determined that, this time, I'd take the correct path from the yard: I'd managed by now to steer properly on to the bush trails above the house but an error-free route to the river still eluded me.

My leaders were Ichabod and Klukshu; we left the yard as the last of three sleds. The first two took the wrong, short route round the corner and over the log. My dogs made as if to follow them. I stamped hard on the brake.

'Gee!' I shouted. The dogs looked round, confused.

'Gee!' I shouted again, and eased off the brake a little. The dogs nudged forward, straight on.

I stopped them again. 'Gee!' I hollered. Ichabod looked round and wagged his tail. I took my foot slightly off the brake once more. Again, they headed straight on.

'Gee!' I shouted, again. The Japanese woman turned round and looked at me as though I were mad.

'Gee!' I hollered in vain. In the end, we had been there too long. Frank and the others would be sitting waiting on the river, wondering what on earth could have happened to us in that short distance. And so I abandoned my hopes for perfection and took the short cut over the log.

'Oh, Ichabod, he doesn't know the commands,' Frank told me later. 'He's just young. I only put him in front because it's the only place he can't chew everything. And I put Klukshu alongside because he's the only one that'll put up with him.'

The temperatures by now had dropped and at last, one day, a fine film of snow once more started to fall. So tiny were the flakes that they seemed more like drizzly sleet, but, as the hours progressed and the snow continued, slowly the boot prints and paw marks that decorated the yard became blurred and then vanished. The light that day was low and greyish blue; the hills surrounding the kennels were enveloped in dark, heavy mist. Even the trees appeared to shiver. They had no snow to cover them after the recent days' thaw and their pale, spindly trunks were exposed now that their thick winter coats had melted.

The days progressed and the temperature fell further, to minus thirty, and then one morning the thermometer dipped almost to forty degrees below. Each time a door was opened from the house to the outside, a burst of swirling, smoky air rushed into the room as if it, like us, was desperately seeking refuge.

The sky was clear now. As I helped scoop poop in the yard, a sun dog glowed bright behind the black silhouettes of the spruce trees. A sun dog looks like a tranche of rainbow: it's formed by light shining through the ice crystals of a cloud. This one was vibrant in colour, a brilliant chromatic spray across the low blue light of the morning.

Now even the dogs were quiet and stayed huddled in their houses. We gave them more straw for warmth – Panda, deliriously happy at any chance for activity, excitedly pulled his new bedding straight back out on to the snow – and added extra oil to their evening feed to counter the fat they'd be burning to maintain their body temperature. But that was all they needed. It was incredible how well these animals adapted to the cold.

More surprisingly, I was starting to adapt as well. I'd been at Muktuk for about a fortnight when one morning I was astonished to find that my fingers no longer felt particularly uncomfortable when I helped to bootie the dogs. Booties generally have to be fitted with bare hands – it's hard to fix the Velcro bindings properly with gloves on – and in cold weather that can involve piercing pain, followed by numbness, and then an excruciating, nauseating agony as the fingers thaw. But, as time went on, my circulation seemed to have improved. My body's thermostat, meanwhile, had undergone a total transformation. My appetite had soared – I was eating second helpings every dinner time, and snacking on muffins, toast and croissants between meals – and, contrary to my tendency of a few weeks ago to feel the slightest chill, now I was working in the yard at thirty-something below and I was almost always warm.

Sometimes we worked indoors – each time the dogs came in from a run, we chained the used booties together by their Velcro straps and hung them in long lines to dry. They always smelt of sweat, as dogs perspire through their pads. Sometimes they were spattered with faeces.

'Always wash your hands after you've touched booties,' Sebastian instructed me earnestly.

In the garage we'd always be accompanied by a number of older dogs and, now, Toby, whose residence indoors had been prolonged. After a few days, his wrist had shown no sign of improvement so Frank had decided he should go to the vet. The vet had diagnosed a broken metacarpal and confined Toby's leg to a cast.

One day, leaving the garage to go into the main room of the house, I left my boots a little too close to Toby's spot by the stairs. A while later, Thomas came upstairs looking despondent.

'Polly, I have some bad news,' he said. I wondered what terrible calamity could have occurred. Thomas blushed.

'I'm afraid Toby has peed on your boots.'

7

By now, I was familiar with Muktuk's routine. The dogs had their breakfast at around eight o'clock in the morning. After that came human breakfast and then, theoretically at nine thirty, it was time for poop-scooping. This was usually followed by a coffee break and a mid-morning chat with Louise and Rocky. The boys would then tend to any other jobs that needed seeing to. One day, I attempted to help Sebastian and Thomas trim the fur on the dogs' paws. When the hair between their toes grows long, snow and ice stick to it and they're more likely to suffer from ice balls.

I was slow and largely inadequate. Each time I finished a dog, I looked up and found that Sebastian and Thomas had progressed six or eight animals ahead of me. The front paws were easy enough; the dogs didn't seem to mind those being trimmed. But the back feet were another matter.

'Don't hold the back leg straight out,' Sebastian told me. 'Hold it like this.' He turned his dog's foot towards its tail. But still my charges seemed to sniff a novice.

'Yes, well, some of them have ticklish feet. That's why they snatch them away,' Sebastian explained.

Terror wasn't ticklish at all. On the contrary, he was wonderfully placid. But Tok, who behaved impeccably while I trimmed his front paws, wriggled uncontrollably when I turned round to tackle his rear. Lady was less compliant still. She just lay on the ground with all four feet tucked under her and refused to move. And then, at last, I arrived at Sue. The same patient dog who had so stoically endured my first fumbling attempt to fit a harness, she just reclined on her back, stuck all four legs in the air, and allowed me to do as I pleased.

Each day around lunchtime, the dogs would have their horsemeat and water. Those who had been out on the trail would be given it when they came back. Then the evening feed of kibbles or fish was doled out at five thirty or six.

Some days, Saul and Thomas would leave on a long training run with the Quest dogs. Sometimes they'd leave in the morning or afternoon; other days they'd go after supper and travel through the night for several hours, camping on the trail before making their way home the following day.

On Sundays, everyone had a lie-in, the routine went back half an hour, and Frank would cook pancakes for breakfast. I'd arrive in the kitchen to find him in his working trousers and merino wool sweater, joyfully measuring ingredients while singing to his favourite tracks: Johnny Cash's 'Ring of Fire' or 'You Are My Sunshine.' He was fond of his music collection. Sometimes, when he was really in DJing mood, he'd pick out songs after dinner. The evening meal was prepared by Simon the cook, and Frank and Anne, their staff and the guests always ate together at the long table in the main room. Frank would dedicate tracks to each of the people present, then dance along like a man having a seizure. Rob, the guest from Texas who'd broken the no-sweating rule in the garage, had proceeded to overstretch himself on the sled and had hurt his back; he was given Bryan Adams's '18 Till I Die'. For me, after that chaotic day's mushing with Stefan and Fraser, Frank chose an appropriately British number: 'Help!' by the Beatles.

Louise would snooze on the floor, always in the same place by Frank's chair at the head of the table. Rocky would wander from person to person, greeting all and sundry and wagging her diminutive tail before taking up her place on the sofa. Sometimes Kato would deign to join us and watch proceedings from the comfort of the pink armchair.

The guests would ask Frank the same questions week after week. He was a masterly storyteller and would always manage to reply with an interest and vitality that suggested he'd never delivered such a spiel before. He'd come into dogsledding by accident, he'd tell them. When he'd moved to the Yukon thirty-odd years ago he'd lived in a cabin in the bush with a dog. Then he'd found a second dog to keep the first dog company. He then took in a third dog – it had been abused and was in need of a home. Little did he know when he did so that this third dog was pregnant. Along came a litter of puppies. And so, somewhat inadvertently, Frank found himself with a dog team. He didn't race his animals at first but used them to haul water and firewood.

And why had he moved to the Yukon at all? Well, he'd smile, soon after he'd graduated from university, he and a friend had decided to go on holiday. Frank wanted to go to Mexico. The friend wanted to go to the Yukon.

They tossed a coin and the friend won. Frank ended up enjoying his holiday rather more than he'd anticipated and stayed on.

He'd talk to his guests about canine behaviour.

'It's as if there are two parts to a dog's brain, the domestic part and the primitive, instinctive part,' he'd explain. 'The domestic part is the wonderful part – the loving, fun part. But when you trigger the primitive part, that's something else.'

Frank believed that the sound of a child's crying could spark aggressive behaviour in a dog. 'I'm convinced that, when you hear about those really terrible incidents with children, the child's crying has triggered the primitive part of the dog's brain. Their instinct, from hunting, is to kill as quickly as they can once they've caught an animal and it's vulnerable.'

Some evenings, Frank would play a video of the Yukon Quest, *The Lone Trail*. The house at Muktuk had no TV connection, but it did have a screen with video and DVD players attached. The film was made on the twentieth anniversary of the race, and Frank and his dogs are a major feature of the footage. He'd stand with the remote control, pausing the action here and there.

'That's Decaf,' he'd say as the dog's face appeared panting in close-up, and then he'd relate the background to each icy scene.

Sometimes, the footage would suddenly disappear and incomprehensible symbols would loom up on the black screen. A stricken look of horror would cross Frank's face.

'Oh shoot,' he'd say, jabbing at buttons in the vain hope that the movie might resume. It never did. Then, 'Sebastian!' Frank would shout in a panicky voice. And

Sebastian would appear from the garage, or from the computer in the annexe where he'd been reading his emails, press a couple of buttons, and the show would continue.

Occasionally, after dinner, Stefan, Sebastian and I would head out to the river for some exercise on our own two feet. Bundled up in long underwear, fleeces, balaclavas and hats, we'd jog along the trail. The surface of the river was speckled sporadically by tracks of deer and foxes, and the snow was cold, crisp and easy to grip in ordinary running shoes. Beneath us, the ice creaked and groaned. As we sweated, our hats and face-warmers froze in heavy white crystals, and our eyelashes became thick with icicles so that when we blinked they stuck together. One evening, a faint display of northern lights appeared above us. Pale triangular cones reached upwards while slight green ribbons smeared across the black evening sky. I was delighted to see them at last but this wasn't a robust show. I'd have to wait a little longer to see the full extravaganza.

Meanwhile, there was brisk action down in the garage. The Yukon Quest was now less than two weeks away and there was a lot more to entering this endeavour than selecting and training the dogs. The race would start on Saturday 11 February; nearly two weeks before, on Sunday 29 January, Saul had to deposit his drop bags. These sacks contained everything he would need at the checkpoints and to resupply his sled for the trail ahead, such as dog food (it's reckoned that a racing sled dog consumes around ten thousand calories a day), new booties, spare parts for the sled, and methyl hydrate for melting snow on the trail so that both he and the dogs would have water to drink between checkpoints. He'd carry the stove and other necessities on the sled throughout the race. It was vital Saul packed everything he'd need because, once the race had begun, competitors wouldn't be allowed to accept any outside help except during the mandatory 36-hour layover halfway through the race at Dawson. For many days, Saul, Fabienne and Thomas had been in the garage laboriously packing and labelling the drop bags while baby Myla slept obligingly in her carry seat.

The Yukon Quest was born in 1984. It was conceived in response to the increasing commercialization of the Iditarod – the more famous long-distance dogsled race that runs between Anchorage and Nome. The Quest's creators designed a course with just ten checkpoints as opposed to the Iditarod's twenty-five. With more than three hundred kilometres of frozen wilderness between some of them, competitors would be alone with their dogs for long stretches, day and night. They'd need an in-depth understanding of the wilfulness and wiles of this cold natural world if they were going to reach the finish line. The prize money would be smaller than that of the Iditarod; the number of entrants would be fewer – but this, said the Yukon Quest's initiators, would be the toughest dogsled race on earth.

Now aged twenty-five, Saul was entering his first Yukon Quest. Although he had never competed in the race before, the event had powerfully influenced his life. His father had entered every one of the twenty-two Yukon Quests since the race's inception. As Frank had predominantly raised Saul as a single parent (Anne was Frank's second wife; they'd met when Saul was a teenager), this meant that many hours of Saul's childhood had been spent riding in the sled basket during Frank's training runs, or following on a miniature sled of his own.

'I often tell people, "I grew up in Toronto, and Saul grew up in a dogsled," ' Frank used to say to his guests.

While all the Quest's competitors had compelling reasons for entering – the challenge, the camaraderie with their dogs, the joy they derived from being out on the trail with their team – Saul had an additional motivation. He wanted to see for himself why his father had dedicated twenty-two years – most of Saul's life – to running this race.

Saul's training had started back at the tail end of summer with twenty-three dogs. Slowly, as the months had progressed, he'd dropped the less able team members. Now he was running a squad of sixteen, all of whom would go in the truck to Fairbanks although only fourteen would finally be selected to start the race. Beyond choosing the members of his eventual team, Saul would need to organize his dogs in the most effective possible way. This would be no mean feat: those who understand numbers better than I do explained that he had 87,178,291,200 different ways of hooking up. (Even more mind-boggling, in the Iditarod, where teams of sixteen dogs cross the start line, a driver has more than twenty trillion combinations to choose from.)

The sixteen dogs left in Saul's squad were in fantastic shape and they were completing their training runs with encouraging times. With less than two weeks to go before the start, there was a sense of nervous anticipation running through the house.

I was looking forward to the race hugely, but I was slightly anxious too. My concerns weren't just for the agonies Saul would have to endure, but also for myself. We'd be on the road for many days. We'd snatch sleep only in the back of the truck; we'd sometimes sit at checkpoints through the night waiting for Saul's team to arrive. The Yukon Quest was a feat of great fortitude for the mushers but, from what I'd heard, the spectators were expected to suffer their own share of discomforts. I fervently hoped that I'd come through it smiling, and that lack of sleep and an erratic diet wouldn't lead to an embarrassing loss of good cheer.

Now, much of our dinner-time conversation centred on racing.

'When I'm racing, the most important thing for me is to have a happy dog team,' Frank explained as we ate our pancakes that Sunday morning of the bag drop. 'They may not be the fastest team, but if they cross the finish line with their tails wagging, looking as if they'd like to do the whole thing over again, then I know I've done it right.'

Twenty or thirty years ago, he went on, drivers used to use whips. They didn't generally strike the dogs (though, no doubt, there were one or two who did) but they believed that the noise of the whip cracking spurred the dogs to run. When the major races outlawed the use of whips, the old hands said the sport was finished. The dogs, they argued, wouldn't run. In fact, the opposite occurred. Without whips, the dogs ran better.

'Fear is not a good motivator,' Frank said. When he'd first started running dogs, he'd been determined not to race. He knew he had a competitive spirit and he didn't want that to interfere with his enjoyment of being outdoors with his dogs. When, at last, a friend persuaded him to enter a short race, he knew very little about scientific training methods. His sole aim was that he and his team should have a good time.

'By rights, I should have been coming in last,' he said. 'But I found I was beating some of those guys who took their training seriously.'

I asked him how a driver makes a large team pace itself in a long race. Obviously a musher wouldn't want his dogs to start too fast as that would both exhaust them and risk injury. But to use the brake pad for long stretches, I debated, would unnecessarily increase the dogs' burden.

A good team, Frank replied, would have covered sufficient mileage to know its own rhythm. Before the Quest of 1995, which Frank won in record time, his team was not raring to go at all. Frank was concerned: usually his dogs became greatly excited and attempted to rush off when he hooked them up, as I had seen. Now they seemed to have lost some of their drive.

'I was really worried there was something wrong with them,' he said. 'I rang a friend of mine who had a lot of experience racing dogs, and asked him what he thought the matter was. And he said, "That means they're ready."'

Over dinner, Saul and Fabienne talked grimly about a local musher whose dog had died on the trail after inhaling vomit.

'You have to stop *before* the dog pukes,' Frank insisted animatedly. 'You can see it coming. Just before it vomits it puts its head down and kind of—' He stood up to demonstrate, raising his shoulders, hunkering down his head, and doing a fair imitation of a dog heaving. 'When you see that, you've got to stop at once.'

Dog deaths are a controversial aspect of long-distance

racing. Occasionally, despite stringent veterinary checks, dogs simply drop dead on the trail. Usually a necropsy reveals that the fatality was caused by a pre-existing but undiagnosable condition in the heart or other organs. The fact of dog deaths raises the ire of animal rights activists, who claim them as evidence that mushing is cruel. (To put things in perspective, some of the animal rights internet discussion groups also complain that it's inhumane to make sled dogs sleep outdoors in the cold.) Realistically, though, very few dogs die in harness. More humans, apparently, die while cross-country skiing. And anyone who suspects the dogs to be running against their will need only visit a dog yard when a team is being hooked up to see their views deafeningly refuted.

In thirty years of driving dogs, Frank had had just one dog die in the harness and that wasn't during a race but in training. He told us the story now. He was running a very large team, and had taught his leaders to double back to him when he called. But on this occasion, as they turned towards him, the line went slack and caught round the neck of the wheel dog. And then the team took off. Frank managed to stop them but when he went to untangle the strangled dog he found she was already dead. And then the team bolted again, dragging Frank along the ground. As he was pulled, the snow hook hit him under the ribs.

'I was yelling at them to stop,' he said. 'Of course I shouldn't have been – that's completely the wrong thing to do. You've got to stay calm. But I was a long way from calm by then. I was hysterical.' He paused. 'It took me a long time to build up the confidence to run large teams after that.'

By now, I'd spent many hours among the dogs. I'd

heard Frank's stories from the trail, seen the video, and looked at the photos. But I still couldn't really figure out why anyone would want to push themselves through an endurance event of such magnitude.

'So what proportion of the time you're on the Quest trail do you really think you're enjoying yourself?' I asked him.

Frank grinned ruefully. 'You've got to get into the zone,' he said. 'If you get into the zone, everything is great. The booties go on easily, all the dogs eat, everything is wonderful. But if you're not in the zone, if you're continually fighting, then it can be horrible.'

The race vet check took place the following Saturday, one week prior to the start. All the dogs were required to be examined by a vet before they ran. Rookies had to attend an official vet check, either in Whitehorse or in Fairbanks, while veterans could use another approved veterinarian if they preferred. Saul had asked if I'd go along with him and Thomas to the Whitehorse vet check to help handle the dogs. I was delighted at the opportunity to see some of the Quest activity first hand.

There had been some worries in the previous couple of days that one or two of the other racing kennels had suffered an outbreak of kennel cough. Kennel cough is highly contagious. While it doesn't pose a severe health risk for pet dogs with low activity levels, it can be dangerous for an infected sled dog to run hard – and these dogs were going to run for 1,600 kilometres. Anne had spent most of the day before the vet check on the telephone seeking advice and tracking down vaccinations and, last night, Frank and Saul had inoculated all the Quest dogs against the disease. But the vaccine wouldn't take effect for several days. In the meantime, they didn't want the dogs to pick up airborne bacteria.

Luckily for Saul, he'd managed to secure the first slot of the day at the vet check and he hoped, this way, he'd be able to prevent his dogs from having contact with any potentially infected animals. He was determined to arrive as early as possible so as to be finished, ideally, before the next musher had even unloaded his squad.

Saul's appointment was at eight thirty a.m. At a little before seven thirty, we started to load the dogs into the truck. Most dog trailers consist of two rows of individual boxes, each of which is separately accessed from the outside. Muktuk's truck was different. It was a customized van inside which the dogs all travelled together: this arrangement was both warmer and more sociable for them. On either side of a central walkway, straw-covered bunks were fitted with cables and clips that allowed the animals to be secured in place by their collars. On the outside of the van, metal posts slotted out horizontally from all four corners. When the dogs needed to be staked out – for feeding during a journey, for example – these posts could be extended, two metal cables with clips would be stretched between the front and rear posts on either side of the van, and the dogs would be tethered to them so they flanked the truck like busby-bedecked sentries alongside a royal carriage. (The major difference, of course, is that royal sentries don't usually pee on their carriage's wheels.)

The Quest dogs were used to travelling; loading them was a speedy business and we arrived at the designated building in downtown Whitehorse in such good time that the place was still in darkness and we had to take a detour via Tim Hortons – Canada's answer to Starbucks – for coffee.

At eight fifteen, shortly after we'd arrived back with our hot drinks, a Quest official named Cathy made an appearance. We unloaded the dogs and staked them out on either side of the van. Soon the vets were ready and, one by one, we took the dogs to be checked.

The dogs were thrilled by the activity. Each time I came out of the door to collect a new participant, those who hadn't taken their turn yet burst into an excited hullabaloo, so eager were they to see what delights lay within those walls.

Once inside, their pleasure didn't cease. They jumped up to greet the officials and licked the faces of those vets squatting on the floor. Each exuberant animal was weighed so that the vets on the trail could check for weight loss if they were worried that any dog was looking too thin. Its pulse, respiration rate and rectal temperature were taken, and its feet, ears, mouth, and overall form were monitored. Saul talked with the medics about a couple of issues that were concerning him – Beethoven had a sore toe; Stanley was a bit thin – but there were no real problems. All the dogs that I took through were awarded full marks.

By the time we left, the narrow Whitehorse back street was choked with dog trucks, curious noses poking from their cubbyholes. These dogs were out-of-towners; they lived in remote spots close to the bush and trails. To their eyes, downtown Whitehorse must have seemed a strange and exciting metropolis.

*   *   *

We'd be leaving for Fairbanks three days later, on Tuesday. Before that, though, we had time for a spot of ice fishing.

I headed out to Fox Lake with Stefan, two guests from California, and Bruce the Australian cattleman. We stopped at the petrol station en route to buy fishing licences, then drove on to our destination.

Stefan had started fishing at the age of four and during the intervening years he seemed to have acquired something of a knack for the sport. Last time he'd come fishing at Fox Lake, he'd recorded on his GPS the spot where he'd been most successful. Now we strode out over the frozen surface to the same location and, laboriously, with a hand-cranked auger, Stefan drilled a hole through the ice. The layer was thick and it was a while before a surge of frigid water gushed up through the saucer-sized opening.

'Ah, my knife!' Stefan smiled just as he'd finished drilling. 'I was looking for that this morning.'

The fish knife lay under a light covering of snow, just a few centimetres from the hole. Stefan must have unknowingly dropped it there on his last visit and the GPS had been impressively accurate in bringing us back to exactly the same place.

I settled in a chair by this first hole. Stefan showed me how to let the line run to the bottom, then raise it about half a metre, and then to jig gently up and down, up and down, up and down. Then he went off to help the others drill their holes.

'You should have caught something in this spot by now,' he said when he returned a short while later.

'Well, maybe the line is feeling a bit heavier – I don't really know,' I said.

Stefan took the rod, hauled up the line, and there on the hook was our first fish, a small but perfectly coloured lake trout.

We each sat by our holes and jigged some more. Sporadic clunking, glugging noises emanated from the black depths. It was a warm day – the thermometer recorded a mere minus two – and every now and then the sun broke through the clouds. The fine snow on the surface of the ice had been contoured by the elements into ranges of flat peaks and shallow craters so that it looked like a moonscape on a miniature scale. In the far distance, mountains, blue-hued beneath the cloud, encircled this vast marble tablet.

We continued to jig. Up and down. Up and down. Half an hour or more passed before I heard rustling movements behind me: over at his hole, Stefan had caught another trout. More time passed. We jigged, then paused and drank hot chocolate. We jigged some more. We ate our sandwiches. Stefan moved over to Bruce's hole – and within minutes was hauling another trout from the lake.

'I reckon this hole's all finished,' drawled Tom, one of the Californians. So Stefan went to investigate, and soon had hooked a fourth.

8

We left for Fairbanks at half past seven on the Tuesday evening. The thousand-kilometre journey would take us around twelve hours, including food and comfort breaks for the dogs. The plan was to drive for five hours to Beaver Creek, a tiny community of about a hundred people just a couple of kilometres from the border crossing to Alaska. We'd grab a few hours' sleep at the Beaver Creek roadhouse, then we'd leave early the following morning and complete the journey to Fairbanks.

'The most important thing you can do at this stage is rest,' Frank instructed Saul.

The moon was almost full that night as we cruised west along the Alaska Highway to Haines Junction and then up along the edge of the Kluane National Park. It blazed lucent white behind a thin gauze of cloud and lit the mountains so that their monumental forms loomed around us like angular white skyscrapers.

The road, too, was white with ice and fine, floury snow. Sometimes an hour would elapse without our seeing another vehicle; then two gigantic transport trucks decked out in glaring yellow lights might drive by within ten minutes. As we passed, their tyres threw up the powder in a great billowing brume so that for a few seconds we were blinded by the swirling whiteness.

I was travelling in the dog truck with Saul and Thomas. We stopped once for the dogs to pee, then continued to Beaver Creek where we met up with Frank, who was driving with Bruce in a separate vehicle. The people at the motel gave us a warm welcome – they were one of Muktuk's sponsors for the Yukon Quest and Frank and Saul had stayed there many times – and gave us a large family room to sleep in.

We fed the dogs, tucked them up in the truck for the night, and turned in ourselves at about one thirty a.m.

The plan was to get up at six thirty, but at six fifteen Frank's animated voice cut into our dreams.

'Come on, let's go everybody! Let's go Saul, let's go Thomas, let's go Bruce, let's go Polly!'

We rolled from our beds as politely as we could manage. Only Saul stayed put.

'It all starts here, Saul,' hollered Frank excitedly a few minutes later. 'During the race, you'll have to get up straight away. There'll be no "five more minutes" on the trail! You've got to get up right away and just wait for your second wind.'

'Yesterday you were saying the most important thing at this point was rest,' Saul argued groggily from beneath the duvet. 'Now it's all "the race starts here".' A sly grin crossed his face before he added, 'Come on. Admit it. You couldn't sleep so you decided everyone else had to wake up too.'

We dressed, dropped the dogs once more and fed them breakfast. Then we ate ourselves – plates of steaming eggs and bacon with mugs of coffee – before driving the few minutes to the American border.

'Oh, God, this woman's horrible,' groaned Saul as we drove up and he saw the official on duty. She was an unsmiling character with blond hair scraped back tightly so that not a single deviant lock could slip through.

Saul handed our passports through his open window. The woman peered intently into the truck, and glared at us. She flicked through our documents.

'Where's the green card that should be in here?' she barked at Thomas.

There was a brief, worried silence.

'Um . . . It had expired, so I took it out,' he replied.

A moment of frozen stillness passed; then the woman unleashed a blizzard.

'You took it out?' she choked. She stared at Thomas with a blend of incredulity and loathing. 'You *took it out*?' The way she said it, you'd think Thomas had told her he'd cut out his grandmother's tongue.

'Yes,' said Thomas. 'I didn't think I needed it.'

The woman was briefly silent; then, to our surprise, she changed tack.

'You got any firearms?' she volleyed.

'No.'

'Any alcohol?'

'No.'

'Cash over the value of ten thousand dollars?'

'No.'

'Any pets?'

We stalled, astonished at the absurdity of the question. We were, after all, in a vehicle emblazoned with pictures of dogs and the words 'Muktuk Kennels' – and dog trucks travelled along this road with sufficient frequency for the border guards not to need to look inside to know one.

'Just what's in the back,' Saul replied with admirable restraint.

'Huh. How many have you got there?'

'Sixteen.'

'Huh,' she pronounced again. 'Well, you – ' she jabbed a finger at me ' – you need to come inside and complete some paperwork. And *you* – ' she glared at Thomas with an expression that most people reserve for confrontations with those accused of the murder of their close family members ' – you're gonna come in and answer a whole lot of questions.'

We were inside for some time. Again and again, she recited to Thomas her hectoring mantra: 'You're not coming in.' Yet still she demanded to know details of his financial situation, the amount of credit remaining on his credit cards; she recorded his hair and eye colour. It seemed a futile exercise given that she was, in any case, turning him away. A cynical soul might imagine this style of interrogation was designed simply to humiliate him.

Finally she finished compiling her report and turned back to Thomas.

'Either you can sign this,' she told him, 'to confirm that you were refused entry because your visa was out of order and because you didn't have enough cash, or we can say that you tried to enter the country illegally as an immigrant – which you *did* – and that's going to give you a whole lot of trouble down the line.'

It seemed an extraordinary choice. Thomas's English was far from perfect and, by now, he was upset and confused. It seemed as though this desperately aggressive woman was taking advantage of the fact that English wasn't his first language. She appeared to be enjoying the opportunity to bandy threats that sounded intimidating, but were entirely irrelevant to the present situation. After all, he had in no way tried to enter the country as an immigrant. His mistake had been to remove a small green piece of paper – that he supposed long expired – from his passport. It was the stub of the visa waiver form that had been stapled there the last time he'd entered the United States; he hadn't known it was necessary for this journey.

Fortunately, he did know where the bit of paper was, as Thomas, Sebastian and Fabienne had discussed this very same remnant just the day before. Fabienne, who was also Swiss, had told Thomas that the visa waiver stub should no longer be in his passport: she'd once had trouble at the border because it hadn't been removed. She therefore suggested he should take it out. Sebastian had voiced the opinion that removing it didn't sound like a good idea. In the end, Thomas had taken the stub out and given it to Sebastian. It was unlikely, given Sebastian's premonition, that he would have thrown it away before Thomas was safely over the border.

We established that, if Thomas were reunited with the green scrap of paper, he would be allowed into the hallowed land. We agreed that he needed to sign the report. I asked the woman about the cash issue: if having insufficient money was one of the reasons for refusing him entry, should he bring a larger quantity with him when he returned to the border? No, she said. It didn't matter how much money he had. Why then, I wondered, had she raised the matter at all?

Finally, she allowed us to leave. We climbed back in

the truck, swung round and returned to Beaver Creek. We were seething with fury and emotion. Saul and Thomas had been training together for months. On Saturday the race would start. It would be the apogee of all their work – and it looked as if Thomas might not be there. Certainly if Thomas's paperwork was out of order, the official had the right to refuse him entry, but her manner had been vicious.

Back at the roadhouse, Saul phoned Anne. She found Sebastian; he still had the paper stub. She would find a way to get it to Beaver Creek. The kindly owners gave Thomas a room in which to wait out his banishment. Finally, Saul and I returned to the truck and, cross and weary, we at last entered the United States of America.

Saul and I drove for a few more kilometres before we spotted Frank and Bruce heading towards us. They'd crossed the border ahead of us and had been waiting in Tok, 150 kilometres away, where we were supposed to meet at Fast Eddy's restaurant. When we hadn't arrived they'd started to worry and, in this land of no mobile phones, eventually they'd had no choice but to come back to find us.

Both vehicles stopped in the road, and Saul and Frank wound down their windows.

'They turned Thomas back,' Saul said tersely.

'Turned him back?' Frank looked astonished.

'He didn't have some bit of paper. We've left him at Beaver Creek.'

We proceeded to Tok. We were all feeling tense; although a couple of hours had now passed, I was still feeling shaken by our border upset. The official's manner had been so offensive, and had left me so distressed, that I felt almost as though I'd been physically assaulted.

We opened the back of the truck to drop the dogs. They had no idea what had happened. They jumped to their feet and wagged their tails in greeting. Closest to the door, Mischief craned his grinning head through the opening, delighted to see human faces. It was comforting, after a dreadful morning, to be reunited with these perpetually chipper creatures.

'You're special dogs,' Frank told them, petting them fondly as he staked them out. 'You're not like all those other dogs back at home. You guys are the special ones.'

We went into the restaurant and ordered food from a waitress so hospitable it seemed impossible she was of the same species as the border guard, let alone the same nationality. Frank and Saul spoke on the phone to Anne. There were two Mexican guests arriving the following day in Whitehorse who would be coming to Fairbanks to see the start of the Quest. Anne had been planning to send them on a bus but now, with the complication of Thomas's rejection at the border, she was trying to make new arrangements. She'd call Colin, who had been a guide at Muktuk the previous year, and ask him to drive them to Alaska. That way, they'd be able to bring the wretched bit of green paper and pick Thomas up en route.

In contrast to our mood, the scenery that surrounded the road as we pressed on towards Fairbanks was idyllic. The weather was dazzling and the sky glowed deep blue over the forests of snow-covered spruce. We crossed streams and rivers, frozen and white. One waterway traversed a windy spot: gusts had blown the snow from the surface so that its icy mirror was left clear to reflect the sky in a shifting medley of turquoise. Beyond the motionless water the mountains of the Alaska Range rose jagged and bluish white. We rocked as gently as we could over the heaves where permafrost had rucked up the road: when the layer above the permanently frozen ground thaws and refreezes, it causes the tarmac to swell and shift, Saul explained. It's a headache for construction engineers in the north, and it's uncomfortable for commuting canines as well.

9

'I'm deaf too,' Bruce hollered across the workshop to Ray.

'*What?*' bawled Ray.

'I said, I'M DEAF TOO!' bellowed Bruce.

'Aw,' said Ray, then shouted, '*Too much gunfire!*'

'Yes, that was my problem too,' yelled Bruce. 'But in my case it wasn't the war. *It was from too many years shooting kangaroos.*'

We were in Ray Mackler's workshop just outside Fairbanks. Ray and his wife Val were close friends of Frank's. Ray had built Frank's racing sleds for most of the last twenty-two years and Frank had called in the morning following our arrival to ask him to make some last-minute adjustments to the one Saul was using; Bruce and I had gone along for the ride. Ray was in his mid-eighties, had just had a knee replacement operation, and was very hard of hearing.

His wife, Val, was also around eighty years old but a great character and still going strong. The house was full of ageing dogs including one enormous Mackenzie husky called Shilo that Val had recently saved from the pound and was looking to find a home for.

Saul's sled had a split in one of its runners and was suffering from a general lopsidedness. Ray reckoned it would take him a while to put it right, so we left him to it and made our way into town. There was to be a handlers' meeting at noon. Thomas should have attended but, more than twenty-four hours after being turned back at the border, he was still waiting out his exile at the motel at Beaver Creek; Colin and the Mexican guests would collect him at about midnight and they'd be in Fairbanks by morning. Frank therefore went to the handlers' meeting in Thomas's place, with Bruce and me as hangers on.

We crowded into a meeting room at the Westmark Hotel and sat at tables with cloths laid out in three sides of a square, as if for a corporate presentation. But this lot, in their outdoor boots and clothing coated in dog hair, were a very different bunch from the power-suited brigade. Frank smiled good-naturedly through the jovial joshing that his demotion from famous musher to substitute handler provoked, and collected his rake with good grace: one of the handlers' duties was to clear up the straw left behind by the mushers where they had staked out their dogs at the checkpoints.

'Only one handler from each team can be in the holding area at a time,' pronounced Mike McCowan, the race marshal. He was a burly, ruddy-faced American you wouldn't want to argue with. He always wore the same green and white polka-dot hat. That handler, he went on, was to help lead the team into its allotted place when it arrived and clear up after it had left – but was not allowed to offer any additional assistance at the checkpoints. Handlers could not help to feed or care for the dogs as the driver was supposed to be self-sufficient.

They could stand to the rear of the team, or at the front of the team, but they could not walk up and down. And they must not, under any circumstances, touch a dog as this would constitute outside help to the musher.

'The hardest thing for you guys is going to be that, at some point, a dog is going to look up at you and go ...' McCowan did a fair imitation of a winsome dog pleading for attention. 'And you must not touch that dog.'

The meeting ended. The handlers wandered off with their shiny new rakes and the race officials geared up for their next appointment. It was a day full of meetings for them. The mushers had to be briefed; the vets needed to convene; the media must be given their instructions. The Westmark Hotel was overrun with dogsledding types, most of whom knew each other. The mushing world was a small fraternity and many of these people were years-old friends. The lobbies and corridors of the hotel had the atmosphere of a reunion as drivers, vets and handlers from across the north stood around in groups and caught up with each other's news while hectic officials scurried around them.

I was to attend the media meeting at four o'clock so I had a few hours to kill. Frank, Saul and Bruce had headed back to the cabin where we were staying, which belonged to a friend of Saul's named Jewel. Jewel had moved to Alaska eight months previously; she had bought the cabin a month ago but had not moved in properly yet. She was in the process of setting up her own dog team and her yard was filled with brand new, gratifyingly empty dog houses. When we'd arrived the previous day, the dogs had been delighted to see their accommodation and had duly peed all over it. Jewel had been at work in her office in town at the time – she

111

worked in the Endangered Species Branch of the U.S. Fish and Wildlife Service – but we'd found the key, as instructed, under the bear skull on the porch. The cabin was half an hour's drive from town, though. It was too much trouble to go back and then return so soon, so I spent the early afternoon wandering the streets of Fairbanks in search of what delights they harboured.

Fairbanks was founded by accident. On 26 August 1901 a trader named E. T. Barnette was steaming up the Tanana River with his wife, Isabel, and four companions towards Tanacross, where the trail that snaked across the Alaskan interior met the waterway. They were hoping to set up a trading post there. But the Tanana was a fickle river and the sternwheeler's captain, Charles Adams, found himself in unexpected shallows. Weaving through the river's channels, looking for a wider body of water, the captain mistakenly digressed into the increasingly impassable Chena River. The water was too low for them to go further and it was already late August. Adams realized he could never reach his destination before the winter set in. Tanacross was still hundreds of kilometres away and within weeks the swarms of mosquitoes would perish and the piercing temperatures of winter would turn the river to ice. And so the frustrated captain dumped Barnette, his weeping wife, and their entire twenty thousand dollars' worth of cargo on the banks of the Chena. He dropped them at the point where First Avenue now meets Cushman Street – at the exact spot where the Yukon Quest would start in less than two days' time.

The Barnettes and company soon found they weren't alone, however. Hapless gold-mining hopefuls Felix

Pedro and Tom Gilmore were camping in the hills above the valley. They had once found a rich stream packed with gold, but unfortunately they couldn't remember where it was. When they saw the smoke of the steamer they ran delightedly down to the encampment, joyful at the chance to buy supplies that would enhance their diet of moose and berries, and to break the tedium of searching for the gold that they knew was there, somewhere.

Barnette intended to sit out the winter there on the banks of the Chena and to move on to Tanacross the following spring. But just as he was preparing to leave in July 1902, Pedro and Gilmore rushed ecstatically into his camp once more: they had found gold! It wasn't a great strike, but Barnette saw his opportunity. He laid out a ten-acre trading site and dispatched his cook by dogsled to Dawson – along the same trail that now served the Yukon Quest – to spread not only the word, but wild exaggerations of it. Such was the feverish enthusiasm of the times that newcomers soon poured into the new town (and, happily, found some more gold as well).

Barnette prospered, adding a number of enterprises to his trading post including the Washington-Alaska bank. The territory's judge, James Wickersham, loaded his records on to a dogsled and moved his base to the town, having struck a deal with Barnette: he agreed to come if the town could be named for his congressional ally, Senator Charles Fairbanks of Indiana. The town grew and flourished. And then, in 1911, the Washington-Alaska bank unexpectedly collapsed and its customers' life savings vanished. Barnette and Isabel disappeared from town. Barnette was tried the following year for embezzlement, but he was found guilty only of

113

misreporting the bank's financial condition. The people of Fairbanks never bought the story, though. Many continued to insist that he'd stolen their money and that he and Isabel were living out their days sipping margaritas in Mexico. In reality, Barnette fell down some stairs in Los Angeles in 1933, broke his neck, and died.

I walked around central Fairbanks where the colourful E. T. Barnette had first established his trading post. The place seemed to have grown in size but diminished in vibrancy since those early prospecting days. There were no very interesting shops or points of cultural interest beyond the ice sculpture museum. Then I realized that the few other people in the street were laughing at me. They'd look straight at me – and chuckle. It didn't just happen once; I noticed it several times. I could only assume that it had something to do with my clothing. I was horribly overdressed. The weather was mild at minus six, but all I had was a huge parka and it was easier to wear it than to carry it. Maybe these people didn't have much else to laugh about through their long cold winter.

I went to the visitor centre. A solitary tourist was in there looking at brochures. He was a fireman from New York.

'What on earth made you want to come *here* in February?' asked the astonished visitor centre staff.

'Well,' said the fireman, 'I'd never been here, and I had a few days spare, and I was interested in coming to take a look.'

The visitor centre staff gawped. I couldn't help thinking that if even they were surprised at seeing a visitor in Fairbanks, it didn't bode well for the place.

From the visitor centre, I headed out to find a grocery store. I had many hours on the road ahead of me and I thought I'd buy some fruit and maybe some good tea bags. I wandered for a while, up and down those same few streets, but I couldn't find anywhere selling food. In the end, I went into another shop and asked.

'A grocery store?' The girl behind the counter looked perplexed. 'Well, I don't know. I'll have to go and ask directions.'

The phone rang in Jewel's cabin at about six a.m. the following morning. There were six of us staying there including the baby – Fabienne had arrived by plane with Myla the day before – and we were ranged on the floor in our sleeping bags. Frank answered the phone. It was Colin: he, Thomas and the Mexican guests, Hector and Malena, had arrived safely in Fairbanks. They were at Hector and Malena's hotel. Colin and Thomas would grab a couple of hours' sleep there, then come out to the cabin. A different border guard had been on duty; he hadn't even asked for Thomas's green paper.

'Oh, and tell Thomas the police want to speak to him. He'd better call the station,' added Frank, jokingly, at the end of the conversation.

He climbed back into his sleeping bag and was just falling asleep again when the phone rang once more. This time it was an officer from Fairbanks police station.

'Is that Frank Turner?' she asked. 'I have a Thomas Arnold on the line. He says you told him to ring but I can't quite work out what he wants.'

For once, Frank's repartee had misfired. In their sleep-deprived, over-anxious state, Colin and Thomas had failed to realize that he'd been teasing. Frank apologized profusely to the police officer who, fortunately, was possessed of a greater sense of benevolence than the border guard had been.

We spent a quiet day at the cabin preparing for the race. Jerry Vanek, the vet for whom Vanek the dog had been named, drove out to join us.

Colin and I brought the dogs in from the yard one by one so that Jerry could look at them, while Frank, Thomas and Bruce ran errands elsewhere. We walked the dogs from their houses on leashes – Saul didn't want them hopping the distance from the yard to the house on just their rear legs – and I found that, what with the snow, the ice, and the immense strength and excitement of the larger male dogs, I was unable to move with anything approaching control. I was terrified that, stumbling and being dragged as I was, I'd slip and stamp on the toe of one of these canine athletes the day before the big race. In the end, I suggested that my dog-handling abilities weren't up to the task and swapped roles with Fabienne. She dealt with the dogs while I took the rather easier job of holding the baby. Given the strength of just one of these animals, I was quietly relieved that I wasn't the one intending to drive fourteen of them through the start chute the following morning.

10

Frank had cooked omelettes for breakfast but my stomach was so knotted with nerves that I had difficulty eating. And all I had to do was watch.

'So are you taking Beethoven or Sakura?' Frank asked Saul. The night before, this final decision still hadn't been made.

'Beethoven,' said Saul, a little grimly. He seemed to be struggling with his breakfast, too. Beethoven was the stronger dog, but he'd had some trouble with a toenail and he'd missed a number of training runs. Now, at last, Saul reckoned his paw had healed sufficiently for him to complete the course.

We finished our food as best we could, cleared up, and drove to a large parking lot on the banks of the Chena River. All of us except for Saul would be back in the cabin in a few hours' time – the first dog drop and checkpoint were relatively close by, so we wouldn't need to pack up our gear for the road until the following day.

It was a clear day with mild temperatures but when we arrived in downtown Fairbanks at nine o'clock, two hours before the start of the race, the sun had yet to rise high in the sky. In the pale lilac-blue morning light, mushers and handlers were busy organizing ganglines and sleds, now packed with gear and adorned with each team's race number and the logos of the sponsors. Officials were checking the drivers' mandatory items – a cold-weather sleeping bag, an axe, snow shoes, spare booties and veterinary records. Vets were clearing up last-minute queries. Television crews were lumbering around with their hefty gear conducting interviews. Alongside the vans, dogs were tethered, then harnessed and shod.

With all the activity, it seemed that just moments had passed before it was time to hook up the dogs. Saul and Thomas jogged with each animal the short distance from the truck to its place on the gangline and clipped its neckline and tugline in place. The dogs were excited now. Stanley was particularly exuberant. Again and again he leapt high in the air, barking with jubilant anticipation, a grinning rictus spread across his face, his tongue lolling long with the pleasure of it all. His antics were a delight to watch. All these dogs had run long-distance races in the past; many of them had run the Quest itself several times. They had a good idea what was in store. Yet, far from feeling morose at the prospect of the long trail ahead, they appeared to rejoice in it. They were exhilarated and full of relish. As they pumped their tails and jumped in their harnesses, it was clear they couldn't wait to start.

The teams were to leave the start chute at two-minute intervals; Saul was wearing bib number five. The time differences would be adjusted at Dawson, where all teams had to rest for thirty-six hours, so that in the second half of the race they'd be racing to the same clock.

Just before eleven o'clock, the first team made its way to that spot on the river where, 105 years earlier, Captain Adams had dumped E. T. Barnette, his distraught wife and their entourage on the mosquito-plagued banks. A few minutes later, Saul and his dogs followed.

Until it was time for them to cross the start line under the Cushman Street Bridge, each team was anchored to a snow machine that thrummed at a slow, controlled chug behind the sled. Additionally, the supporters – in Saul's case Thomas, Frank, Jerry, Colin and Jewel – trotted alongside holding leashes to keep the dogs in order. The countdown began; the leashes were unhooked; the team took its position; the rope attached to the snow machine was released – and at last, after months of preparation and thousands of dollars of expenditure, a slightly tense Saul and his utterly joyful dogs hurtled in a blur across the start.

The dogs were eager to get going, and we had no time to lose ourselves. The first dog drop on the course was at North Pole. It was about fifty kilometres away by the race trail and the teams would take only a few hours to arrive there. North Pole was not a checkpoint: mushers were not required to register there. But if they had any early problems with their dogs, this was a place where they could leave them. Vets would be on hand to care for them and their handlers could collect them and return them to the straw-filled sanctuary of their trucks. Once a dog had been dropped from a team, though, it could not be reinstated or replaced with another animal for the duration of the race. The rest of the team would have to continue under reduced power.

North Pole makes the best of its name. The appellation

119

was the brainchild of the Dahl and Gaske Development Company which bought an area of land there in 1952. Having sold off the property in lots, Dahl and Gaske came up with a money-making masterplan: they'd change the name of the existing settlement to North Pole and thereby attract a major toy manufacturer who, they thought, would be so thrilled at being able to stamp its product with the words 'Made in North Pole' that the inconveniences of operating through sub-Arctic winters thousands of kilometres from home would be as nothing.

The toy factory never came. But still, the festive folk of North Pole have tried their hardest to give their town a year-round holiday feel. There are streets named Santa Claus Lane, Snowman Lane, Kris Kringle and Saint Nicholas Drive. There's even a Santa Claus House – it's Santa's official home apparently, and he receives more than a hundred thousand letters there each Christmas. In a show of goodwill, the U.S. Postal Service even delivers letters to Santa that have no stamp.

Thomas, Jerry and I made our way in the dog truck along the highway and into the town. We passed a gaudy building from whose yard beamed a giant plastic Santa. It seemed almost eerie. Here we were in the middle of Alaska, in February. We had, until that moment, all been quietly relieved that Christmas was a whole ten months away. Imagine living here in North Pole, and being faced with beaming Santas and ho ho hos every day of the year.

'People travel here to North Pole just so they can post their Christmas cards and have them stamped with the name of the town,' Jerry cheerfully informed us.

'God help them,' I muttered.

We parked a five-minute walk from the trail – it's vital during the race that the dog truck is out of sight and smell of the dogs – and strolled down to the river, whose course the race followed for its first section.

It was beautiful weather – for humans. The sky was clear, the sun was shining, and the temperatures had crept a fraction above zero. For the dogs, though, it was a different matter. Running in this heat, they'd be too warm.

Basking on the riverbank, we watched the first mushers come through. The teams had only been in action for a little over three hours but already there had been considerable jostling for position. First through North Pole was the second driver to leave Fairbanks. Hans Gatt was a 47-year-old Austrian now living in Canada; he won the Quest for three years running from 2002 to 2004. He passed through the dog drop without stopping. Fifteen minutes later came Eric Butcher, with bib number seven, and Lance Mackey, number six. Starting numbers eleven, Hugh Neff, and twelve, Paul Geoffrion, followed just a couple of minutes later. All of them trotted straight through, waving at the small group of cheering spectators. They had no problems yet.

With great anticipation, we waited for Saul. Two female mushers arrived almost neck and neck: Kyla Boivin, who'd grown up running dogs on her father's trapline and who, at the age of twenty-three, was making a comeback after an absence of two years following knee surgery; and Michelle Phillips, at whose kennels Stefan had worked the previous winter. A couple of minutes passed; then a trickle of teams appeared. But none of them was Saul.

Just before three o'clock, Saul appeared in his number five bib. He only had thirteen dogs in harness.

'I'm dropping a dog,' he said quietly as he drew to a halt. Journalists and photographers kicked into excited action; it was the first real event of the afternoon.

'This is why we're here!' a volunteer worker standing close to me called out with glee as he ran grinning towards the sled. I nobly resisted the temptation to trip him up.

Beethoven was sitting in the sled bag. He looked quite perky and altogether pleased to be the centre of such attention.

Saul looked less happy. He quietly completed the necessary documentation, passed Beethoven to Thomas, and went on his way.

'He wouldn't pull,' Thomas told us when he rejoined our group with Beethoven trotting cheerfully alongside. 'Saul says he just lay down in the snow and refused to run.' The vets had checked him over: there was nothing the matter with Beethoven's toe. He'd just missed too many training runs. He had lost fitness and mental strength and, in this warm weather, the desire to run had left him.

'Oh dear, Beethoven.' Frank smiled at the dog lovingly before loading him into the comfortable straw of the dog truck.

The first checkpoint of the trail was at Angel Creek. It would only take a couple of hours to drive there by road from Jewel's cabin which was on the same side of town. On the trail, however, Saul was expected to keep a conservative pace. He wouldn't arrive until eleven o'clock or so in the evening. We went back to the cabin, ate supper, and had a couple of hours' sleep before heading out.

Angel Creek is not a big place. In fact, the lodge that serves as the Quest checkpoint is its only major building.

The owner of the lodge was a tiny woman with a very large character.

'One year, I was just so tired, I put my head in my hands and drifted off at the table,' Frank told us. 'I'd just fallen asleep when—' He smacked his head with his palm. 'She just came up behind me and slapped me on the head!'

Jerry laughed ruefully. 'She did that to me too one year.'

It transpired that it is against the law to sleep in a bar in Alaska, and this woman took her duties seriously.

The lodge was a log cabin; the pelt and head of a black bear decorated one of the walls. I wondered whether the proprietress had whacked the bear on the head, too, thereby bringing about its demise. Neighbouring wall space was adorned with antlers and skins of other beasts long deceased.

The centre of the room was dominated by a huge, cylindrical, cast-iron stove. Square tables with red-and-white check plastic cloths filled the remainder of the middle of the room while, round the sides, more tables were flanked by mustard-coloured faux-leather banquettes. A group of locals sat and drank at the table next to ours. The women swigged beer and laughed raucously. They wore faded, baggy sweatshirts and jeans, and walked with a cowboy's swagger. Their hair was long and lank; their faces seemed raddled beyond their years.

The menu consisted of burgers, chicken nuggets, Budweiser, Labatts, Alaska Amber and Old Milwaukee. Side orders came small – a few onion rings whose onions may or may not have emerged from the ground this decade; a meagre smattering of weak, limp little fries.

On one wall, beyond a pool table, a white cardboard poster recorded in black felt-tip pen each musher's time out of Fairbanks and their times in and out of Angel Creek. Lance Mackey had come in first, at twenty-four minutes past eight. Mackey had something of a Lance Armstrong story about him: in 2001 he was diagnosed with cancer and went through extensive surgery and radiation treatment. He took time out to recover, then returned to the circuit and won the Yukon Quest in 2005. He came from impressive dog-racing lineage: his father, Dick Mackey, was one of the founders of the Iditarod, which he won in 1978. Lance's older brother, Rick, had kept the torch alight with an Iditarod win five years later and a Quest victory in 1997.

Just a minute behind Mackey was Kelley Griffin. Griffin was a Quest and Iditarod veteran but she was not expected to place high in the final rankings.

'She's going too fast,' said Frank as he examined the board. 'Most of them will camp on the trail on the way here. She's just run straight through.'

The question of when and where to rest is one of the major tactical issues in long-distance dogsled racing. At this early stage, it meant little who came in first, second and third. Competitors might camp just out of sight of the trail and, while the apparent leader was resting at the checkpoint, simply roll through, stopping only a few minutes for the formalities. Dogs could rest more peacefully out in the bush than they could amid the bustle of the checkpoint – though, at the checkpoints, there was straw to make them more comfortable in cold weather, mushers could take water from a tap rather than having to laboriously melt snow over a methyl hydrate stove, and hot meals were provided. At Angel Creek, however, mushers didn't have to battle against the temptation of a tasty burger: everyone had to stop for a minimum of two hours as there was a mandatory vet check.

We stood in the cold night under a full moon, a huddle of perhaps twenty or thirty handlers and spectators. For long periods, nothing happened at all. Then an official standing up on the trail would call, 'Team!' The anticipation would rise – who was coming? – but for a few moments we'd see nothing. A headlamp would appear, glinting feebly through the black. We'd hear the soft patter of paws on snow and, almost soundlessly, a sled would glide to a halt. Now we'd see which musher was driving. The team's handler would rush to take the leaders' neckline and run the dogs to their allotted parking place. Volunteers would grab the ganglines and run alongside. And then they'd be gone.

The dogs' work was now finished for a few hours, but the mushers enjoyed no such respite. Even those who were planning to stop here for more than the mandatory layover would enjoy little sleep. They had to fetch water for their dogs, examine and treat each animal's feet, go through the vet check, and eat themselves before they could retire for a couple of hours' rest. Then they had to tear themselves from their too-short slumber, feed their dogs and fit fifty-six booties if they still had a full team running. With all these tasks to be completed, a six-hour stop only allowed about two hours' sleep for the driver.

We stood and watched as the teams jogged in, then trotted to the resting area. Many of the front-runners would stay just three or four hours, preferring to rest on the trail: at this early stage in the race, when the teams were bunched close together, the checkpoint was a busy and crowded place. Saul was intending to stay six hours here, though, and get some sleep.

We waited some more. The temperatures were dropping now and even Thomas, with his incredible heat-generating body, began to feel the chill.

'I'm just going to run to the truck and get my hat,' he said at a little after eleven o'clock. He took off his handler's armband, which allowed him access to the holding area, and gave it to Fabienne on the off chance that Saul should pick the next two minutes to arrive. Thomas jogged just out of earshot and then, 'Team!' The shout went up, and Saul and his dogs appeared from the night.

'Here! Frank!' shouted Fabienne excitedly, waving the armband at him. She couldn't do much to help, after all – she had a newborn baby strapped to her chest.

'What? Where's Thomas?' Frank jabbered.

'He's gone to get his hat.'

'Oh! Quickly, put it on me,' Frank cried.

Hurried, fumbling hands fixed the armband in place and Frank rushed towards the team, but they'd started to move without him.

'Whoa! Whoa!' Frank shouted at the dogs.

From the back of the sled, Saul rocked with mirth.

'Hey, you gotta try and keep up!' he shouted at his veteran father as the small crowd of spectators erupted into laughter.

Frank returned to the lodge a short while later with a worried expression. Stanley had a sore wrist; Val had vomited on the trail, and Mischief had diarrhoea – though these last two ailments were probably due to the warm weather, and would soon right themselves. The dogs from Muktuk were larger than many other kennels' racing dogs. They were great at going up hills and they were fabulous in the cold but, when temperatures rose, they suffered.

Some time later, Saul arrived in the lodge, his tasks at last completed.

'Eat as soon as you can,' Frank instructed him. 'That way the food can work through your system and you can have a good shit before you leave. Otherwise you'll have to do it on the trail.'

I went back to the truck to have a couple of hours' sleep while Saul was resting. I climbed into the front and reclined the seat. The engine was running and the heating was on, so it was a comfortable refuge from the sub-zero night. I soon dropped off and my subconscious drifted into the strangest of nightmares. I dreamt that the truck's brakes failed as I slept. The vehicle rolled away, down a peculiarly English suburban close, and finally crashed into a small red-brick semi, knocked down the wall, and came to a halt in an unknown woman's kitchen. The woman was furious about the destruction to her property. She was just working herself into a terrible rage when: bang, thump, slam. I woke up. The noise that had pierced my dreams was not the collision of a dog truck with a semi-detached house. It was the opening and closing of the truck's doors. The rest of the crew were climbing in. Saul had just left. He was tired and discouraged, they said: Stanley's wrist had still been sore so he'd dropped him from the team. Now we had two dogs in the back of the truck. Saul's team was down to twelve. This had not been his plan for day one.

11

On either side of the Steese Highway overflow glistened. This water, forced up and over the sides of the streams' icy lids by pressure from beneath, was coloured the palest jade, then a glorious, translucent aquamarine tinged with orange from the iron deposits in the water. Once, we passed two towering stalagmites tinted green and pink. This was the water the miners used for sluicing that had fountained from the earth and frozen.

Again and again, we saw gold mines, out of use in the winter months when the ground was too stiff to work. Rusting machinery – JCBs and cranes – lay by the side of the road. They were probably long out of service but, here in the north, disposal was difficult and expensive.

We were driving now to Mile 101, the second dog drop of the trail. It's named for its distance along the Steese Highway from Fairbanks and lies just before the race's most fearsome peak, Eagle Summit. I was in the dog truck with Thomas and Jerry, Beethoven and Stanley; Frank was behind with Bruce, Hector and Malena in the pick-up. Fabienne and Myla had stayed in Fairbanks, this part of the route being deemed too difficult for a tiny baby. The winding road climbed high, giving long vistas through the trees over the snowy peaks of the White Mountains. These hills were gently rounded in shape, and speckled with spruce and birch. From a distance, the trees looked like tiny iron filings sprayed across a sheet of white paper, attracted by a magnet all to point the same way.

In places, the spruce was reduced to sparse, blackened sticks that soared into the sky with dry, twiggy claws for branches. At their feet, lithe green shrubs with plump needles sprouted. This was where the land had fallen victim to forest fires.

Wildfires are a big issue both in Alaska and in the Yukon. They're caused by lightning and by human error and, though fire is vital for the regeneration of forests, it poses a threat to human communities. In 1990, a fire raged for eight weeks around Tok, where we'd eaten at Fast Eddy's during our drive to Fairbanks. It burned four hundred square kilometres of forest. It was assumed that the town itself would perish, but as the flames reached its outskirts the wind changed and the settlement was saved.

Fire management authorities attempt to control wildfires; they tread a fine line between encouraging the rejuvenation of natural ecosystems and protecting human property, but sometimes the force of the flames overpowers them. Over the last decade, Alaskan fires had burned an average of nearly 17,500 square kilometres each year; that's to say, in ten years a total area considerably larger than the whole of England, Wales and Northern Ireland put together. In 2004, the worst year on record, 26,400 square kilometres were burned across the state of Alaska, plus more than 17,000 square kilometres in the Yukon – that's a total area larger than the whole country of Switzerland. That year, according to the National Center for Atmospheric Research, wildfires across Alaska and Canada generated more than 30 million tons of carbon monoxide, roughly equivalent to the total man-made emissions from the continental USA over the same time frame. The researchers also concluded that the fires may have raised ground-level ozone concentrations by as much as 25 per cent in the immediate area, and by 10 per cent as far away as Europe.

As we drove through the blackened forests, we passed every now and then sections of another environmentalists' talking point: the trans-Alaska pipeline. Permafrost dictates that more than half the pipeline is raised above the ground – if the pipes were buried, the warmth they generate would cause the ground to melt and shift. This pipeline carries oil 1,300 kilometres from Prudhoe Bay on the Arctic Ocean to its terminus at Port Valdez on the Gulf of Alaska. A massive silver tube, it slices through the length of the state in zigzags designed to allow for the metal's expansion and contraction in changing temperatures. It was built between 1973 and 1977 and it changed the face not just of the sliver of land it traverses, but of the whole of the forty-ninth state.

When the American government purchased Alaska from Russia in 1867, many Americans thought the transaction utterly absurd. Although William Seward, the Secretary of State at the time, had negotiated a price of just 7.2 million dollars – a mere two cents an acre – the new territory was scathingly derided as 'Seward's folly'. It was a terrifying place and few 'civilized' people would dream of going there. There was an Indian population, of course, and there were a few white traders who scraped a living from the area's valuable supplies of fur. But the north was in general seen as a harsh, unprofitable land.

That was before they found the oil.

Since the development of the Prudhoe Bay oil fields, royalties and taxes on oil revenue have generated more money than all other Alaskan industry combined. They constitute almost 90 per cent of Alaska's general fund income. Because Alaska's constitution dictates that mineral reserves belong to the people as a whole, all the money the state earns from oil is channelled back into public works and even directly into the Alaskans' bank accounts. Oil pays for the state's schools, roads and welfare. Oil means that Alaskan residents don't pay state sales or income tax. Additionally, each resident receives an annual payout from an oil-related investment vehicle called the Permanent Fund: a quarter of the state's income from oil is invested in stocks, bonds and real estate and a dividend given to everyone – including children – who's lived in the state for twelve months or more. In recent years, this has hovered around the thousand dollar mark having reached a peak in 1999 of $1,963. This dip in revenue is due in part to the reduced oil production at Prudhoe Bay. In 1988, almost two million barrels a day were being drilled; today the output is under a million.

Needless to say, the environmentalists and the oil giants don't agree on the effect of the oil industry on Alaskan wildlife. The pipeline was constructed with more than five hundred crossings for animals – places where the pipe is either buried or raised high above the ground – so as not to interrupt the migration routes of caribou herds. Oil industry experts point out that the population of the Central Arctic caribou herd has dramatically increased since the building of the pipeline; conservationists counter that this has nothing to do with the pipeline but is due to near-perfect natural breeding conditions in recent years.

Certainly, the welfare of Alaska's wildlife is carefully monitored. But one convincing argument from the environmental lobby is that, however rigorously the oil companies strive to maintain habitats, accidents sometimes happen. The case in point is the *Exxon Valdez* oil spill: in 1989 the tanker of that name struck Bligh Reef in Prince William Sound and spilled more than 42 million litres of crude oil. Although it was by no means the largest oil spill in the industry's history, it was probably the one with the most serious environmental impact. Because the area was so unspoiled, it was rich in wildlife – fish, birds, otters and seals. Because it was so remote, the clean-up response was slow. For the first few days very little action was taken and the contamination spread.

Subsequently Exxon instigated a massive clean-up operation costing a reported 2.1 billion dollars but, still, some wildlife groups have never recovered. The *Exxon Valdez* Oil Spill Trustee Council, which was created to oversee the environmental restoration with the money Exxon was required to pay in damages by the courts, estimates that several thousand sea otters died in the immediate aftermath of the spill and that the population continues to be diminished. Numbers of harbour seals, whose population was in decline before the spill, have fallen in affected areas by nearly 50 per cent. Populations of several bird species including the common loon, the pigeon guillemot, the cormorant and the harlequin duck, thousands of which died immediately after the spill, have never recovered. Perversely, of course, the spill pumped more money into Alaska's economy with thousands of workers involved in the clean-up operation over a number of years.

Now, there is a move to increase oil output by drilling further to the east. The proposed new site is highly controversial: it falls within the boundaries of the Arctic National Wildlife Refuge. The oil industry wants to drill on the coastal plain, on the Refuge's northern coast, which is an important calving ground for the Porcupine caribou herd.

The oil lobby argues that the Refuge is vast; that this area constitutes less than 8 per cent of its total; that wildlife and oil drilling can co-exist; that the quantities of oil extracted would be substantial. Conservationists counter that, unlike the Central Arctic herd, the Porcupine caribou have no place to go if they are displaced; that drilling would be likely to disrupt the herd's migration and therefore its access to vital calving grounds; that its numbers are already diminishing due to changing weather patterns, among other factors. The coastal plain is boggy terrain, difficult for wolves and unpopular with bears. If the caribou were forced to recreate their nursery in a spot more favourable to its predators, calf survival, which is already precarious, would very probably diminish.

We left the pipeline to its controversies and climbed higher into the hills. At one point, we passed a man with his two teenage sons on the side of the road. Their truck and trailer were buried in the deep snow of the ditch. Knowing that Frank and the others were just behind us in the pick-up, and given that we had dogs in the truck, we left it to them to tow the man and his sons from the ditch. Frank wouldn't much want to stop – he was eager to see Saul – but the unwritten rules of the north dictate that you never drive past anyone in difficulty.

It didn't take them long to haul out the vehicle and within a few minutes we saw them cruising behind us once more. Still, by the time we arrived at Mile 101 Saul was already there and sleeping. It was a remote place where few people were spending time; the couple of tiny cabins were reserved for the use of officials, vets and mushers. The trail, the mushers said, was in dreadful condition and the going was rough.

'It's the worst I've ever seen it,' one of them, Paul Geoffrion, told Frank. Shortly after that conversation, Geoffrion decided to withdraw from the race. It was a decision he may later have been thankful for.

The weather was closing in and Frank and Jerry, veterans of the route, were worried that the high road around Eagle Summit might be closed if conditions worsened. Frank and Thomas, therefore, stayed at Mile 101 to check in with Saul when he woke up while the rest of us proceeded over the hills to relative civilization at Central, the next checkpoint.

Eagle Summit peaks at 1,105 metres, though the road doesn't stretch to the top. In the summer, it's said to be a beautiful drive. In winter, however, this was a desolate piece of highway.

'Don't drive over Eagle Summit at night,' the media had been warned in their pre-race briefing. It was still daytime as we made our way over but the sky had darkened to a heavy bluish slate. Beneath, the road was white. The beige patches on the surrounding hills

135

did little to warm the atmosphere. They were sparse and windswept, a constant reminder of the brutal environment. We were above the tree line here; a few spiky shrubs provided the only meagre signs of life.

'The Eagle summit is one of the most difficult summits in Alaska. The wind blows so fiercely that sometimes for days together its passage is almost impossible,' Hudson Stuck wrote in his book *Ten Thousand Miles with a Dogsled*. Stuck was an Episcopal missionary who travelled constantly between the Indian villages and remote mission stations of Alaska from his arrival in the north in 1904 until his death in 1920.

Frank, too, had many stories to tell about this mountain. It's not only the highest but the steepest hill on the Quest trail, and the slope is much more sheer on one side than on the other. When the race runs from Whitehorse to Fairbanks – it goes in opposite directions on alternate years – teams have to climb the vertiginous incline and, going uphill, a musher helps the dogs by running or walking behind the sled and pushing it.

'I was going up and I was breathing like this . . .' he had told us, making awful rasping noises. 'My heart was pumping boom-boom-boom-boom. I just couldn't go any further, so I did a terrible thing. I stood on the runners.' This meant that the dogs had to drag not just the weight of the loaded sled up the hill; they had to haul Frank as well. 'I felt this big.' He held his forefinger and thumb a centimetre apart. 'And then, one of the dogs turned round and looked at me. And then I felt this big.' The thumb and finger closed in.

Then Frank had taken one of the riskiest decisions of all his time running the Yukon Quest. Instead of driving from behind, he'd walked to the front of his dogs. He'd whistled to them, and they'd followed him up the hill. Had the dogs decided they'd had enough, had they turned round and headed back down, he'd have lost his team on the mountain and the steepness of the incline would have presented a serious risk to dogs harnessed to a loaded sled without a driver to control its speed. But, luckily for Frank, those dogs trusted him so totally that they arrived at the top unscathed.

As the race was running from Fairbanks to Whitehorse this year, Saul wouldn't have to climb that remorseless slope; instead he'd have to go down it, an undertaking which presented its own terrors. And he wouldn't be able to adopt the methods used by Stuck in the early 1900s:

The descent was as anxious and hazardous as the ascent had been laborious. The dogs were loosed and sent racing down the slope. With a rope rough-lock around the sled runners, one man took the gee pole and another the handle-bars and each spread-eagled himself through the loose deep snow to check the momentum of the sled, until sled and men turned aside and came to a stop in a drift to avoid a steep, smooth pitch. The sled extricated, it was poised on the edge of the pitch and turned loose on the hardened snow, hurtling down three or four hundred feet until it buried itself in another drift. The dogs were necessary to drag it from this drift, and one had to go down and bring them up. Then again they were loosed, and from bench to bench the process was repeated until the slope grew gentle enough to permit the regulation of the downward progress by the foot-brake.

We arrived in Central as had Hudson Stuck and his dogs a hundred years before us. It was a charming little place with a school and a post office to serve its winter population of just fifty people. At one time this town had been the pulsating heart of the Circle Mining District, and now there's a tiny museum here to explain just what all the fuss was about. It was closed for the winter, but great hunks of antiquated gold-mining machinery lay beneath thick canopies of snow in the grounds outside.

The checkpoint was at the Steese Roadhouse whose restaurant, bar and shop formed a focal point for the community. It was not long before the first teams appeared. Hans Gatt was back in the lead; he came in at five thirty and went straight out again after a pause of just a few minutes. He had time, though, to speak to the thronging media before he left. The trail over Eagle Summit was abominable, he told them. Somebody could die out there tonight.

Twenty minutes later, Sebastian Schnuelle arrived. Schnuelle was a 35-year-old German, now living near Whitehorse. He was hard-core racer; just a week after the Quest finishing banquet, Schnuelle – together with Gatt and the other front-runners – would be at the start line of the Iditarod for nearly another two thousand kilometres of fun. Like the Turners, he also ran a tourism operation although, with his racing commitments, the running of that was mostly left to others. With his long wild hair, which usually stuck upwards, and his bushy beard, he looked as though he didn't have much time for hairdressers either. Schnuelle opted to rest at Central and to enjoy the juicy steak that the roadhouse laid on for competitors. A few minutes behind him came Lance Mackey, who stoically forwent the meatfest. He checked in, then headed straight back out to the trail.

Frank and Thomas arrived at about seven p.m. Saul had left Mile 101 at six. The run over the summit usually took five or six hours so we expected him to arrive at Central between eleven o'clock and midnight. I ate a 'Quest burger' in the restaurant and then, at eight o'clock, I retired to the back seat of the truck for a couple of hours' sleep.

At ten thirty, I emerged from the truck and rejoined the activity of the Quest. More teams had come in. Drivers tended to their dogs, bedded them down in straw, and then came into the restaurant. By now the weather on the summit was worsening and the mushers' stories were dire. The trail, they said, was atrocious. There was no snow – the ever-strengthening gales had blown it away leaving just ice, rock and moss which they couldn't brake on. Visibility was so poor they couldn't see their own teams. The wind was so ferocious it had blown away the trail markers.

Nervously, we wondered what Saul was going through out there. Quietly but regularly, we all checked our watches. Eleven o'clock came and went. Then it was midnight and there was still no sign of Saul or of Yuka Honda, a Japanese rookie who had left Mile 101 within ten minutes of him. With Yuka's handler, Todd, we hung around outside the roadhouse, staring intently at the road on which the mushers ought to be approaching, willing a dim headlight to appear in the distance. But nobody came.

By one o'clock, Saul and Yuka were indisputably late. Frank asked the officials what plans they had to deal with this kind of situation. They said they had no plan.

Frank burst into a brief tirade, then calmed down and tried to get some sleep on the floor of the media room, leaving us with strict instructions to wake him with the slightest snippet of news. I sat in there too, using the opportunity to check my emails. For a short while, all was silent. Then: 'Dogs! There are dogs!' somebody bellowed through the door.

'Saul?' shouted Frank, leaping to his feet. 'Is it Saul?'

We rushed outside, but the call had been a false alarm. The dogs in question were a team leaving, pressing on to the next checkpoint at Circle.

I sat outside with Thomas. He had taken up residence on one of the bales of straw that were piled along an outside wall of the roadhouse. He had scarcely moved from there since ten thirty the previous night. He was wearing a puffy neon-green parka that had once belonged to Frank. I told him he looked like a Teletubby. He almost smiled.

For the next couple of hours, virtually nothing happened. No team arrived. The last driver – Wayne Hall, a trapper from the remote Alaskan community of Eagle, with his band of working dogs – had come in at five to ten the previous evening and had reiterated what the others had said: conditions were shocking. He would have lost the trail had his headlamp not picked up a reflector at the last moment, he said. Since Wayne, there had been nobody.

Every now and then, a team that had finished resting went on its way: Kelley Griffin at a quarter to two, Michelle Phillips forty minutes later. Almost silently, mushers and dogs pattered off into the blackness, safe in the knowledge that the most feared hill of the course was behind them.

Still we sat outside. The weather in Central was peculiarly mild: while we knew from the mushers' stories that the mountain was being battered by a blizzard, at the checkpoint things were deceptively calm. We, too, were quiet. Conversation had more or less ceased as a sober acceptance had settled in: something had gone wrong.

At three o'clock, I went to get some sleep in the truck. Rest didn't come easily. I lay awake for a long while, then slept fitfully until at eight forty I heard the clinking of aluminium bowls outside. Thomas was feeding Beethoven and Stanley. I stuck my head out of the door.

'What's the news?' I asked.

'No news,' said Thomas.

No news? I could scarcely believe it. I had felt certain that Saul would arrive while I slept. By now he ought to have been bedded down in the mushers' cabin, his stomach full of steak.

'There's no news of Saul,' Thomas went on. 'But three mushers just came in – with two teams.'

The awful story was this: one of the mushers, Randy Chappel – not from the Quest itself, but from the shorter Yukon Quest 300 event that left Fairbanks eight hours after the main race – had lost his dogs on Eagle Summit. Three mushers – Chappel, Brent Sass (who went on to win the 300-mile race) and Regina Wycoff, a Quest rookie – had banded together to travel through the storm. They'd been lost, but had managed to find the trail again. Then Chappel, sliding down a steep and difficult section, had lost control and let go of his sled. When he righted himself, he could no longer find his dogs. The buffeting snow reduced visibility to virtually nothing and the dogs' barking was drowned by the wind.

The three mushers had decided that their priority was to get the rest of the dogs and themselves off the mountain and so Sass had broken the trail ahead. Or more accurately, his stalwart leader, Silver, had done so. In the blasting wind and swirling snow, the mushers said they hadn't been able to make out the trail, but Silver had led them to safety. Behind Sass, Silver and company, Chappel rode on the runners of Wycoff's sled. They'd hoped to find Chappel's team as they descended but they hadn't caught a glimpse of them. Now the team was loose on the mountain and, while sled dogs are hardy creatures and the cold wouldn't be a problem, the fact that they were unsupervised while attached to sled and lines could be highly dangerous. When he arrived at Central and walked into the checkpoint, Randy Chappel was fighting back tears.

I ate breakfast, drank coffee, and waited some more. Three boys in neatly ascending size had been volunteering at the checkpoint overnight. They each wore matching overalls the colour of French mustard.

'Thanks for all your help,' I heard one of the officials say.

'It's been great,' the tallest of the kids enthused. He was probably about twelve. 'It gave me an excuse to stay up all night!'

Thomas had been up all night too, but he was wearing a rather grimmer expression. He was still sitting on his bale of straw. Frank had become increasingly withdrawn. His only child was missing in a howling blizzard, in sub-zero temperatures, on a mountain that he knew from his own experience to be perilous. His eyes had taken on

142

an intense, round, frightened look and he was by now spending most of his time in the back of the dog truck with Beethoven and Stanley.

The morning progressed and still no mushers appeared at Central. Nor had they returned to Mile 101. The information coming through was patchy and perpetually changing but it now seemed that there were at least five or six teams unaccounted for. Some reports claimed that there were as many as thirteen stranded in the storm. In the car park outside the roadhouse, TV crews set up. They had a story on their hands.

Mid-morning, Mike McCowan, who had previously moved on to Circle but had come back to deal with the deteriorating situation at Central, delivered a briefing to everyone present: handlers, media, and hangers-on. We should under no circumstances try to drive from here to the next checkpoint at Circle, he said. The snow was deep from the storm. Already that morning two vehicles had gone into the ditch. And we couldn't go out in the other direction either: the road over Eagle Summit was closed and would not open until the following day.

I sat in the restaurant. The phone rang.

'Is Frank Turner in here?' the man behind the bar shouted. Frank wasn't in the building, so I took the call; it was Fabienne. She was with Jewel in Fairbanks, desperate for news, and her terror was now turning to fury that nobody had been in touch to update her on the situation. But the horrible reality was that we had no news. We may have been just a few kilometres from the mountain, but we had no more idea what catastrophes might have occurred there than she did.

Now that we had daylight, a small group of local men went out on snow machines to look for the missing mushers. These were the most skilled trappers in the area. They knew the terrain better than anyone. With nervous anticipation, we waited for them to deliver news. An hour or so later, they returned. The weather was so bad they'd been forced to turn back, they said. Visibility was zero. The winds were raging. Time and again, they'd had to dig their machines from the drifting snow. In the end, they'd had no choice but to abandon the search. They had, however, seen a musher.

'What was his name?' everyone clamoured. They didn't know. He had been male. He'd be in Central in an hour.

How could they have come back without a name, we all wondered. But people did things differently up here. The musher was safe. He was on his way. The details would be revealed soon enough.

We stared intently down the road waiting for the solitary team that we'd been promised. Privately, handlers and spectators all prayed it was the musher to whose team they were attached. Finally, at one forty, the shout went up: 'There's a team!'

The musher and his dogs pattered down the road that cut through the tiny community. We peered to see who it was. But it wasn't Saul. It was a musher from the Quest 300. The officials crowded round his sled, then came back with disheartening news: he'd left Mile 101 that morning and had come straight through. He had seen nobody and heard nothing. The missing mushers, then, were no longer on the trail.

We sat in the roadhouse and watched the NBC news. The story had now gone national and every seat and most of the standing space in the small room was taken as we listened to the news report that was being broadcast, rather bizarrely, from the car park outside via a sleek city studio.

The well-coiffed anchor sat behind a stylish, minimalist desk. 'Thirteen mushers are lost in the middle of nowhere,' she solemnly pronounced.

An indignant voice piped up from behind the bar. 'This isn't the middle of nowhere!'

By early afternoon a small crowd had gathered as local families wandered to the roadhouse to see the action – or, rather, the terrifying lack of it. Hairy-faced fathers carried small children; it appeared that there was no barber near here and the men solved the problem by cutting neither hair nor beard seemingly for decades.

By now, the number of lost teams had been whittled down to six: the others had either made it over the summit or had turned back to Mile 101. More snow machines went out and returned having found nothing. And then a new rumour reached our ears. The state troopers were putting a plane in the air. If they couldn't find anything, they'd call in the military with its more sophisticated search-and-rescue capabilities. And then, just a few minutes later, the news changed again. It would be dark in a few hours. The missing mushers might well be facing a medical emergency; it would be too dangerous to risk their spending a second night on the mountain. The state troopers had decided to call in the military right away. The army was sending a Black Hawk and a Hercules.

I walked round the side of the building to where Thomas was still sitting on his straw and related this development.

'Really?' he asked disbelievingly. 'Are you sure?'

A few moments later, there could be no doubt. The thrumming of an aircraft grew louder and then, as we craned our necks upwards, a Hercules circled a couple of times overhead, then roared off into the hills. We all laughed a little anxiously. For this tiny outpost to feature on the television news had been extraordinary enough; now the drama seemed to have mutated into a Hollywood disaster movie that was scarily for real.

My emotions were somersaulting. The Hercules that cut through the clouds seemed at the same time magnificent and melodramatic. It brought profound relief – it was kitted with high-tech gear so, however dire the situation on the mountain, we knew that our wait for news would soon be over. Yet, as is always the case moments before a desperately important pronouncement, this sense of deliverance was darkened by intense fears. Would the news that we expected any moment now grant salvation from our anxieties – or would we, in the days, weeks and months to come, look back upon these fraught minutes as the last bright moments before we were blown apart by a terrible truth?

It didn't take the military long to carry out their mission. Only half an hour or so passed before the sickening news crackled over the radio. They had ordered six medevacs. We were horrified: this, we thought, implied that there were serious injuries. Then, forty-five minutes later, the news changed again. These were not medical evacuations but ordinary rescues. What's more, they'd found the driverless team. All were unharmed. In two hours, the Black Hawk evacuated six mushers and eighty-eight dogs from the mountain and transported them back to Mile 101.

We couldn't go there, of course. The road would be closed until the next day, so we went back into the restaurant and drank a beer in tired, muted celebration. Our elation was dampened, however, by the knowledge that Saul was now out of the race. The Quest rules forbade competitors from accepting outside help of any kind. They couldn't so much as take a cup of tea from a bystander; to take a ride in a Black Hawk was clearly a major transgression. So, while we were truly delighted that all the drivers and dogs were safe, and profoundly grateful to the Quest officials, volunteers and military airmen who had effected their rescue, we were none the less sorely disappointed that after all that time, effort and money, Saul's race had lasted less than three days.

We ate dinner. Fortunately the owners of the Steese Roadhouse had been blessed with the foresight to buy in plenty of supplies. Then we managed to secure two bedrooms for the night – they had all been rented out the previous evening, but today two had come free as their occupants had moved on to Circle. Hector and Malena took one and, as there was a double bed and a single, invited me to share their accommodation. The others took the second. We were wrung out by the emotional demands of the last twenty-four hours and now a deep exhaustion set in. I went to bed at nine p.m. and slept through till eight the following morning.

The road maintenance men had been up before we were and already the highway had been cleared. I went with Frank, Bruce, Hector and Malena to collect Saul's drop bags from the checkpoint at Circle. Having picked up the bags, we'd proceed back to Mile 101 where we'd meet up with Thomas and Jerry with the dog truck, and collect Saul and the dogs.

The road surface had been packed but all around us deep snow from the storm thickly blanketed the ground and trees. Arriving in Circle, we parked the truck and walked, quite literally, to the end of the road. Here, the Steese Highway met the banks of the Yukon River and stopped. There was only one road that led to the next checkpoint on the race trail, Eagle – the tiny township to which Roald Amundsen mushed from Herschel Island in the Beaufort Sea in 1905 in order to telegraph the news that he had navigated the Northwest Passage – and that road didn't connect with Circle but with Dawson and Tok. In any case, it was only open from April to October. During the winter, Eagle's hundred and fifty or so inhabitants could leave town by air, skidoo or dogsled. Or they could just stay put.

Circle City may have had year-round road access, but those final kilometres of the Steese Highway attracted fewer inhabitants even than Eagle. According to a painted information board on the bank of the river, the population stood at a meagre seventy-three.

Back before the Klondike gold rush, Circle's population had swelled to twelve hundred. The town was nicknamed 'the biggest log cabin city in the world'. It had its own newspaper and was home to a number of government officials including a customs inspector and a tax collector. The commander of the military in Alaska was stationed here with eighty men and a number of officers. Disputes were settled by miners' meetings: a complainant would post notice of a meeting, the miners would convene and hear the arguments, and justice would be immediately decided by a majority vote. This simple legal system was widely accepted by northern folk as fair, and simpler and more effective than the courts that took its place.

Jack McQuesten, a one-time prospector who with his partners Alfred Mayo and Arthur Harper set up a series of trading posts along the Yukon River, ran an Alaska Commercial Company store in Circle. McQuesten was known for his generous terms of credit as well as for his ingenious homemade thermometer, which served the whole community as there were no conventional mercury thermometers in Circle at the time.

'This consisted of a set of vials fitted into a rack, one containing quicksilver, one the best whiskey in the country, one kerosene, and one Perry Davis's Pain-Killer. These congealed in the order mentioned, and a man starting on a journey began with a smile at frozen quicksilver, still went at whiskey, hesitated at the kerosene, and dived back into his cabin when the Pain-Killer lay down,' Arthur Walden wrote in his memoirs *A Dog-Puncher on the Yukon*.

Before the Klondike stampede, Circle also boasted an opera house, eight dance halls, twenty-eight saloons, a library, a hospital, a school and a church. In 1896, the nearby Birch Creek produced gold worth more than a million dollars. But by the end of that glorious year, Circle City lay abandoned. Rumours had reached its inhabitants of an extraordinary strike upriver.

News of the Klondike discovery was brought to Circle by Arthur Walden; he worked as a dog driver and made his living carrying mail, freight and paying passengers on his sled. Walden was employed in the winter of 1896 to take a passenger to Fortymile, which at the time was the nearest settlement to the Klondike River. Gold had been discovered in the creeks around the Klondike a few months previously but the news had not yet filtered to Circle. Arriving at Fortymile, Walden heard of the wondrous riches being taken from the ground a short distance away and decided to continue his journey to the Klondike creeks to see the activity for himself.

'As a large proportion of men working at the diggings had partners in Circle City, they were very anxious to get letters down to them, and, as I happened to be the first man to go down after the new discoveries, I went back with quite a large mail, each man howling to his partner to throw over everything and come up and be rich for life,' he wrote.

The scene that ensued when Walden arrived back in Circle has become the stuff of Klondike legend. Walden walked into Harry Ash's saloon and dumped the stash of mail on the bar. Another musher had arrived from the Klondike just ahead of Walden and had spread the rumour of riches, but he'd brought no mail and nobody quite knew whether to believe him.

Ignoring Walden's request for a drink of beef tea, Ash riffled through the letters till he found one addressed to himself. When he finished reading it, he jumped over the bar calling out to his customers, 'Boys! Hughie is right! Help yourselves to the whole shooting match! I'm off for the Klondike!'

'Then began the wildest excitement, as man after man got his letter and thought he was rich for life. Harry's invitation was promptly accepted and a wild orgy began. Corks weren't even pulled, and necks were knocked off bottles ... The next morning Harry Ash pulled out, and the big stampede to the Klondike had started. My batch of mail had killed Circle City in less than an hour.'

More than a hundred years later, it was still pretty dead. As in so many of these northern settlements, the gold rush had left its ghosts and little else. Even by 1905, when Hudson Stuck stopped here on one of his missionary journeys, the place had wilted.

'Spread out in the foreground were the little, squat, huddling cabins that belonged to no one, with never a light in a window or smoke from a chimney, the untrodden snow drifted against door and porch. It would be hard to imagine a drearier prospect, and one had the feeling that it was a city of the dead rather than merely a dead city,' he wrote in *Ten Thousand Miles with a Dogsled*.

Not much seemed to have changed. The settlement's atmosphere felt as drab and melancholy the day we were there as it had been when Hudson Stuck had visited a century before. It was curious how different the mood was here from that of Central just a few kilometres down the highway. There was hardly a soul in sight: the town's seventy-three inhabitants were either lying low or out of town. Many of the buildings were shuttered. In their driveways, vehicles lay covered in thick snow half as high as they were. At one end of the tiny settlement, a couple of small aeroplanes stood grounded beneath coverings of snow. On the side of the road, a skewed yellow signpost warned: 'Aircraft Xing'. But they weren't.

The mushers who were still in the race had left the checkpoint long ago. Like the gold prospectors of more than a hundred years earlier, they'd harnessed their dog teams and headed along those historic trails towards Dawson. They hadn't even stayed long enough to finish the chocolate cake.

'Would you like some cake?' asked a solitary stranger in a pick-up. 'Margaret down at the checkpoint made it. But I've already had a piece. I can't manage two.' He gave me a polystyrene bowl filled with the rich, light dessert. I offered to share it with the others but they turned it down, so I was forced to eat it all myself.

Like the mushers, Saul's bags were no longer there: somebody else had already come by, collected them, and hauled them back to Central. So we climbed into the truck and turned around. We picked up the bags, filled the tank with petrol, and at last retraced our steps to Mile 101.

It's strange what a day can do. Mile 101 was now covered in deep snow. And there, outside the cabin, sat Saul and the other five mushers, their race over almost as soon as it had begun. They were munching on snack bars and looked surprisingly cheerful after their adventure. The dogs were ensconced in the truck, snoozing happily in their straw, all in good health.

Frank and Saul greeted each other with an understated hug.

'Oh well, there's always next year,' Frank told the assembled group in an attempt to be positive.

There wouldn't be a next year, said Phil Joy, a 33-year-old American biologist. There was no way he could afford it. He'd spent all his savings on training for and entering this year's race.

Frank nodded in muted understanding. He'd previously revealed that it cost Muktuk between twenty-five and thirty thousand dollars to enter a team in the Yukon Quest. One could do it a lot more cheaply if one wasn't aiming for a high place in the rankings – one could spend less by using normal dog food instead of expensive, high-nutrition rations, for example. Frank's own status enabled him to attract sponsors, and his tourism business helped. But still, the Yukon Quest was a massive undertaking, and for a rookie without resources the commitment was more difficult still.

Conversation moved on.

'What did the dogs make of the Black Hawk?' we asked.

'Well, they obviously didn't know what it was, but they seemed to realize that, whatever it was, it was going to get them out of there,' said Saul. 'They didn't seem too worried. The guys just pitched them in so they were all in a kind of a huge dog pile.'

Now we learnt the details: they had followed the markers but had somehow gone slightly to the right instead of to the left. They'd ended up on the wrong side of the summit. Then the storm had really kicked in and they'd decided to hunker down until it diminished. The winds had been so strong they hadn't been able to unzip their sled bags without filling them with snow. They couldn't put on a parka, let alone light a fire. They had managed to crawl into their sleeping bags, though Saul's had later blown away.

'I felt really small, as if there was a satellite looking down on me, like I was a tiny speck of dust. For the first time, I realized how insignificant I really was,' he said.

The six mushers had been in two groups. Saul had been with Yuka and Jennifer Cochran, an effervescent 33-year-old rookie. ('Doesn't she ever get miserable?' I asked Saul as Jennifer bounced around Mile 101 in unfathomably good spirits. 'Oh yes, she had a few bad moments during the night,' he said.) They'd been very

153

close to the others: Kiara Adams who at just eighteen-years-old was the youngest competitor in the Quest had been with Phil Joy and another competitor from the 300 race. But neither group had known the other was near by.

We waited for a volunteer on a snow machine to bring Saul's sled down from the mountain. And then, finally, reunited even with his errant sleeping bag, we piled into the trucks and made our way back to Jewel's cabin where a much relieved Fabienne was waiting with Myla and a supply of food and beer.

There was an incredible sunset as we made our way back along the Steese Highway. First, the sky paled to a delicate pastel blue as the sun dropped towards the horizon. Then tinges of purple crept among the clouds, and the snowy hillsides glowed magenta. Gradually, the sun dipped lower and the snow-packed road shifted from bluish white to rich lilac, while the sky blazed brilliant, fiery gold behind the spruce and the contours of the mountain. We'd had a bad couple of days. Nature had seemed cruel and bad-tempered, furiously hurling its winds and snow. But now, as the setting sun cast the clouds into deep, hot crimson, a fierce beauty reigned over this capricious northern land once more.

12

'Huh-huh-huh-huh-huh,' went the truck.

'Darn,' said Frank.

'Huh-huh-huh-huh-huh-huh-huh-huh-huh,' went the truck.

'Oh shoot,' said Frank, and he slapped the steering wheel.

We were back at Fast Eddy's in Tok, partway through the twelve-hour haul back to Whitehorse. I was in the pick-up with Frank, Bruce and Jerry. We'd stopped in Tok for fuel, had eaten plates of outstanding halibut and chips, and were now ready to set off again – but the truck seemed to have taken a liking to Alaska. The others – Saul, Thomas, Fabienne, Myla and the dogs – had already left and were by now some way ahead.

Luckily, we had Bruce with us and he had been tinkering with diesel engines in the Australian bush for decades. He stuck his head in the bonnet, fiddled around, pumped a little by hand, and blurted out occasional instructions to Frank in his broad Aussie drawl.

'Try her now . . . a little more . . . Stop!' Finally the engine sputtered to life and we made it over the border and to Beaver Creek where we stopped to refuel once more.

'Everyone go to the bathroom!' Frank told us. 'We're not stopping at all from here. We're going to drive straight through.' It was still five hours to Whitehorse; obediently we emptied our bladders as Frank filled the tank.

As we approached Whitehorse, the low, almost-full moon began to rise. At first it was an opulent amber globe. It climbed higher in the sky, the gold blanching gradually to silver. Then, as it finally turned a searing white, the faintest traces of grey-green aurora borealis began to finger their way up from the horizon.

Later, the northern lights put on a spectacular display. After we'd eaten a late dinner and everyone else had gone to bed, I stood outside and watched as a banner of pale green light spread across the sky. At first it was barely discernible, like a strip of sheer chiffon weaving across the blackness. Then it grew stronger in form until its green shell and dark-red underbelly undulated adagio between the stars. Next the arc faded out and a series of pointed green spires grew up from behind the trees like a row of long tapering teeth, converging into fine pinnacles. Then they too weakened and died, and slowly swirling tornadoes spiralled upwards, finally petering out into tips high in the night sky.

For an hour or more I watched them. Every now and then they would lose their lustre and creep away, and I'd think the show was over, but just as I headed to the cabin door for bed a smear of green would seep from another side of the sky and the lights would rouse themselves for yet another brilliant encore.

*   *   *

Of the original twenty-two teams at the Yukon Quest start line in Fairbanks, only thirteen were still in the competition. But those thirteen were progressing fast. By the Thursday morning, when we woke up after a good night's rest at Muktuk, the sleep-deprived leaders of the remaining pack were approaching the Fortymile River dog drop.

The race was now being led by Lance Mackey. He arrived at Fortymile at five to nine. William Kleedehn followed at ten twenty. The fact that Kleedehn was in the race at all, let alone running in second place, was inspirational as he only had one leg: he lost the other in a motorcycle accident when he was a teenager. Now he wore a prosthetic but he was still unable to bend his left knee properly. Currently in third place, Hans Gatt passed the dog drop twenty minutes after Kleedehn.

Fortymile, too, is rich in gold-mining history though there's not a lot there now. It was the first real gold-mining community in this region: prospectors, accompanied sometimes by their wives, drifted there from the late 1880s. At that time little was known of the Yukon in the outside world.

'In London, globes of the world were still being issued showing the Yukon River flowing north into the Arctic Ocean instead of west into the Bering Sea. And there were stories told – and believed – of prehistoric mammoths that roamed the hills with jets of live steam issuing from their nostrils, and of immense bears that prowled the mountain peaks in endless circles because their limbs were longer on one side than on the other,' Pierre Berton wrote of the early 1880s in his book *The Klondike Fever*.

The settlement of Fortymile was cut off from the rest

of the world for three-quarters of the year, yet there were saloons and dance girls, an opera house, and a library. There was even a bishop, one William Bompas, 'a giant of a man with a high dome, a hawk nose, piercing eyes, and the flowing beard of a Moses', according to Pierre Berton. 'I feel so long dead and buried that I cannot think a short visit home, as if from the grave, would be of much use,' Berton quotes him as having written from his Fortymile diocese.

The population of Fortymile plummeted after 1896, however, when gold was found in the creeks of the Klondike. Like moths to a lustrous flame, the Fortymile inhabitants flocked to this richer land and Dawson City sprang up to house the stampeding prospectors.

That Thursday morning, the posse of surviving Yukon Quest mushers was flocking there too. The journey from Fortymile to Dawson by dogsled would take them only six hours (and the first in would win four ounces of Yukon gold). The trip by car from Whitehorse would take the same. If we wanted to see the rest of the race, we'd have to turn around fast and head up to the bright lights and boardwalks of that legendary gold-mining town.

Bruce had now decided to hire a car of his own so I travelled with him; Thomas, who was out of a job and could enjoy a few days' holiday, made his way in the dog truck with Elmer, a recently arrived client from Virginia who had a white Father Christmas beard and a round belly in perfect keeping. Frank would drive with another new client, Dick, in the pick-up once it had been fixed by the garage.

Bruce and I left Muktuk mid-afternoon and headed

up the Klondike Highway. The road was good, but the snow on the surrounding land was horribly sparse. Whole hillsides glared brown and rocky with just odd, sorry-looking remnants of half-melted snow. Where did the trail run, we wondered. We hoped it didn't go over these hills, or the mushers would need to fit their sleds with wheels rather than runners.

We drove through huge swathes of starkly beautiful, charred forest – a massive fire had raged here during the terrible summer of 2004. Occasionally, a pure-white Arctic hare lolloped over the road in front of our tyres.

At nine thirty, we reached Dawson and the unambiguously named 5th Avenue Bed & Breakfast to find that Thomas and Elmer had arrived just before us. The bed and breakfast was a turquoise-painted weatherboard house on a street corner. The outside may have been in keeping with tradition, but inside Tracey and Steve's spacious home embraced the twenty-first century with newly decorated bedrooms and en suite bathrooms. To us, after several nights sleeping on floors and in the back of the truck, all this seemed like seven-star luxury.

We were strangely demob happy. Every one of us, of course, would infinitely rather have been facing a sleepless night down at the checkpoint waiting for Saul to come in, but that option was off the menu. In the circumstances, there was nothing for it but to drop our bags and head straight back out for a couple of beers.

We trudged along the snow-packed 5th Avenue. Dawson is colder and darker than Whitehorse in winter. It lies more than five hundred kilometres northwest of the Yukon capital and just over two hundred and fifty kilometres as the crow flies from the Arctic Circle. In December and January, they have almost perpetual darkness here; in midsummer, Dawson basks beneath the midnight sun.

Tonight, though, the temperatures were not too biting and we only had a couple of streets to go to Diamond Tooth Gertie's, where Tracey had suggested we'd find plentiful food, drink and entertainment. The building was an old one – it was originally built in 1901 as the Arctic Brotherhood Hall – though now the music was not two-steps and waltzes but cover versions of sixties hits performed by a band of middle-aged men with neatly parted hair and clean, pressed shirts tucked into their jeans.

Diamond Tooth Gertie herself was probably a little more raucous. A celebrated dance-hall queen of the Klondike gold rush days, she was named for the diamond she had inserted between her two front teeth.

In the last years of the nineteenth century, it wasn't just Gertie's diamond that glittered in Dawson. After the discovery of August 1896, an estimated hundred thousand hopeful prospectors flooded to the region from North America and across the globe in a bid to get rich quick. Many never completed the treacherous journey over arduous mountain passes and down the rapids of the Yukon River. Thousands of those who did make it to Dawson found the best claims had already gone and turned right round and headed for home. Still, in just a couple of years, Dawson was transformed from a muddy, unpopulated moose pasture to a dazzling gold rush town. By 1898, the nearby gold towns of Circle and Fortymile were home only to ghosts while Dawson bulged with a population of nearly forty thousand miners, dance-hall girls, entrepreneurs, teachers, nurses and clergymen. The town had a telephone service, running water and steam heat in its glamorous hotels, theatres and dance halls.

The discovery was made by an American named George Carmack and two relatives of his Indian wife, Skookum Jim and Tagish Charlie. Carmack was an easygoing man who lived contentedly with his wife's tribe. He wasn't much interested in gold; he preferred to live as an Indian. He'd been drying salmon on the banks of the Klondike River when, in the summer of 1896, a prospector named Robert Henderson had come by in his poling boat. Henderson had stopped to talk to this white man the miners scathingly called Siwash George because of his tribal ways. He'd been mining a profitable creek he'd named Gold Bottom, he said; he suggested Carmack might try his luck too. Carmack ventured that he'd like to prospect there with his in-laws once he'd taken the fish in, but Henderson wasn't keen.

'There's a chance for you, George, but I don't want any damn Siwashes staking on that creek,' popular legend reports him as having replied.

Carmack's Indian relatives were offended, and when some days later the three made their momentous discovery – not at Gold Bottom but a short distance away at Rabbit Creek – and staked their claims, contrary to the gold miners' code they never went back to tell Henderson what they'd found.

Rabbit Creek was renamed Bonanza. Carmack recorded his claim at Fortymile and within a fortnight ecstatic miners from that settlement had staked the whole of the creek and were starting to spread to neighbouring land. And so, about three weeks after Carmack's initial Bonanza strike, three men came wandering towards Henderson's camp and told him the news from which he would never recover: Carmack had found gold, and hadn't let him know.

Through the winter of 1896, miners toiled on their Klondike claims, burning fires to melt the permafrost until they reached the bedrock. From there they dug out the gravel and heaped it into huge piles above ground. When spring came and running water was available, they sluiced the gravel piles to extract the gold. It was only then, in the warmer weather, that most miners knew whether their shafts had hit the paystreak – or whether they had toiled all winter for naught.

A few struck ground so rich that the gold was plain to see even in winter. One such legendary miner was Clarence Berry. He had headed to the Yukon in 1894, a penniless victim of the depression. He had been working as a bartender in Fortymile when Carmack came into the bar and tipped his nuggets on the counter, announcing his discovery on Bonanza and sparking the beginnings of the stampede. Berry staked a claim – and found a fortune.

'When Mrs Berry needed pocket money, she merely walked to the dump and with a sharp stick smashed apart the frozen clods and pulled out the nuggets,' Pierre Berton wrote.

While most had been tearing towards the creeks, their hearts ablaze with dreams of gold, a businessman named Joe Ladue had staked out a townsite at the point where the Klondike and Yukon Rivers met. Ladue owned a sawmill at a tiny settlement upriver; he quickly loaded his lumber on to a raft and floated it to the boggy pasture he named Dawson City after George M. Dawson, director of the Geological Survey of Canada, who had explored the region a decade earlier. He subsequently moved his sawmill there, too. In October 1896, twenty-six people lived in Dawson. In July the following year, five thousand people had set up home there. By the summer of 1898 the population had ballooned to more than thirty thousand people (and one milk cow, which arrived to great fanfare that July), and the town had sprawled across the river on to the Yukon's western shores.

Dawson's west bank was sparsely populated these days, but it was still home to the government campground and that was where we made our way the morning following our arrival in the town. In summer this spot would be full of vacationers putting their feet up; today, the bays were dedicated to canine rest and relaxation.

Nine of the thirteen mushers still in the race had arrived here now. Mackey, Kleedehn and Gatt had arrived within a few hours of each other the previous afternoon. Gerry Willomitzer, Sebastian Schnuelle, David Dalton, Michelle Phillips and Hugh Neff had appeared at intervals through the night, while Kelley Griffin had come in shortly before ten o'clock in the morning. The exhausted competitors, for the first time in nearly a week, had headed off to a shower and a bed while their handlers cared for their dogs.

We walked along Front Street and past the Yukon Saw Mill Company, an imposing two-storey construction the colour of clotted cream. This building dated from 1900; the company once incorporated the largest machine shop north of Vancouver, a foundry and a lumber yard that stretched over three city blocks. We crossed the ice road – a smooth, wide highway that traversed the Yukon River. As we ambled, a couple of dog trucks with spare sleds strapped to their roofs glided past us. Occasionally the wet nose of a dog peeked out from behind a grille: these were animals that had been dropped from their teams and would complete the course with the aid of a diesel engine.

There have been bids to build a bridge in Dawson though, so far, all efforts have been quashed by the high costs involved. The town has the ice road in the winter and a car ferry in the summer, but during the busy tourism months the queue for the boat stretches long. Additionally, there is no way of crossing from the main town to West Dawson, on the opposite bank, while the river is freezing up in the autumn or breaking up in the spring. Some of the West Dawson residents relish this. They love the isolation. But others find the privations of those periods – which can last up to six weeks – too great. The turn-of-the-century miners may have been cut off for months during their long, harsh winters but, in this day and age, six weeks is a long time to go without fresh groceries.

In July 1898, two society ladies set up home on Dawson's west bank, but they ensured that, during the course of their stay, they wouldn't need to do without groceries or any other of life's considerable comforts. Mary Hitchcock and Edith Van Buren had decided to 'do' the Klondike as a pleasure trip. They brought with them 500 kilograms of supplies including a portable bowling alley and an animatoscope that showed films, and lived in a tent that covered 260 square metres.

The mushers' encampments that lined the river bank now were not quite so grand in style. Each cosy nook set back from the river featured a small tent whose chimney puffed out convivial trails of white, puffy

164

smoke. Outside the canvas hotels, mushers' supply bags sat in neat lines. Bales of straw, piles of firewood and scuffed old cool boxes were heaped in each clearing. The dogs themselves, though, were for the most part out of sight: the mushers had bedded them down as far as possible from the path that ran in front of their camps. The priority was for the dogs to rest, not to become distracted by passers-by.

'At Dawson, it's vital that the dogs rest and eat,' Frank explained as we walked along. 'If a dog doesn't want fish, you give it chicken. If it doesn't want chicken, you give it pork. If it doesn't want to eat out of a bowl, you feed it by hand. But it is the handler's job to stay there and to keep on trying until he finds out what the dog wants.'

We finished our tour and crossed back over the ice. It was colder walking in this direction. A biting wind blew down the river's course with no obstacles to break its path, and we were happy to arrive at last at the checkpoint, a large, log building that serves as Dawson's visitor centre in the summer months. In a back room, locals had set up a cafeteria selling piping-hot moose stew, quiche, soup, pizza and an array of biscuits and cakes. The chefs were raising money for the Percy de Wolfe dogsled race, which celebrates the life of the man they called the Iron Man of the North, who carried the mail between Dawson and Eagle during the winters of 1910 to 1949. He was known as a man who would risk his life to protect the mail. During freeze up and break up, he battled crashing cakes of ice. On one journey, his horses broke through the ice; de Wolfe managed to throw twenty bags of mail from the sled before it too was submerged and the horses drowned.

The checkpoint was buzzing with gossip: there was to be a drivers' meeting at lunchtime and then, at two o'clock, a meeting would be held in the checkpoint that all – media, handlers and spectators – could attend. Rumour had it that the race officials were worried about the lack of snow on the trail between Dawson and Whitehorse and were keen to devise an alternative route.

At two p.m., the mushers filed into the large main room of the visitor centre, accompanied by Mike McCowan, the race marshal, in his distinctive green and white polka-dot hat, and his fellow officials. It was a curious gathering. Faces were serious and intense; everyone assumed an air of gravitas in anticipation of the earth-shattering news we sensed was to follow. Yet, realistically, there were only a few dozen of us in that room, including a handful of eager-faced journalists dressed in an odd assortment of winter hats and parkas. McCowan paused while they thrust their microphones towards him. He was a rotund, slightly puffing man, with a neatly trimmed grey moustache and beard. Then he cleared his throat and, with no drama whatsoever, came straight to the point.

'The Yukon Quest will not be finishing in Whitehorse this year. It will be finishing in Dawson City,' he told the assembled hotch-potch. 'We will launch teams out of Dawson, run them to Pelly Crossing, turn them around and run back to Dawson.'

And so, once again, my plans changed. Frank and the others decided they wouldn't wait to see the end of the race. They would return to Whitehorse tomorrow. Jerry was no longer needed by Saul so he chose to stay in Dawson and help out the vet team there. I wanted to see the finish, so I opted to stay in Dawson for the next week. I'd try to hitch a lift down to Pelly to see the teams come in there, but rather than hopping from checkpoint to checkpoint, grabbing sleep in the back of the truck when I could, I'd spend this second week of the Yukon Quest comfortably ensconced in the 5th Avenue B&B, with occasional jaunts round town and into the checkpoint to entertain me.

That afternoon, I went into the internet café a few doors down from the checkpoint. Immediately I recognized the man behind the counter: he was the singer from the band in Gertie's the previous night. His name, it turned out, was Ron, and he also had a third job driving the school bus. Dawson was a small town and its inhabitants were masters of multi-tasking. Tracey from the B & B wore many hats, too. She told me that, in addition to running the guesthouse, she worked at the Riverwest Restaurant and Coffee Shop and also did some shifts as a dancer at Diamond Tooth Gertie's during the tourist season. One summer she'd danced there six nights a week, worked all day in the café, and taken on half the job of running the B & B while her husband, Steve, did the other half. By the end of the season, she said, if someone just looked at her the wrong way she burst into tears.

'So what are you doing here?' Ron asked me.

I told him about my trip and about my intention to write a book about the Yukon and sled dogs. I'd be here for several days yet, I added, given that the Quest's finish line would now be on the river just outside the café's window.

'Dick's an author, too,' he said, nodding towards

the only other person in the room, an elderly, slightly stooped man who was typing at a keyboard. The older man looked up.

'What kind of stuff do you write?' I asked him.

'*What?*' he shouted.

'*She said, "What kind of books do you write?"*' hollered Ron. This man, I considered, would make a good friend for Bruce and Ray.

'Ah, lots of stuff,' the man replied rather quietly. '*Arctic Exodus. The Mad Trapper of Rat River. The Lost Patrol.* Some other ones too.'

He listed the titles nonchalantly. But to my astonishment, I recognized them.

'But I've read *The Lost Patrol*!' I said. It was a book about a group of ill-fated Mounties who, during the winter of 1910–11, had lost their way in the Richardson Mountains as they travelled by dogsled between Fort McPherson and Dawson. They'd been forced to eat their dogs one by one until, in the end, they all died – three from starvation, one from suicide.

This, then, was Dick North, one of the most renowned authors of Canada's north. He lived right here in Dawson – I later discovered there was even a street named after him on a hill behind the town – and I'd bumped into him after less than twenty-four hours in this tiny outpost.

'Ah yes,' he said, not sounding remotely surprised. 'Well, I'm in here every morning. Come in and have a chat any time you like.'

And so I settled into my unscheduled week in Dawson. It was a fabulous little town bursting with character and not at all a difficult place in which to spend a few days by accident.

The touristy main drag lasted only a couple of streets but incorporated a handful of interesting shops. Like the people, the stores frequently held down more than one job. For example, Maximilian's Gold Rush Emporium on Front Street was the bookshop, newsagent and CD store, and also sold jewellery, souvenirs and clothing.

The liquor store was a definite part-timer. It only opened on Tuesdays, Fridays and Saturdays. If you wanted alcohol the rest of the week, you had to buy it at one of the hotel bars because the grocery stores weren't allowed a liquor licence. Canada was turning out to be surprisingly puritan in that respect: even once I'd tracked down a bottle of wine at the hotel, I was obliged by law to carry it out wrapped in a brown paper bag so that it didn't sully the eyes of innocent passers-by on the street.

But as I left the town's very tiny centre the place became arguably more interesting still. Building regulations in Dawson dictate that construction complies with the town's heritage and the houses were low-rise painted timber, many with picturesque verandas that sometimes served as storerooms and junk depositories. Every now and then, a green plaque fronted one of the buildings and explained its historical significance.

On the corner of 5th Avenue and King Street St Mary's Church still stands, but it isn't the original building. That was a log construction which, together with a hospital, was erected down on the waterfront by the Jesuit priest, Father Judge. Father Judge was a much-loved figure of the gold rush days. Frail in body but bounteous in mind, Judge had travelled to the Klondike from Alaska during the earliest days of the rush; he was convinced that the stampeding prospectors would soon be in need of medical care. To save his single dog from the strain of pulling his medicine-laden sled alone, he joined the animal in the harness and pulled alongside. Judge worked tirelessly for the sick and even gave up his own bed for them. It was not long before his generosity took its toll: he died from pneumonia in 1899. His hospital burned to the ground in 1950, and the church was moved to Mayo – but the distinctive steeple remained in Dawson and tops the new church on 5th Avenue.

A short distance away, a sombre, unornamented hall built from dark-stained wood announced itself as the warehouse where food for the winter was cached before the town had access to outside supplies during the frozen months. A tall flat-faced construction lurched drunkenly to one side. Its tilt, the noticeboard said, was due to the effects of permafrost heaves. A little further along, St Andrew's Church teetered. It was an attractive building; one wall would once have been dominated by a magnificent arched window. But now both windows and doors were boarded up.

'Danger. Keep clear. Unstable structure,' warned a sign posted to the entrance.

Dawson City had shrivelled since its boom time: in 1898 the population may have been forty thousand but a hundred-odd years later a mere two thousand people had their homes here.

And this was winter. The tourist trade was dormant and, even with the Quest in town, a white silence hung over those icy streets that had seen so much wealth and scarcity, such splendour and utter distress.

13

That momentous winter of 1896–7, Dawson was a strange settlement. In January 1897, none of those historical edifices that I visited – the churches, the warehouses and the dance halls – existed. Dawson still only had a handful of houses; almost everyone lived in tents. There was as much gold as one cared to pull from the ground, yet food was terrifyingly scarce. Salt was selling for its weight in gold. Nails were so hard to come by that one prospector, desperate to build a sluice box, paid eight hundred dollars for a tiny pot of bent, fire-charred specimens. While the river was frozen, supplies couldn't come in – and news of the staggering riches that were being dug from the earth couldn't be taken to the outside world.

The Canadian government surveyor, William Ogilvie, did try to warn the authorities in Ottawa about the tremendous commotion that was soon to be unleashed. During those winter months he sent out two messages by dogsled, but the faraway officials took little notice.

Then, in the middle of May, the ice broke on the Yukon River and boats could pass once more. Two months later, on 14 July 1897, a steamer named the *Excelsior* docked in San Francisco. She had journeyed from the tiny port of St Michael on the coast of the Bering Sea. Her passengers were the ragged, grizzled miners of the Yukon. Their cargo was gold. By the time another ship departing the same port, the *Portland*, docked in Seattle three days later, the news was out. At six o'clock that morning five thousand people crowded the Seattle docks to see those tattered folk who carried tens of thousands of dollars' worth of gold in their battered bags and boxes. America was in the grip of a depression and these sacks of Klondike gold fired the imagination of a weary public. By nine thirty, the streets were swarming with prospective Klondikers.

'GOLD! GOLD! GOLD! GOLD!' shouted the headline of the *Seattle Post Intelligencer* on 17 July 1897. 'Sixty-eight Rich Men on the Steamer *Portland*. Stacks of yellow metal.'

'All that anyone hears at present is "Klondyke",' the *Seattle Daily Times* reported six days later. 'It is impossible to escape it. It is talked in the morning; it is discussed at lunch; it demands attention at the dinner table; it is all one hears during the interval of his after-dinner smoke; and at night one dreams about mountains of yellow metal with nuggets as big as fire plugs.'

Storekeepers closed up shop, clerks resigned their posts, policemen left their beats and teachers deserted their classrooms. Within weeks, thousands had left for the north.

The hopeful prospectors took various routes. None was easy. The wealthy could journey by steamer to St Michael, then continue along the Yukon River to Dawson itself. But even this supposedly simple journey

172

was fraught with difficulty due to the shortness of the navigable season, and the majority of those who set out were forced to return to their homes in the south before winter set in.

Most travelled instead by ship to Skagway. Skagway was on the American side of the border, and so fell outside the jurisdiction of Canada's North-West Mounted Police. Though the town had a sheriff, it was actually ruled in the late 1890s by the notorious villain 'Soapy' Smith and his gang of crooks who tricked, robbed and sometimes even murdered the new arrivals until a vigilante put a bullet through Soapy himself.

The town of Skagway at this period of its existence was about the roughest place in the world. The population increased every day; gambling hells, dance halls and variety theatres were in full swing . . . Robbery and murder were daily occurrences; many people came there with money, and next morning had not enough to get a meal having been robbed or cheated out of their last cent. Shots were exchanged on the streets in broad daylight, and enraged Klondykers pursued the scoundrels of Soapy Smith's gang to get even with them. At night the crash of bands, shouts of 'Murder!', [and] cries for help mingled with the cracked voices of the singers in the variety halls.

So wrote Sam Steele, the superintendent who headed up the Yukon's division of the North-West Mounted Police during the gold rush years, in his memoirs *Forty Years in Canada*. If they survived Skagway, stampeders proceeded under their own steam either over the White

Pass from Skagway or by the Chilkoot Trail that started five kilometres away in Dyea.

The Chilkoot Trail was the slightly shorter route, but it was so demonically steep in parts that pack animals couldn't climb the whole route and travellers therefore had to carry their own luggage. In 1898, following a winter of near starvation in Dawson, their journey was made more arduous still by a new regulation: the Canadian authorities insisted that those crossing the border carried enough food and other supplies to last them a full year. The weight of these supplies dictated multiple journeys as prospectors were forced to trek back and forth. It took at least ninety days for a person to cross into Canada in this way. The trails became so crowded that the men crammed in along them in a never-ending procession.

'Above towered the storm-beaten Chilcoot. Up its gaunt and ragged front crawled a slender string of men. But it was an endless string. It came out of the last fringe of dwarfed shrub below, and drew a black line across the dazzling stretch of ice . . . And it went on, up the pitch of the steep, growing fainter and smaller, till it squirmed and twisted like a column of ants and vanished over the crest of the pass, ' Jack London wrote in his first novel, *A Daughter of the Snows*. 'Men who had never carried more than parcels in all their lives had now become bearers of burdens. They no longer walked upright under the sun, but stooped the body forward and bowed the head to earth.'

London was one of the thousands who rushed to the Klondike when gold fever gripped America in July 1897. He had been living in Oakland, San Francisco, toiling ten hours a day in a steamy laundry, earning a

174

paltry thirty dollars a month. Thrilled by the prospect of adventure, he convinced his sister and brother-in-law to stand him his grubstake. London was only in the Yukon for a year, from August 1897 to July 1898, and he didn't find his fortune in gold. He did however take home with him rich stories of the rugged, romantic gold rush that, in the end, made him a wealthy man.

Although London travelled to the Klondike via the shorter, steeper Chilkoot Pass, heaving his outfit with the help of Indian porters, it is his description of the White Pass crossing that is the better remembered. White Pass was the lower of the pair – its ascent was gradual enough, theoretically, to allow pack animals to cross. But its demands were deceptively gruelling. Of the three thousand horses driven over the pass in 1897 almost none survived. The brutality of the White Pass became infamous, and London incorporated its gruesome stories into his writing.

> The horses died like mosquitoes in the first frost, and from Skagway to Bennett they rotted in heaps. They died at the rocks, they were poisoned at the summit, and they starved at the lakes; they fell off the trail, what there was of it, or they went through it; in the river they drowned under their loads, or were smashed to pieces against the boulders; they snapped their legs in the crevices and broke their backs falling backwards with their packs; in the sloughs they sank from sight or smothered in the slime, and they were disembowelled in the bogs where the corduroy logs turned end up in the mud; men shot them, worked them to death, and when they were gone, went back to the beach and bought

more. Some did not bother to shoot them, stripping the saddles off and the shoes and leaving them where they fell. Their hearts turned to stone – those which did not break – and they became beasts, the men on Dead Horse Trail.

From 'Which Make Men Remember'
by Jack London

There were other ways in too. 'All American' routes came via Prince William Sound and over the Valdez glacier. Those choosing these trails suffered even more horribly than the tortured souls attempting the Chilkoot Trail and the White Pass; many died. Some patriotic Canadians and British opted for all-Canadian routes, such as the dreadful Ashcroft Trail through British Columbia, or the equally agonizing Edmonton Trail.

An English peer named Lord Avonmore was among those to arrive in Edmonton intending to take the latter route. He brought with him a large team of friends and servants and 5,000 kilograms of supplies, which included 50 kilos of lavatory paper. Avonmore's expedition didn't make it out of Edmonton, though. Berton explained: 'One of the party, a Captain Alleyne, died of pneumonia contracted in the twenty-below weather. Another, a Dr Hoops, sprained his ankle and had scarcely recovered from this misadventure when he stumbled across a dog sleigh and cracked his ribs. A colonel in the party meanwhile broke his arm, while a Captain Powell froze his feet so badly that he died. A Captain O'Brien assumed leadership of the group and, as his first official act, arrested a compatriot, a Mr Bannerman, on a charge of embezzlement. Before he could pull things together, however, he was himself jailed for trying to stab his manservant, and the expedition tottered to a standstill.'

Almost certainly, the one piece of luck that the Avonmore group did enjoy was that they never left Edmonton. Of the thousands who did set off, only a handful ever made it to Dawson and those that did arrived so late – the journey took some of them a staggering two years – that scarcely any of them found gold.

Late on Saturday morning I walked back through those streets that the early prospectors had so tormented themselves in trying to reach. The front runners of the Quest – Lance Mackey, William Kleedehn and Hans Gatt – had completed their layover and had left Dawson under cover of darkness in the early hours. The next two, Gerry Willomitzer and Sebastian Schnuelle, were due to set off at around midday, with David Dalton and Michelle Phillips heading out a couple of hours after that. Hugh Neff would not be leaving Dawson via the trail but under the power of his dog truck. By the time he'd arrived at the halfway point he'd had to drop six dogs and the vets weren't happy with the condition of the remaining eight. They'd insisted he stay in Dawson for a while longer to allow his team to recuperate; furious at their intervention, Neff had pulled out of the race.

With a small group of fellow spectators, I watched from the eastern bank of the river as those teams whose time was up trotted fresh from their rest back to the wilderness of the trail. At first, each appeared as a tiny speck, crawling like a minuscule black caterpillar from the government campground on the opposite shore. The overcast weather created a monochrome spectrum – the snowy river was pure, chilling white, the sky pale grey, and the rocky cliffs that sliced into its clouds were unforgiving black. Beneath them, the shadowy spots that were musher, sled and dogs gently, rhythmically, perpetually pattered along. It wasn't until I had this time to pause and consider the scene that I realized how broad this great river was. Now, more than ever, the magnitude of the teams' undertaking glared bright amid the muted landscape. The hills that enveloped the river appeared gargantuan and foreboding and, before them, mushers and dogs looked infinitely vulnerable.

At Sunday lunchtime Lance Mackey was still in the lead, and was resting his team at the Stepping Stone checkpoint just a few hours' run from the turnaround at Pelly. I was again in the checkpoint at Dawson, and was working my way through a generous slab of sensational vegetable lasagne. I was sitting at a table with Gary Chamberlain, a bush pilot who had in previous years worked for the Yukon Quest, and a couple of guys from Sorel, the race's sponsor and the company whose winter boots I was wearing since I'd given Frank back his loaned bunny boots.

The Sorel duo and Gary were earnestly discussing the pros and cons of various types of footwear, and looking at some prototypes for new boots that Sorel had designed. Gary was just expatiating about the little cleat that stuck out from the heel of his bunny boots – not all bunny boots had it, he said, but it was hugely useful to be able to tread down on it with the other foot when he wanted to take them off – when Wendell Carey, one of the race managers and a good friend of Gary's, rushed through the door.

'I'm going to Pelly,' he told Gary a little breathlessly. 'You want to come?'

'Sure,' said Gary, and then turned to me. 'Do you want to come?'

Ten minutes later, I was disappearing at breakneck speed down the Klondike Highway in the back seat of Wendell's truck.

Gary was a gentle bear of a man with white hair, a white moustache and kindly eyes. He seemed to move through life at a relaxed, measured pace. Wendell was quite the opposite. It could just have been the anxieties of the race combined with the effects of sleep deprivation but Wendell, with his ice-blue eyes and assortment of blue clothing to match, appeared to like life fast.

The journey from Dawson to Pelly is generally reckoned to take three hours. We made it in two, and that included a stop at the side of the road for me to take a picture of a gambolling cow moose and calf.

We screeched into the tiny town and immediately came upon Mike McCowan in his own truck, looking slightly thunderous. Wendell hopped out to talk to him, then bounded back into the driver's seat, fired up the engine, and roared into action once more. The boss, he said, was unhappy. The rangers hadn't marked the trail along the road to Pelly Farm. This would be the mushers' return route out of Pelly: they would come into the checkpoint via the Pelly River, then turn round and go back not the way they came but on the little-used, snow-packed back road that ran just above the river and led out to the very remote farm near Fort Selkirk. The first of the teams would be arriving at Pelly within hours so the new route needed to be marked right now.

We came to a stop outside the house of one of the rangers. Wendell bounced from the driver's seat and returned a couple of minutes later with an armful of trail markers – simple wooden sticks with reflective tape on their upper tips.

Pelly Crossing struck me as a dispiriting place. It perches to the side of the Klondike Highway, roughly midway between Dawson and Whitehorse. The settlement was originally a ferry crossing; then, when the Klondike Highway was built during the 1950s, it became a construction camp. After the highway was completed and the camp emptied of labourers, the Selkirk First Nation – one of the Yukon's fourteen First Nations communities – moved its base here from near Fort Selkirk, which wasn't on the new transportation route.

Now, fewer than three hundred people live at Pelly. Unemployment is rife. The people struggle with displacement issues; the community has a problem with domestic abuse. The cost of living is high, jobs are few, and young people with ambition soon move away.

Many of the First Nations' problems can be traced to the residential schools system: for five generations, from the late nineteenth century, First Nations children from across Canada and the United States were taken from their families to be forcibly educated. Placed in schools where they were forbidden from speaking their own language – unable to talk in English, many spent years in silence – and even from associating with their siblings, the system effectively severed the children's ties with their own language and traditions. Abuse ran rife through these institutions, whose staff were not effectively monitored. This attempt to 'civilize' the Indian children, which was not officially abandoned until the 1980s, leaves a dark legacy and deep scars across communities today.

And so the government pumps in money – the Quest's checkpoint was in a spangling new recreation building that all two-hundred-odd inhabitants could have fitted into several times over; there's a school, a heritage centre, a health centre, and three policemen. There's a possibility that the community could develop Pelly's tourism potential given its convenient situation on the highway and its proximity to areas rich in wildlife.

Frank lived and worked in Pelly for a decade. He was the town's social worker and still has great fondness for its people. He helped get funding for these community projects, he later told me, but then he lost heart because they didn't really change anything.

It took us around an hour to drive from Pelly Crossing to Pelly Farm – I later found out the journey takes everyone else an hour and a half – plunging markers into the snow as we went. At one point, Wendell braked suddenly and pointed at the river to our left. On its white surface trotted a solitary black wolf.

'And it's in range!' Wendell exclaimed to Gary. But neither man was carrying a gun.

They told me later, over ill-advised tequilas in the Eldorado Hotel, that they would usually both carry a rifle but as we'd been in a rental vehicle and they'd been crossing the US–Canadian border they weren't carrying firearms on this trip.

Would they have shot the wolf if they'd had a rifle handy, I asked them.

181

Wendell looked astonished. 'For sure!' he retorted. 'You'd get five hundred dollars for that pelt.'

'But really, do you think you'd have got it?' asked Gary, grinning.

'I like to think I'd have been in with a good chance.'

And the meat? They'd compost it, they said. It would go back into the earth. They'd eat it if only wolf didn't taste so darned awful.

We continued along the road to Pelly Farm. Wendell pointed out the claw marks on the trunks of poplar trees where bears had shimmied up. It seemed amazing to me that those lumpish creatures could wriggle up such spindly limbs.

'They go up them like monkeys,' said Gary.

'And not all bears sleep through the whole winter,' added Wendell. Older bears, he explained, don't hibernate as successfully as younger animals. They have trouble putting on enough weight to last the winter and so may well wake up early.

The whole issue of bears in the Yukon struck me as mildly worrying. Two types roamed here – grizzlies and black bears – and, should you meet a belligerent specimen in the bush, it was important to know which of the two you were dealing with. To this end, the government department Environment Yukon, alongside numerous books and articles (the book shop in Whitehorse had an entire shelf dedicated to titles such as *Bear Encounters and How to Deal With Them*), sets out the differences for visitors. The black bear, says Environment Yukon in its leaflet, *Into the Yukon Wilderness*, has dark-coloured front claws which are relatively short and well curved. In profile, it has a long, straight muzzle, and the highest point of its back is over its hind legs. The grizzly, by contrast, has front claws that are light coloured, ten centimetres long or longer, and only slightly curved. In profile, the grizzly's face has a concave look, and the highest point of the back is over the shoulders.

The leaflet goes on, 'If it's a grizzly that you've surprised at close range, and it's accompanied by cubs or has a carcass near by, it's probably attacking in self-defence. If it's a black bear, it's probably seeking food.' Having figured out which kind of bear it is, and its personal circumstances, you should then react accordingly. If a bear is seeking food – that's to say, if it's a black bear or a grizzly without cubs and so on – you should fight back.

'You need to fight back with all your energy with whatever you have,' says the writer at Environment Yukon, who is no doubt sitting safely behind a sturdy government desk as he types, expending energy only to walk to the nearest coffee machine every now and then. 'Kick, punch or hit the bear with a rock, chunk of wood or whatever is handy. A bear's nose is a good place to strike.'

But if the bear is acting in self-defence, that's to say if it's a grizzly with cubs or a carcass to protect, it's important that you don't fight back but play dead by dropping to the ground, face down, knees drawn up to your chest, and hands clasped tightly over the back of your neck.

It seemed to me that there was an awful lot to work out in the second or two one might have spare for decision-making. I was glad it was winter and most of the bears, at any rate, were asleep.

We continued our journey, past a native fishing station which consisted of a huddle of log cabins at the water's edge. The First Nations people would put their nets out for salmon in the summer, then smoke and dry their catch, Wendell explained. Many of the Selkirk people still depended on fishing and hunting for a good part of their food. And then, finally, we arrived at Pelly Farm.

The entrance to the property was an incredible junk yard. Seemingly endless heaps of decrepit, rusting tractors and trucks lay alongside countless other slowly oxidizing objects. It looked as though nobody had thrown anything out here for decades or more. And there was a good reason why: in these northern parts, there was no municipal tip. There was no council lorry to whose crew these people could pay a small fee and in return see their outsized rubbish removed to an overstretched landfill site. To dispose of old vehicles and machines was costly. Additionally, it was expensive to ship new parts here. And so, when a truck or a washing machine expired, these resourceful northerners tended just to hold on to it if they had the space. At a later date, if they needed to replace something on another machine, they might be able to source the part from a broken-down model. Some people actually operated commercial junk yards: when someone needed a part, they'd call the junk supplier before attempting to order and ship goods from the south.

Even the piles of rusting metal couldn't detract from Pelly Farm's magnificence, though. This isolated spot on the banks of the Pelly River surrounded by resplendent nature and wilderness would not be everybody's home of choice, but for those who don't rate a Saturday-night social life high on their list of needs there could be few more heavenly locations.

Dale Bradley, who lived here and ran the farm with his two elderly uncles, came out to greet us.

'Mackey went by about twenty minutes ago,' he said. We stuck in a few final trail markers, and headed for home.

It was dark by the time we left Pelly Farm. As we drove back towards Dawson, fat flakes of snow swirled yellow in the headlights' beam, and coated the road with a soundless cladding.

14

From White Horse to Dawson was six days by open sleigh. It was then I realized the vastness of the land and its unconquerable reservation. The temperature was about thirty below zero. With bells jingling, we swept through a fairyland of crystalline loveliness, each pine bough freighted with lace and gems, and a stillness that made silence seem like sound . . . Our breath froze on our fur collars; our lashes and eyebrows were hoar; our cheeks pinky bright, as we took shallow breaths of the Arctic air. Every now and then the driver would have to break icicles out of the nostrils of his horses. Sometimes the sleigh would upset, and often we would have to get out and push through waist-high snowdrifts.

From *Ploughman of the Moon* by Robert Service

Robert Service travelled from Whitehorse to Dawson in 1908 when the Klondike Highway had not yet been conceived of. Rather than flying along a maintained road in a truck with Wendell Carey at the wheel, Service made the journey via the Overland Trail that lay a little to the west of today's highway.

Although Service wrote extensively about the Klondike gold rush years, he didn't actually arrive in the Yukon until 1904, well after the rush had stampeded to goldfields new. He was not a miner but a bank clerk; he remained in the territory for just eight years, and spent much of the remainder of his life in France. None the less, his verse captured the raw adventure and rich personalities of the Yukon during the gold rush he never himself witnessed, and it's for his Yukon collections that he's still best known.

Service had been transferred from his Whitehorse bank to the Dawson branch. He didn't last long in his new job, though. Within a year, his second volume of poems had been published and his royalties were paying him far more generously than his employer was. And so he quit.

Until then, Service's digs had been provided by the bank; when he left his job he needed to find a home of his own. He found a cabin high on the hillside whose doorway was decorated with a pair of moose horns that, Service wrote in *Ploughman of the Moon*, looked to him like the Winged Victory.

The little cabin on Eighth Avenue still stands: it was just a few minutes' walk up the hill from the 5th Avenue B&B. And so, on Monday morning, I headed up there in the company of two new friends, Susan and her seventeen-year-old daughter Hilary.

Susan and Hilary came from Kenora, in northwest Ontario, and had come to the Yukon to work as volunteers for the Quest. Susan was just starting out in the dog-mushing world. She had a small team of dogs which she took on purely recreational outings on the trails around her home. For her it was fascinating to be immersed in the big league for a few days and she entered into all available activities with boundless enthusiasm.

Susan and Hilary were staying at the 5th Avenue B&B as well – in fact, by this time, we three were the only remaining guests – and, now that the race had been rerouted back to Dawson, they'd be staying on to watch the winners cross the finish line.

Susan, it turned out, was not only keen on dog-mushing; she was also an avid Robert Service fan. Indeed, she had across the years so cruelly tormented her children with recitals of his poetry that it was hard to convince Hilary that she'd like to visit the bard's cabin at all.

'But look, Hilary, it's right there!' Susan exclaimed, gesticulating towards the wooden signboard that stood directly outside the B & B's window and pointed up the hill. 'How can you come all the way to Dawson and not go to see Robert Service's cabin?'

Hilary relented. We left the B & B and started to walk up the hill. It was a glorious, sunny day, and the previous night's snow crunched satisfyingly underfoot.

'I wanted the gold and I sought it; I scrabbled and mucked like a slave . . .' Susan burst into verse the moment we set foot on the road.

'No! No! Stop it!' shrieked Hilary, clapping her hands over her ears.

A short stroll later we came to the cabin. In summer, they recite Service's verse here during the long, light evenings. Fortunately for Hilary, though, in winter the cabin is closed. Still, we stood and stared at it for a while. It was a tiny space, perched on a snowy hill behind a meandering log fence. A few steps led up to the off-centre door. Above, a thick canopy of snow blanketed the slightly pitched roof and, in the gable, the smooth white moose horns still sang quietly of success.

Our literary tour didn't end with Service, though. Just round the corner stood a shrine to Jack London.

Jack London's cabin was not originally built on this spot. The structure that stood here now had been brought by Dick North in the late 1960s.

North had long been fascinated by London and by the idea that, somewhere out in the Yukon wilds, there might still stand a cabin that the young prospector had lived in. It was known that London had spent the winter of 1897–8 in a cabin on Stewart Island. Poor nutrition had led to a severe bout of scurvy and, as soon as the river had thawed in spring 1898, London and his companion had torn down their cabin and floated with the logs to Dawson. They'd sold the timber for six hundred dollars and London had taken himself and his money off to Father Judge's waterfront hospital.

But North discovered that there had been a second cabin on whose log wall London was reckoned to have scrawled his name; two local trappers had once found the hut up on the left fork of Henderson Creek. They had cut out the slab of wood that London had autographed as a memento, but years had since passed and the cabin's whereabouts had been forgotten. North dedicated himself to finding it and it is the story of this journey, alongside London's own, that forms the thread of his book, *Sailor on Snowshoes: Tracking Jack London's Northern Trail*, the manuscript of which North had been making final revisions to the morning I'd met him in the internet café.

North's own adventure was an exciting one. In the spring of 1965, he mushed and snowshoed out into the remote wilds of Henderson Creek where he and his companions duly found a cabin with a slash taken out of its wall. There followed some considerable research: North had to locate the original slab of wood, have the signature verified by handwriting experts, see if it fitted into the slash on the wall of the cabin, and find an expert to tree-ring date the logs of the cabin. But finally all the facts fell into place and, in spring 1969, an expedition was launched to carefully dismantle the cabin and to build *two* identical constructions using both the old logs and new. One of those cabins was sent to Oakland, the town of Jack London's birth. The other still stands in Dawson City.

In the afternoon I went shopping, Dawson style. Given the dearth of stores that were open, and the fact that I had several days to spend in Dawson, shopping was an activity that needed disciplined pacing: it would be a mistake to exhaust all the delights in one day. That afternoon, then, I'd scheduled in a visit to Wild and Wooly. Jerry Vanek, the vet, had introduced me to its owner, Romy, a couple of days earlier. She'd said I must drop in and have a cup of Baileys coffee with her.

Romy was an elegant blonde woman who wore stylish, narrow-fitting leather boots that surely would not have survived an hour in the snow outside. This was the first such footwear I'd seen in the Yukon, and it made my own Sorels, in which I had started to feel really very comfortable, look hideously clumping.

Romy had made many of the items for sale in her shop

herself: she painted pictures, created pretty bracelets and necklaces, and took photographs of wildlife which she then transformed into cards. She showed me beautiful images of an Arctic fox and of some caribou which, she said, she'd taken along the Dempster Highway just a day or two earlier. She sold her own wares alongside imported items – ornaments, elegant spoon rests, glorious pewter moose, tasteful children's toys, clothes, hats, boots, scarves, charm bracelets featuring moose and dogsleds, and much more.

Originally from Switzerland, Romy had moved to Dawson twenty-six years previously with her Dutch husband.

'We were living in Zurich,' she told me, 'and my husband decided he wanted to buy me a diamond ring.'

He had taken her to one of the most expensive jewellery stores in the city and shown her the piece he wanted to buy. It cost fifteen thousand francs.

'You're crazy!' Romy told him. 'We don't have the money for that kind of ring. I don't want you to spend everything we have on a stupid rock! If you really have to blow all our savings, let's go to the Himalayas, or float down the Yukon or something.' And with that she flounced out of the shop.

The next day she came home from work to find their apartment full of maps of the American north.

'What on earth is all this?' she demanded of her husband.

'Well,' he said, 'I decided we weren't fit enough for the Himalayas.'

And so they came to the Yukon, and they never left. Now they have a seventeen-year-old son, a couple of businesses, and a second home in Mexico.

I asked Romy about winter tourism in Dawson: why was there so little? Romy threw up her hands in horror.

'We have tried!' She grimaced. 'But nobody comes!'

About twenty years ago, she went on, a local musher built a beautiful tourism lodge. He brought over representatives of all the major airlines in Europe. He kitted them out in winter gear, took them on a wonderful week's expedition into the bush, and lavished upon them fabulous meals every night. At the end of the week, the airline reps were entranced. They loved Dawson in the winter, they said. They would have no problem filling their planes with tourists. Then they went home – and not one tourist came.

'It's too expensive,' said Romy. 'And there's too little daylight – in December and January, we only have about two hours' light a day.' At this time of year, in February, the days were lengthening in Dawson by six minutes every day; the hours of daylight increased by nearly three-quarters of an hour from one week to the next.

Romy and her husband had tried to set up their own winter tourism business, she told me. They'd invested in a number of snow machines, intending to rent them out to visitors. But the business had failed.

And so she dedicated her energies to her beautiful shop and her own stylish handicrafts. In the winter she stuck a notice on the closed shop door asking customers to phone her at home if they wanted to look round.

'I used to sit here,' she said, 'but in the end I realized it was a waste of time. Now, in the winter, I just open when there are customers.'

That evening, I tried to buy a newspaper. It was seven

o'clock; the only place near to the B & B that was open was the petrol station on 5th Avenue.

'I'm afraid we don't sell newspapers,' said the young, brown-eyed man behind the counter very politely. 'You'll need to go to Maximilian's on Front Street.'

'But they'll be closed now, won't they?' I asked.

'Yes, you'll have to go tomorrow, and at this time of year they don't open till noon.'

'Oh well, never mind,' I said. 'By that time today's papers will be long gone. I'll manage without.' I'd wanted that particular issue for a story that had run about the Quest.

The man behind the counter assumed an earnest expression. 'Oh no,' he said very sincerely, 'in this town you'll never find a paper that's less than three days old.'

Lance Mackey left Scroggie Creek, the last checkpoint on the course, at two forty-five on Tuesday morning. At the final checkpoint of the race there was a mandatory eight-hour layover that was designed to prevent over-eager competitors from exhausting their dogs in a flat-out push for the finish. Hans Gatt and William Kleedehn had decided to rest their dogs for longer, however: although Gatt had arrived at the checkpoint three-quarters of an hour ahead of Mackey, he didn't leave until six o'clock in the morning, giving his dogs a full twelve-hour break. Kleedehn left two hours after him. Even given that extra rest, all three teams were expected to cross the finish line the same day.

The talk at the checkpoint had it that Mackey ought to win, and that he should cross the finish line between two and four o'clock in the afternoon. Susan, Hilary and

193

I were at the checkpoint at one. We'd waited in Dawson for five days solely to see the winner of the Yukon Quest take the number one bib. There was no way we were going to miss it.

For a short while, we stood down on the river where a finish chute had been set up. A handful of people were down there with us. A couple of kids played on toboggans. A few folk whirled around on skidoos. But it was cold and I had forgotten to bring my parka and snow pants from the B & B. The others too were feeling chill so we soon went back to the checkpoint. After all, the building was just a few minutes from the finish line and we'd have good warning before the first team reached it: the Quest had arranged with the Bonanza Gold Motel, on the shore of the river a short distance away, that when the first sled passed the motel owners would telephone the checkpoint. The checkpoint would alert the town authorities and they in turn would sound the town siren, whose klaxon was generally reserved for the portentous moment when the river ice broke each spring.

Two o'clock came and went, then three o'clock, then four. It was growing colder outside and I really needed my parka and insulated trousers if I was going to spend long in the evening air, but it would take me twenty minutes to run to the B & B to fetch them. If I went, would Mackey choose that moment to cross the finish line and, after this long wait, would I miss the climax of the race?

In the end I decided to chance it. I sprinted up the hill, retrieved my clothing, and rushed back down again.

'Is there any news?' I breathlessly asked a couple of people standing outside the checkpoint as I returned.

There wasn't.

We waited some more.

The Mackey clan was now here in force. Lance's wife, Tonya, had been following the race throughout as his handler but now a whole gaggle of other relatives had assembled including Lance's Iditarod veteran father, Dick. He was an amiable, white-haired man.

'I hate this part,' he said. 'I'm no good at waiting.'

As the minutes, then the hours, ticked on, conversation dwindled, then took an obscure twist.

'What noise does a moose make?' I asked, for no good reason at all. Presumably it didn't say moo.

'A moose doesn't make much noise at all unless it's rutting,' replied Alex, a Quest volunteer from Fairbanks. Alex wore a scarlet-and-black plaid shirt and had a chubby pink face and soft blue eyes. His red hair was long and curly, almost falling into ringlets that framed his bushy red beard and moustache.

He went on to explain one technique for attracting a moose when hunting.

'We take a can, like a coffee can, poke a tiny hole in the bottom, and run a wet string through it. The hole's got to be really small, so it's tight. When you pull the string it makes a kind of *oooooh* noise with the friction. That's supposed to sound like a cow moose in heat.' He paused for a few moments before adding, 'It's never worked for me though.'

Every now and then the checkpoint's telephone would ring and the room would fall silent, all eyes fixed on the volunteer who picked up the call. And then, when it was clear that this was not the Bonanza announcing a musher, the hum of time-killing conversation would start up once more.

195

At six thirty or so, I had some supper. And then I waited some more.

Then we heard it! A siren! The whole room leapt to its feet. Chairs screeched across the floor, frantically we grabbed hats and coats and surged excitedly for the door. The first person to get there yanked it open – and stopped. An ambulance passed by outside. We giggled foolishly and shuffled back to our seats.

At eight o'clock Susan, Hilary and I managed to borrow a pack of cards and embarked on a game of Crazy 8s. I didn't really understand the rules and lost decisively. I am always dreadful at cards.

Perhaps my substandard performance at Crazy 8s was due to the fact that I wasn't fully concentrating. Rather than focusing on my hand, my mind was continually repeating the one question that by now plagued us all: where on earth was Lance Mackey? Even allowing for the spectators' over-enthusiastic projections, he surely ought to have been here by now. The Mackey clan sat increasingly silent round their table.

Dog-mushing wasn't turning out to be much of a spectator sport, I thought to myself. I didn't like to voice my ideas out loud but really, this was supposed to be the most exciting part of the race and we'd been ensconced in this building, doing pretty much nothing, for seven hours now. It wasn't like any other sport. With ball games, you see the whole shebang. Even when watching long-distance races such as cycling or marathon running, of whose courses enthusiasts usually only manage to observe a tiny section, one can follow the action through coverage on the radio or TV when the race is out of sight. But with dogsledding, nobody knew what was going on out there. From the moment a musher left one checkpoint until he or she reached the next, no one else had any idea what was happening.

For the competitors, of course, that was the beauty and the challenge. For the race's founders, that was the whole idea. Driver and dogs were out there alone, surviving in this harsh land without outside help. If a team met a moose on the trail, if a musher lost dogs, or soaked boots and clothing in freezing overflow, there was no support crew just round the corner offering a warm van and a change of clothing. The team was on its own.

When finally the telephone rang just before half past eight, nobody took much notice. We'd settled into a kind of underwhelmed torpor and when the volunteer at the desk rather timidly called out to the weary assembly, 'Musher!' there were a few moments of spellbound disbelief before anybody reacted at all. Even the Mackeys took a while to register and it wasn't until the much-relieved spectators were out of their seats and running, at last, for the door that Tonya, Lance's wife, called out, 'Do you know the number?'

'It's number six,' said the volunteer.

The Mackey group whooped in celebration and rushed to greet their team.

Several minutes passed before, at last, a tiny head-lamp appeared in the distance down the long, dark river. Slowly it grew stronger until, finally, still looking fresh after their 1,600-kilometre run, Lance Mackey's dogs trotted quietly but cheerfully over the finish line and drew to a stop. We were a thin crowd that cheered them – there were maybe thirty of us, including Mackey's crew and the media corps – but we clapped as noisily as we could. Lance fed his dogs some snacks, then took them off to rest. And that was the end of that.

It turned out that Mackey had taken a wrong turning on the final stretch into Dawson.

'I didn't even know I'd won until I crossed the finish line and got that bib,' he said later as he sat in the warmth of the checkpoint and ate his supper. 'I tell the dogs all the time, "Hey, pay attention, goddammit!" This time they were probably saying the same thing to me.'

Hans Gatt and William Kleedehn came in a little more than an hour later with just six minutes between them. The run had taken Kleedehn, in third place, almost four hours less than it had taken Mackey – but then, he had taken the right trail.

'Is it true Lance went the wrong way?' he asked Mike McCowan as he stood in the finish chute. When McCowan confirmed that it was, Kleedehn didn't even pause. 'It's good he got here in time,' he said.

In the checkpoint, the exhausted mushers submitted to interviews as they spooned bowls of stew into their spent bodies. Why did Gatt choose to rest twelve hours in Scroggie, the hungry media pack wanted to know. Given Mackey's wrong turn, Gatt could have won if he'd left after the mandatory eight-hour layover.

'Half of my team were three-year-old dogs and I just decided in Scroggie that I wasn't interested in racing for first place,' he explained. He was very quietly spoken: I was sitting right next to him and I could scarcely hear what he said. He looked predictably dreadful – they all did with their unkempt facial stubble, red, weather-beaten skin and fatigued, staring eyes. 'If I hadn't waited, it would have created a mad dash for the finish line over a hundred miles. For me, the health of my dog team was more important than winning the race. Making one final push – that's not something for young dogs.'

'Are you looking forward to the Iditarod?' a perky journalist asked. That race would start in less than a fortnight.

Gatt grimaced. 'Right now, I don't even want to think about it.'

William Kleedehn gracefully signed autographs for one or two children who were still about at ten forty p.m., and picked bits of ice out of his beard as he talked.

'I wouldn't mind winning this race one day,' he said gently, 'but I wouldn't be happy at all if I won it because Lance took the wrong turn. It's good that he made it in time. The mandatory eight hours at Scroggie was not enough for my dogs. So I waited for twelve hours, and then waited an extra hour to let Hans get away so that I wasn't even in this race any more. I figured I had the third-best team, and for me the race was over.'

He ate another mouthful of stew before adding, 'It's a dog race, you know. Maybe the wrong turn was Lance's fault, but my idea is that the best dog team should win.'

15

I headed back to Whitehorse a couple of days later. Susan and Hilary were driving there – they'd be at the finish banquet in Whitehorse on Saturday night, and they generously offered me a lift all the way to Muktuk.

We stopped en route at Braeburn. The roadside lodge there is famous for its outsized cinnamon buns. These communities on the second half of the Quest route – Carmacks, McCabe and Braeburn – had suffered as a result of the race's rerouting. They'd bought in supplies and expected to make money as the race rolled through but, now, nobody had come. Our purchase of two cinnamon buns can't have done much to help, but we bought them anyway. They were the size of dinner plates, yet surprisingly moist and tasty. They could have fed us for days.

Finally, we turned off the highway and began to descend the steep winding driveway towards the kennels. There was fresh snow: about six inches had fallen over the last two nights. Frank had been out with his plough so that small white mounds banked to the side of the road and the spruce gleamed with Christmas card prettiness.

It was good to be back, to spend time in the yard scooping poop, talking to the dogs, and helping to harness and bootie them when their turn came to go out for a run on the river. I had by now become strangely competent around these animals. The booties I fitted no longer fell off. The dogs seemed more eager to do as they were told.

I was now living in a cabin rather than in the house. The Muktuk cabins were scattered along the lower part of the driveway. When they'd first bought this piece of land six years previously, Frank and Anne had brought the two older, larger cabins with them. While the house was being built the staff had lived in one cabin and the family – Frank, Anne, a stepdaughter and Frank's father – in the other. In the end, though, the cosiness had become unbearable and Frank and his father were sent to live in a camper van.

Now one of those older cabins was inhabited by Stefan, Sebastian and Thomas. They slept in its upstairs loft section while downstairs there was a kitchen area and a living space featuring a couple of sofas, an armchair, a table scattered with unwashed mugs and half-eaten chocolate bars and, at night time, a small pile of sleeping dogs. I was staying in the smaller cabin next door. It was a comfortable, rustic place, heated by a wood stove. Water came from a large plastic container; light glowed dimly from oil lamps. If I wanted a shower, I walked down the drive to the house.

On Saturday evening the Quest finishing banquet took place at the High Country Inn in Whitehorse. A rolling slide show ran through the evening featuring photographs of that year's race taken by two local photographers, Derek Crowe and Ed Vos. Now we

201

could see just how horrifyingly bald Eagle Summit had been, and how terrifyingly steep its descent. We could see the magnificence of the landscapes – the sparse mountain tops, the pastel pink sunrises and blazing amber sunsets. We could understand the treachery of the overflow ice; we witnessed the camaraderie of the mushers laughing and sharing a hot drink. Above all, though, we could appreciate just how incredibly those sled dogs had performed. Through dense bush and on rocky summits, in the black of night and the brilliance of day, photograph after photograph showed them trotting loyally along, their tails wagging and their long, pink tongues hanging out of their mouths in broad, lopsided grins.

But now, after more than six weeks of immersion, I was going to take a few days' rest from all things canine. Early on the Monday morning after the finishing banquet I was back at Whitehorse airport. I was heading to Inuvik and Tuktoyaktuk on the shores of the Beaufort Sea.

Thomas and Ira, his German shepherd, were leaving for Switzerland the same morning. Their flight left just an hour before mine and both Stefan and Sebastian came along to say goodbye. We bade fond farewells to Ira who peered dubiously out of the cage in which she'd be transported across the continents, and then to Thomas. We bought coffee and were sitting waiting for my flight to be called when we bumped into John Overell.

John was heading to Dawson where he was the resident vet. I'd met him during the weeks of the Quest as he'd been working on the veterinary team. John and I were taking the same flight: the plane to Inuvik touched down in Dawson on the way. He flew often between Whitehorse and Dawson, and between Dawson and Inuvik where he held veterinary clinics every few months as Inuvik had no vet of its own.

'Make sure you push to the front of the queue. You must get a window seat,' John told me as we sat sipping our scalding coffee from paper cups in the airport's single room, which served both arrivals and departures. The view from the air between Dawson and Inuvik, he said, was particularly spectacular. As there was no allocated seating for this flight, and there were no proper boarding passes (at the check-in desk I'd been given a piece of laminated orange paper which had the information '#6 – BOARDING PASS' printed on one side, though the number six didn't appear to refer to anything) the first in line took the best places on the plane.

The call came for our flight to board – that's to say, a uniformed woman stood at the end of the room and shouted that we were leaving now – so I jumped up and made my way as near to the front of the queue as I could manage without upsetting any of those laid-back Yukon folk.

I handed my laminated orange card to the smiling woman as I walked through the door on to the airport tarmac. Not only did I have no printed boarding pass, I had no proper ticket, either: I'd made the reservation over the phone and, when I'd checked in, the ground staff had simply looked at my ID and ticked my name on a list. There were no hand luggage X-rays or security questions. It was refreshing, for a change, to board a plane as one might board a bus.

This plane behaved like a bus, too, with its various

stops – at Dawson, then Inuvik, Old Crow and finally back to Whitehorse. And it wasn't a great deal larger than a bus, either. This was a Hawker-Siddeley 748 with twin propellers. It had room for around forty passengers in cramped seats with no space for overhead luggage. We squeezed in, squashing our bulky parkas and other detritus into whatever crannies we could find: in the north in winter there was no such thing as travelling light. The cabin steward then did a quick head count to make sure nobody was missing, the pilot fired up the engines, and we careered down the runway and into the air.

We touched down at Dawson an hour or so later and all piled out into the terminal building, whose size made the Whitehorse airport seem like a small metropolis. Then those flying onwards reboarded.

John was soon proved right. The view from the plane window between Dawson and Inuvik in itself made the journey worthwhile. The flight path ran directly over the Ogilvie Mountains. To start with, they were round and smooth like perfectly pregnant bumps. Then the hills rose higher and became dramatically sculpted. Now the ridges looked razor sharp while the slopes beneath were carved into dramatic concave hollows.

Then the land began to flatten once more. Rivers wound white, tight and curly, the frozen water surrounded by low trees which, from this height, were not individually visible but threw the sections of land into a muted green hue. Sometimes several rivers slithered alongside each other like a team of bleached anacondas while others wriggled towards one another until they joined to form one great, unmoving waterway.

*   *   *

It was in the area below me now that, in early 1932, Canada's most famous manhunt unfurled. In temperatures that dipped into the minus forties the fugitive, then known by his alias Albert Johnson, was unable to shoot game for food or openly to light a fire for fear of detection. Yet for weeks the 'mad trapper of Rat River' evaded capture by police and hundreds of volunteers.

I'd heard about the mad trapper's exploits; his wiles and fortitude had at the time gripped the world and Dick North, the author I'd met in Dawson's internet café, had mentioned that he'd written a book about him. Now, as I looked out of the aeroplane window at the gelid landscape below in which Johnson had outwitted his pursuers, I could scarcely believe that he had survived for so long.

The episode opened on Christmas Day 1931 when a native trapper went to the Royal Canadian Mounted Police (as the North-West Mounted Police had by then become) post at Arctic Red River and complained that Johnson, who was living in a cabin on Rat River slightly to the west, was tampering with his traps. On 26 December, therefore, two constables set off by dogsled from the police post towards Rat River to ask Johnson some questions: he ought to have had a licence if he himself was trapping there. It took the police two and a half days to mush to Johnson's cabin. Such was the beat of Mounties in the northern bush.

When they arrived, smoke was puffing from the cabin's stovepipe, which suggested Johnson was home. The Mounties called to him but he didn't answer. They saw him peek from a window, but he wouldn't communicate with them. Sensing trouble, the constables decided to mush to the larger RCMP base at Aklavik

– in the Mackenzie Delta just to the west of present-day Inuvik and another night and two days' round journey by dogsled – for a warrant and reinforcements.

On New Year's Eve the Mounties returned to Johnson's cabin. Their numbers had now doubled to four. The trapper still refused either to speak or to emerge from his tiny fortress; when one of the policemen went to knock on the door, Johnson shot him in the chest. The wounded man's desperate companions strapped him to a sled and mushed 130 kilometres back to Aklavik with already-tired dogs in debilitating cold, stopping frequently to rub their unmoving colleague's flesh to prevent it from freezing. They completed the journey in twenty hours and the constable's life was saved.

Now the mission was really under way. The commander at Aklavik dispatched nine men, forty-two dogs and a good supply of dynamite to bring in Johnson. But still the trapper held out. Even when the police dynamited the shack, blowing off its roof and caving in its walls, Johnson kept up such a fearsome volley of gunfire from a fox hole that he'd dug under his floor that, after fifteen hours, police supplies ran low and they had to return to base. When they came back to the cabin, Johnson had gone.

The manhunt that followed lasted, incredibly, for more than a month. The Mounties and the volunteers who joined them were all tough men, experienced at operating in the Arctic bush. They travelled with dogs. They had supplies, food, and fires for warmth. Johnson could eat only the small animals he managed to snare, for the report of a gun would have given away his location. He could only build a fire under a snow bank where the plume of smoke would not announce his whereabouts. Yet still he managed not only to evade capture but, starving after thirty days on the run, to cross the formidable Richardson Mountains. Those who knew the land pronounced this feat to be all but impossible.

It wasn't until mid-February that the RCMP, by then with the help of a plane and pilot, finally killed Johnson in a shoot-out. During the course of the manhunt, they had lost one of their own men and two others had been injured.

Even though the mad trapper was dead, however, a question remained as to his true identity. 'Albert Johnson' was certainly a pseudonym: people who recognized his face from the death photographs claimed to have known him over the previous years under a variety of names. He had been taciturn and wary of strangers, they said. Nobody knew much of his past. The police found no identification on his body. In his cabin there were no letters, photographs or clues of any kind.

In the end, Dick North took up the mystery with a near-obsessive interest. He spent more than twenty years researching Johnson's true identity and even tried to have his body exhumed for fingerprinting. It would have been well preserved as it was buried in permafrost. ('If the reader gets nothing else out of this book, he or she will at least learn the procedures for digging up a body in Canada's Northwest Territories. Granted, the information might not be of much practical use but, if employed as a conversation opener, one could be assured of being one of the few persons knowledgeable on the subject,' he wrote in *The Mad Trapper of Rat River*.) In the end, with the help of a newly discovered photograph, he concluded in the 1990s that the 'mad trapper of Rat River' was an outlaw from the American West named Johnny Johnson. The case, for North at least, was closed.

An interesting side effect of the mad trapper drama was that it secured the importance of the radio as a news medium. Before the manhunt the radio had, according to Dick North, been considered as little more than a mild curiosity. But during those weeks when the story unfolded, the public became transfixed. North explains: 'For days on end the listening public remained with their ears glued to their radios, and, as a consequence of this interest, radio sales boomed throughout North America.'

I flew over the Mackenzie Delta now, close to Aklavik where the police hunt for the mad trapper had been based, and the view from the window changed one last time as solid land gave way to pools, lakes and lagoons. Though the water's surface was perfectly still at this time of year, the pools' forms seemed yet to undulate like misshapen basins, bathtubs and U-tubes moulded from hard, white porcelain. On and on they went, and between them snaked those pallid rivers that pointed, ultimately, towards the great white ocean.

At Inuvik airport a man stood in the car park wearing Teva sandals and socks. Did he not realize this was the Arctic? But the weather was sunny and the temperatures mild – it was only minus twenty-two – so maybe he was making the most of the balmy conditions.

My taxi driver was a hospitable man who insisted on pointing out Inuvik's every landmark as we made our way to the bed and breakfast I had booked.

'This is the town's only traffic light,' he announced as it turned red and we drew to a halt. 'That's the hairdresser's,' he explained, pointing to the right as we set off again, 'and over there's the video rental place. Back there is the visitor centre, but in winter it's closed.'

Inuvik is not in the Yukon, but just over the border in the Northwest Territories. It was founded in the 1950s when the Canadian government decided it needed to establish an administrative centre in the Western Arctic and Aklavik, the largest existing settlement, was considered too prone to flooding and erosion. Construction of the new town began in 1955. It was a complicated project. Because of the permafrost, every building had to be raised on piles, otherwise its heat would thaw the top layer of ground and the building would sink. In 1970, oil was found in the Mackenzie Delta. Natural gas was discovered the following year. Since then, oil and gas extraction have become the town's principal industry.

For the first decades of its existence, Inuvik had no overland access. Even now, there's only one road that leads here from the south. The Dempster Highway, like the town, had to be built on an insulating gravel pad because if the permafrost melted the road would sink. It runs 736 kilometres from just outside Dawson, over the mountains and across the Peel and Mackenzie Rivers. Both these waterways have to be traversed by car ferry during the summer – there are no bridges – and the highway closes altogether for six to eight weeks in the autumn while the rivers freeze and again in the spring when the waters thaw. At these times, Inuvik can be reached only by air.

The Dempster Highway opened in 1979. By this time Val, who owned the bed and breakfast I was staying in, had already lived in Inuvik for six years. She was originally from Ottawa but moved to Inuvik when she was fifteen-years-old because her father, who was in the military, had been posted there.

'I arrived on 17 December 1973,' she told me. 'It was minus fifty-two degrees. I was wearing vinyl high-heeled boots and a miniskirt. My hair was big, my nails were painted. I told my father I hated him.'

The family had arrived in the depths of winter. They would not see daylight for several weeks, for Inuvik has a full month of total darkness each year.

'The first thing I saw at the airport was this really fierce husky. It just looked at me and growled. And my mother said to my father, "What kind of hellhole have you brought me and the kids to?"'

In those days there was no fresh bread or milk in Inuvik's stores, Val told me. Bread had to be made by hand; for milk they used reconstituted powder. There were no paved roads. When residents didn't need snow boots, they needed boots for the mud.

Val had stamped angrily off to school. On her first day, she wore her miniskirt.

'It was like going to jail – you know, when they make inmates walk the mile, or whatever. The boys were just, "Waaah!" and the girls were like, "Ugh!" None of those kids had ever seen a miniskirt before.'

Now, thirty-odd years later, Val is still there, married to Gord, and they have two children of their own.

'The things I miss are the theatre, and opera, and museums,' she told me. 'It's not that you can't get stuff here – now we can get most things – but you can't always get them when you want them. Most of all, though, I miss fresh produce. Down south people take things like cherries and blackberries for granted. Here we don't. When I go south I just go wild buying fresh food.'

My major mission on my trip into the Arctic Circle was to visit Tuktoyaktuk, an Inuvialuit (part of the Inuit family) community on the shores of the Arctic Ocean. Tuk, as it's more commonly known, can be reached by land only during the winter when a 194-kilometre ice road is forged along the Mackenzie River and, finally, across the frozen ocean itself. In the summer, Tuk is accessible only by boat or by air.

I was spectacularly nervous about the prospect of hiring a truck and driving along the ice road all alone. During my weeks in the Canadian north I'd not yet taken the wheel of a car. I'd seen plenty of vehicles sunk in snowy ditches and I'd heard enough terrible stories to put me off attempting to drive in these icy conditions myself.

I asked Val if she thought my idea preposterous. She said I should be fine: I should make sure I hired a decent four-wheel drive, I should go slowly, and I should leave her a note to say where I'd gone and when I was planning to be back. That way, if I ran into trouble, she'd know when to call the RCMP and where to direct them.

And so on Tuesday morning I headed to the Norcan rental depot. I told the woman behind the desk that I wanted to go to Tuk, that I had no experience of driving on snow and ice, and that I wanted the simplest, safest vehicle they had.

'All our vehicles are four-wheel drive,' she said. 'Just take it slow and you should be fine.'

She told me to come back in an hour when she'd have

211

warmed up the car. I had coffee in town, then returned to take temporary possession of a navy-blue Chevrolet Blazer.

'Where are you going?' asked the manager. He hadn't been in the office the first time I'd called. He was a lean, grey-haired, mustachioed man.

'Tuk,' I told him.

'Uh-oh! We'll never see her again,' he joked to the woman.

'Yes, that's what I'm afraid of,' I replied in rather humourless tones.

'She'll be snatched up by an Eskimo!' He winked.

'That's the least of my concerns,' I said.

'So what are you scared about?'

'Well – I've never driven on ice and snow before.'

'Ah, just go slow,' said the man. 'The thing is, it's all white out there. Everything is white, so you can't see the stuff coming up. If you go too fast, you can't see the bends until they're right in front of you, and that's when people get into trouble. But if you go slowly, you'll see everything in plenty of time.'

I nodded anxiously.

'A couple of weeks ago, we had this Swedish guy come in,' the manager continued. 'I told him, like I'm telling you, "You've got to take it slow." But he hadn't gone fifty kilometres before he turned the car. He came back and I said, "What happened?" He admitted he'd been speeding. I said, "Didn't I tell you to go slow?" And he said, yes, he knew I'd said that but then he'd thought it was getting late and he wanted to get there quickly. I said to him, "But look now. Now you didn't even get there at all. And there's five thousand dollars of damage to the vehicle."'

The woman smiled sympathetically while I signed in various boxes, taking out every form of insurance on offer.

I loaded my gear into the car – parka, snow boots, enough food to last me for days, a big bottle of water and then, because I was in survival mode, two spare pairs of socks and some extra long underwear. I had to run back into the office to ask the woman how to get the car into reverse – it had one of those gear sticks attached to the steering column, which I'd never come across before, and in my state of terror clear thinking was out of the question – and then, painfully slowly, I was off.

'Just drive past the Esso station there – ' the woman had pointed through her office's glass door ' – then you'll come to the ice road. You'll need to turn right.'

I drove past the Esso station, reached the ice road, and turned left. After a couple of minutes I passed a huge metal ship frozen into the side of the road. Such was my awe at the surroundings and so great was my concern with making the car go forwards and keeping it the right way up that it wasn't until five minutes later, when I reached the end of the road at the far side of Inuvik, that I realized my mistake.

I turned round, and drove, and drove.

'So what kind of speed would you consider appropriate for the ice road?' I'd tentatively asked the woman in the office before leaving.

'Well, I went to Tuk with a friend a couple of days ago, and I'd say we did between seventy and eighty kilometres an hour most of the way,' she'd told me.

I decided that, given they were locals, between sixty and seventy ought to be about right for me.

'Tuktoyaktuk: road closed,' said a signpost. Adrenalin surged. But nobody had told me this: the people in the rental depot would have known, and so probably would Val – the closure of the very few roads that led to Inuvik was hot news in this isolated spot. What's more, I'd overheard a conversation in the Norcan place: 'He's coming back from Tuk this morning,' someone had said, referring to I don't know whom. 'He's on his way now.'

Tentatively, I pressed on. It was very silent out there amid all that white. But every twenty minutes or half-hour, a car would roar past in the opposite direction at speeds much more daring than mine. There was only one place they could have come from. The route had to be open.

The road was wide – as broad as a dual carriageway – and maintained so that it was smooth and polished like an ice rink. In parts, a light sprinkling of snow took the glare from the surface; in others the sheer ice glistened. But the four-wheel drive seemed to have the conditions under control. It was a glorious day, the sun was shining, and visibility was good.

To begin with, spindly little trees stuck out from the grey and white river banks. Then, about a hundred kilometres into the journey, the trees disappeared and the banks became stumpy and flat.

After a while, my anxieties diminished sufficiently to enable me to fiddle with the radio controls. There seemed only to be one station, which played hits from the sixties and seventies about once every half-hour. The rest of the time, a lilting voice rambled on in a language I could neither understand nor identify.

Then the land levelled out completely. The only features of the bright, white tundra were pingos

– mounds of earth that have been pushed upwards when underground water, trapped by permafrost, has frozen and expanded. They looked like giant, congealed molehills that were perhaps the height of a person, perhaps many times that. It was hard to tell when surrounded by so many kilometres of blank, featureless flat. I later found out that some of those pingos around Tuktoyaktuk were 50 metres high – that's to say they were the height of almost thirty men standing one on top of another – and 300 metres in diameter.

The last stretch of road carved into the sea itself. Now the landscape was incredibly beautiful, and more astonishing than anything I had imagined. The light was perfect that day. The soft blue skies turned a dusky coral pink as they met the incredibly distant horizon. The manager of the car rental depot had not been entirely accurate: the seemingly endless sea was not all white. It was palest lavender and washed-out cornflower, deepening into a rich inky blue where the banked roadside snow cast shadows on to its own haphazard form. The sun reflected primrose yellow off the sheer, glaring ice of the road that now seemed to lead to eternity. The ocean was not totally flat, either. Instead, it rose and dipped in little crests and troughs that absorbed and reflected the low Arctic light in subtle hues. It was truly extraordinary to be out there all alone amid those myriad muted colours, driving a jeep across the Beaufort Sea.

Then, suddenly, I saw a row of spindly poles sticking out of the road as a barrier. I hit the brakes – too hard. The anti-locking mechanism screamed and the car cruised on. I stamped on the brakes again, to no avail. The poles were almost upon me now. I had no idea where they'd come from. I'd been driving slowly; I'd been concentrating, or so I thought. And now, so close to Tuk yet so far from civilization, I seemed to be just fractions of a second from utter catastrophe. I had no idea what lay beyond: was the road really closed? Was this why? Would the smooth icy highway now tumble into the frigid ocean and silently expire?

I touched the brakes a third time, more gently now, and the vehicle started to slow. But the barrier was too close. I had no chance of stopping in time.

'Just go for a gap,' said a little voice in my head. I steered the car between two of those wispy sticks and for a few moments I entirely forgot to breathe. In my mind's eye I saw a banner stretched across the clear blue sky marked with the words 'The End' as in an old-fashioned film.

There was a loud thud. And then the car, miraculously, sailed on. I touched the gas; the engine picked up a little. Remarkably, all seemed well. The barrier had marked a crack in the road's ice where the ocean had shifted. I was supposed to have steered round to the other side.

Shaking violently, my heart thumping, I continued at an assiduous crawl until, at last, minute black specks appeared on the horizon. I drove on and on as, infinitesimally slowly, the buildings grew larger. It was astonishing how long it took me to reach them, even given my slow pace. With no other landmarks, perspective was thrown out of all known proportions. I wasn't alone in finding that my powers of perception were destroyed this far north. A Swedish explorer in the Arctic once wrote an in-depth description of a distant piece of rocky headland featuring two symmetrical white glaciers before realizing that he was, in fact, staring into the face of a walrus.

It was supposed to be a two-hour journey, but I'd been on the ice road for two hours and forty-five minutes before finally, thankfully, I arrived at Tuk. What with the wait for the car to be warmed and my detour in the wrong direction, I hadn't left Inuvik till twelve thirty. I was eager to be back in town before nightfall – to add darkness to my challenges for the day seemed unwise – and this left me, sadly, with just an hour to spend in Tuk. I was sorry. Now I was here, the town seemed much larger and more interesting than I had anticipated. Rows of beige, boxy, metal-walled cabins perched above the permafrost. They were identical in design: a few steps led up to the door; each had one rather beaten-up window in its front. Other houses were made of wood, but they retained the same functional appearance. Yet, under this low blue light, with the tremendous expanse of frozen ocean engulfing them, even rows of pre-fabricated metal emanated a strange beauty.

There was a hotel in Tuk where I could have stayed the night. I went in and asked to use the loo. The people were delightfully friendly and seemed entertained by the thought that an odd British woman, who had never driven on ice before, should have rented a vehicle and made her way out to their very remote home.

I drove to the end of the village where a clearing looked out on the ice that stretched unimpeded to the very top of the world. A couple of picnic tables had been set up for those summer visitors who flew here to dip their toes in the Arctic Ocean. I unwrapped the sandwich I had bought in Inuvik and ate it as I stared out at the frozen peaks and troughs.

Just next to this clearing, a red-bottomed boat sat grounded. A peeling, white-painted plaque was attached to its varnished wooden bow announcing in black capitals its name: *Our Lady of Lourdes*. This tiny mission schooner once transported goods between the Arctic camps and, for decades, ferried Inuvialuit children to residential church schools. The missionaries weren't the first white men to influence the lives of the Tuk people, though. The Roman Catholic Mission first established a station here in 1937, the same year as the Hudson's Bay Company set up its local base. But as early as the 1890s, whalers had visited Tuk, and had brought with them the influenza that decimated the native population.

About halfway along the main street, a cemetery sat at the water's edge.

'Eternal rest grant to them O Lord, and let perpetual light shine upon them,' read the painted words over a white wooden archway, with an Inuvialuit transcription beneath. The light was shining on them that day. It was a remarkable shade of lilac-blue and cast the mounds of snow over the graves into the palest indigo.

Behind the white picket fence, beyond the mishmash of wooden crosses, some tall, some small, some lurching forward like stooping geriatrics on the shifting permafrost, lay the mesmerizing, immeasurable, ice-bound ocean. If one must die and be buried, I thought as I stood there on the side of the road, there can be few more glorious spots for it than this.

I drove back down the main street. There was a gentle bustle to Tuk: vehicles chuntered up and down, snow machines roared, pedestrians sauntered. The weather wasn't too cold: it was a mere minus thirty-one beneath that gentle, Arctic sun. I'd have liked to have spent longer at the ramshackle hotel with its musty carpets, to have sat and chatted with the friendly old Inuvialuit woman who was watching TV in the living room. But I'd purposely told Val and Gord I'd be back that evening. It seemed too complicated to change my plans and risk a search party's being sent out. So I stopped at the gas station, filled my tank with petrol, and headed back along that astonishing, otherworldly road.

This route along the Mackenzie River had been used not just by the Inuit but by white explorers and traders for centuries.

Alexander Mackenzie, a fur trader with the North West Company (at that time the principal rival of the Hudson's Bay Company) navigated the river that would be named after him in the summer of 1789.

'Hardly a Shrub to be seen,' he wrote in his journal on 11 July, from the exact same stretch of river that I drove along as I made my way back to Inuvik. 'Close by the land is high and covered with short Grass and many Plants, which are in Blossom, and has a beautiful appearance, tho' an odd contrast, the Hills covered with Flowers and Verdure, and the Vallies full of Ice and Snow. The Earth is not thawed above 4 Inches from the Surface, below is a solid Body of Ice.'

Mackenzie and his men may not have found trees this far north, but they did come across Inuit tribes.

'The Natives made a terrible uproar speaking quite loud & running up & down like perfect Madmen . . . I made them Presents of some small Articles but they were fonder of the Beads than anything else I gave particularly Blue Ones . . . There were 5 Families of them but I did not see them all as they kept in their hiding Places.'

John Franklin journeyed along the same route in June

1826. It was Franklin's second Arctic expedition (and not the fatal one – it was on his third visit that he and his men disappeared).

It was surprising, really, that Franklin had been allowed to make a second expedition at all for his first foray to the north, in 1819–22, had been utterly disastrous. He had from the start been an unlikely choice of leader for such an undertaking.

'John Franklin was a beefy, genial giant who literally could not hurt a fly. He was formal, painfully shy and abnormally sensitive: to order, let alone witness, a flogging made him tremble from head to toe,' wrote Fergus Fleming in *Barrow's Boys*. 'It can only have been Franklin's charm that won him the leadership of the 1819 Canadian expedition because he had nothing else to recommend him. Aged thirty-three, he was overweight and suffered from a poor circulation that left his fingers and toes cold even in an English summer. He was unfit and had no experience of land travel. He could not hunt, canoe or trek. Three meals a day were a must; he could not move without tea; and even when he could move he could manage no more than eight miles a day unless he was carried.'

That first expedition had ended in the starvation to death of more than half his party. In their desperation, Franklin and his men ate lichen from the rocks, which gave them dysentery. When there was no lichen, they ate their spare shoes.

Remarkably, Franklin had returned home a hero. His triumph over adversity (even if that adversity had been partly his own fault) won the admiration of a public high on the romantic notion of the gentleman explorer. Franklin was the man who'd eaten his boots. He did at least have the sense to learn from his mistakes. When he set out to chart new ground a few years later, his planning was meticulous. He and his men practically skipped up to the Delta, then mapped a thousand kilometres of coastline before returning to spend the winter in the comforts of Fort Franklin on the shores of Great Bear Lake.

One of the most controversial of Arctic explorers, Vilhjalmur Stefansson, spent time exploring the Mackenzie River area too. Stefansson was not his original name: he was Canadian of Icelandic parents, and they had called him William Stephenson. But he thought that name insufficiently exotic for a polar explorer and so he changed it. Stefansson's first expedition took place in 1906–7, when he made his way to the Arctic via the Mackenzie Valley and Herschel Island. The expedition, which aimed to see if there was an undiscovered continent in the Arctic, was a failure. However, Stefansson's love for the north was born and he spent most of the years from 1908 to 1918 among the Inuit. He became known for his assertion that men could survive in the region's pitiless conditions by adapting to the ways of the natives and by living off the land. While he proved that he could stay healthy by subsisting on a diet of just meat and fat, he was criticized for exaggerating the ease of existence in his so-called 'Friendly Arctic' where, after all, even the Inuit regularly starved to death.

Following in the tracks of these explorers I drove on towards Inuvik, looking forward to spending the night tucked up not in an igloo as Stefansson would have insisted but in a soft bed in Val and Gord's comfortably heated house after supper at the local Chinese. The woman on the radio still gabbled in her strange tongue.

The men at Tuktoyaktuk's petrol station had seemed to think I'd come from a different planet. Indeed, I felt as though I had. That village at the end of its river road had been a long way from anything I'd ever known. And yet, it was still Canada.

Back at the bed and breakfast, I found Gord. He was home from the office – he worked as a petroleum products officer for the Northwest Territories government – and was now going swimming. Would I like to go with him? So I grabbed my costume, hopped in his truck, and took a ride to Inuvik's leisure centre.

The leisure centre had been opened just the previous year, and was a fabulous complex for such a small town. There was not just a swimming pool but a water slide, a 'wild river' in which you could either float with the current or work your leg muscles by walking against it, a hot tub and a steam room. I swam for a while, then joined Gord in the hot tub with a sixty-something-year-old man called Nick. Nick was in Inuvik for just a few days; he was travelling round the north with a ridiculously large quilt whose patches were meant to represent the rich tapestry of ethnic groups that made up the modern Canadian nation. We talked about the quilt for a while; then we screeched down the water slide – a man in his fifties, a man in his sixties and me – and I promised to visit the Very Big Quilt in the morning.

I'd been feeling slightly cynical about the quilt, but as soon as I walked into the large hall of the leisure centre in which it was exhibited the following day, I changed my mind: this was a remarkable display. The concept was inspired by an artist named Esther Bryan.

In the 1990s Bryan travelled with her parents from their home in Canada to Slovakia to find the family that her father had left behind: he had been a refugee, and the only member of his family to have escaped his war-torn homeland. It was a profoundly emotional journey and from it Bryan drew a powerful sense of the trauma of migration. She devised this project as a result.

The 36-metre-long Quilt of Belonging is made up of 263 patchwork blocks. The first row represents all the First Nations peoples of Canada, because they lived in the land first. Then in row upon colourful row come the embroidered squares of Canada's 192 immigrant nationalities: St Kitts and Nevis and New Zealand; Syria and Somalia; Botswana and Belarus; Denmark and Djibouti.

The overall effect was one of blending and of harmony, but a closer look at each individual square demonstrated each group's unique character. The Inuvialuit square was made from grey and white sealskin, sewn with sinew, and depicted a traditional northern sport in which contestants try to kick a stuffed sealskin hanging from a rope. The Burundi patch illustrated an African village scene and was embroidered with stitches that replicated the texture of the banana leaves and straw thatch typical of that country.

I left the quilt and went to the town library to check my email. The library was another great facility. It had a huge collection of fascinating northern books, almost all of which had been donated by one man. Out of school hours the building swarmed with children clamouring for their turn to play computer games. While they waited, they sat at tables with colouring books.

'Please could you take your boots off and leave them by the door?' the woman behind the desk asked me as I tramped in. I stopped and apologized before turning round to do as she asked.

'I know it seems crazy.' She laughed. 'When I first got here I thought, "What? You want me to take my shoes off?"' But in this town where everyone wore boots caked in snow, it was normal to leave one's footwear at the door.

Boots duly stowed, I chatted with the woman for a few minutes. I commented that the library seemed well used. She sighed.

'Lots of people treat us as day care,' she said.

'Oh well,' I said, 'one or two of them might look at a book by accident.'

'I try!' said the woman. 'And I'd much rather they were in here driving me crazy than outside on the pavement throwing rocks.'

The librarian knew all the children by name; indeed, she soon knew my name too.

'So you're new in town?' she asked.

When I explained that I was just passing through, she brought out the visitor book for me to sign. 'Usually I only have it out in summer,' she said. Then she turned to one of the children hanging round her desk.

'No you can't go on a computer,' she told him firmly. 'You've already had two goes today.'

I wrote my inscription in the visitor book. A girl aged nine or ten came up to the desk and asked if her friend could play computer games.

'Well she can,' said the librarian. 'But you know that you're banned. Is the computer for her or for you?'

There was a general shrugging.

'You're banned from using the computers till May twenty-eighth. You know that.'

There were sad expressions from the two girls.

'So do you still want a go?' The librarian turned to the second child.

'I guess,' the child replied morosely.

I'd only been here a few days, but already I was starting to feel comfortable in Inuvik. The temperatures may have been cold, but the people here were warm as whale blubber. There was a sense of community to the place. The facilities – the leisure centre, the library, the community greenhouse – were buzzing. While the cars in the yard of the building labelled 'Inuvik Auto' were so buried in snow that just chinks of their side windows peeped from the drifts, the streets were thrumming with trucks and snow machines and, on occasion, dogsleds. 'Dog team crossing,' the yellow-metal signposts stuck into the snow at the side of the road announced.

These civic-minded folk seemed to have more time to give than their southern counterparts. They were happy to take a few moments to chat to a newcomer. Noticeably, many of the people I talked to came from somewhere else. Gord from the B & B came from Calgary; the woman in the library had moved here from BC. They lived here from choice, because they liked it. If they didn't, they could leave. And so, despite the tremendous problems – not just the challenging environment but the cost of living, and the domestic issues and alcoholism suffered by the native communities – these northern towns seemed to me to be well balanced and cheerful places.

*   *   *

I flew back to Whitehorse a few days later. I was heading to Muktuk, but only for a couple of days: almost as soon as I arrived I'd be embarking for a week or more on a dogsledding and camping trip along a section of the Yukon Quest trail with Stefan and Sebastian, and four of Muktuk's guests. We were going to start from Dawson, then travel along as much of the route towards Whitehorse as the snow and our own capabilities would allow. I was greatly excited about this upcoming adventure. For the last couple of months I'd watched the clients come and go on their shorter camping expeditions and I'd seen them return, some exuberant after their adventure, others surprised by the intense labour that winter camping required. I was eager to find out how I would respond to its challenges, and fascinated, too, by the opportunity to mush along the Quest trail having followed the race just a couple of weeks before.

Once again, the plane crossed the Mackenzie Delta with its voluptuously curving lagoons. It headed over those rivers and mountains where the Mounties and volunteers had tracked the mad trapper, and where so many other dramas had been played out.

It was in these mountains, the Richardson range, that Bishop Isaac Stringer and another Church of England missionary, Charles Johnson, lost their way in the autumn of 1909. They were heading from Fort McPherson to Dawson by canoe: Stringer's diocese covered both the Yukon and the Mackenzie River and he was making the journey as part of his regular episcopal rounds. Stringer was experienced in Arctic travel: he had been based at Herschel Island for five years before moving south to Dawson. The trip should have taken five days. The men packed provisions for eight. But their departure was delayed for a week by illness and, that cold September, the water through which they were paddling started to freeze.

Stringer and Johnson decided to abandon their canoes and to retreat to the missionary post at La Pierre's House to the west. When they failed to find that, they attempted to push on instead back to Fort McPherson, but snow and fog obscured familiar landmarks and soon they were lost. Stranded above the tree line with little fuel for a fire and almost no food, the bishop hit on an idea. Knowing that in times of desperation the Indians boiled beaver skins with the hair removed and drank the soup, he proposed that he and Johnson apply the same cooking method to their spare boots, which were made from seal skin with walrus skin soles. They chopped the footwear into pieces and boiled it for many hours before baking the hide on hot stones. Stringer recorded the results in his diary:

October 17 Travelled 15 miles, made supper of toasted rawhide sealskin boots. Palatable. Feel encouraged.

October 18 Travelled all day. Ate more pieces of my sealskin boots, boiled and toasted. Used sole first. Set rabbit snares.

October 19 No rabbit in snare. Breakfast and dinner of rawhide boots. Fine. But not enough.

October 20 Breakfast from top of boots. Not so good as sole.

Finally, after fifty-one days, Stringer and Johnson stumbled emaciated into an Indian fishing camp. They were so thin that the Indians didn't recognize them. It was only on hearing Stringer's voice that one of them ventured, 'I think it must be the bishop.' From this point forward, Stringer became known as 'the bishop who ate his boots'.

Between them, Franklin and Stringer seemed to have made the consumption of one's footwear almost fashionable in these parts, I considered as the plane cruised over the mountains. I was happy not to have been driven to such a recourse myself. My own Sorels, made from plastic and felt, would not have made nearly such a nutritious dinner. In any case, such dangers seemed remote: while men may have frozen on the trail that ran below us, the plane in the sky was far too hot.

'Usually you freeze on these planes, but today they seem to have turned the heating up way too high,' the man sitting across the aisle from me commented.

'Yes, I'm going to turn it down just as soon as I can get to the back,' said the sweating steward, barred in by his trolley. 'I know, everyone's boiling in their thermals.'

As we waited for our perspiration to evaporate, I started talking to the man across from me. He asked what I was doing; I explained my trip.

'Are you from Inuvik?' I asked him in return.

'Yes,' he said. 'I'm going to Whitehorse for the film festival. They're showing my movie tonight.'

His name was Dennis Allen and he was a film director. His movie *My Father, My Teacher* was being screened as part of the Yukon Film Society's Available Light Film Festival.

'You should come along,' he said. 'It's at the Beringia Centre at seven thirty.'

I went.

'You made it!' Dennis exclaimed when I bumped into him in the foyer.

'Aren't you Gerry's brother?' asked Stefan, who had come to see the film with me.

It turned out that Dennis's brother Gerry was a friend of Frank's – not to mention a major character in the film. He'd be helping Frank and Stefan with a mushing trip to Herschel Island later in the season.

The film was both touching and fascinating. It depicted the upheaval experienced by Dennis's Inuvialuit family as they moved from their base in the Mackenzie Delta to the new town of Inuvik where they had to abandon their tradition of living from the land and adapt to the white man's ways.

'Everyone was saying, OK, you know, they're going to build this new town and there's going to be jobs and prosperity, we're going to have electricity and we're going to drive cars and we're going to watch TV and listen to the radio,' Dennis explained in voice-over as the now-familiar streets of Inuvik panned across the screen.

'I used to go to meetings and listen to all this "what's going to happen in the future",' Dennis's 77-year-old father, Victor, said of his early days in the town. He moved to Inuvik when it was first founded because the new school was there, and he and his wife preferred to create a home for their children in town than to let them live in the residential hostel. 'The kids were just small then. We were talking about their future. What they're going to be. And it sounded simple as that. But it didn't work that way . . . because they had to struggle in order to survive the new system.'

229

There was nothing overtly political about the film – really, that was the beauty of it. It was a personal story. Much of it was shot at Baby Island where the family still goes each year to hunt whales for muktuk.

'I had to educate myself too,' Victor said. 'I had to learn to work, you know, be on time and this kind of stuff . . . It was hard. Lots of times it was hard for me. Really hard. Because all of my mind was hunting, the hunting season's come round, all my mind is out on the land.

'My kids were in school. They got no time to learn their own mother tongue because we were all too busy trying to make a living. We have to go along with the trend. We have to go along with what's happening. We cannot fight it. I used to try to fight it but I found out it was not worth it. You have to go along with it because your kids are in it.'

Victor was old now and rather toothless, but he was wise and gentle and almost always smiling, even when he recounted the most traumatic displacements of his community.

'The thing they left out of the school system is that they didn't have anything about the land. That's a big loss right there,' he said.

Dennis told of his own struggles with addiction, the way he chose as a young man to cut himself off from his culture because he was ashamed of it, and then drank heavily and took drugs to numb the pain. 'At that time, a lot of people drank. It was just part of moving into the western civilization,' he said.

'We can't go back to that culture because it's gone and this is why young people have a lot of problems today. Their mind is on the land but they don't know how to get there,' said Victor.

I later read that Victor, with his cheerful willingness to adapt to Inuvik's ways, had been the town's first Santa Claus.

'There were no chimneys on the houses for Santa to climb down, and he did not use reindeer; he arrived instead on a sled pulled by a team of huskies,' Jane Stoneman-McNichol related in her book on Inuvik's history, *On Blue Ice*. 'Victor Allen was the town's first Santa Claus. He made his début in front of the school to a cheering throng of children.'

'His dogs didn't want to run that day,' an elderly Inuvik resident remembered. 'Someone ran ahead of his team pulling at the dogs. What a sight! All the little children standing on the steps of the school shouting, "Here comes Santa Claus!" and there was Santa with his dog team that didn't want to run. He made the children so happy.'

16

We were sliding backwards down the steep, snowy hill.

'Maybe you should put on the brakes,' suggested Stefan, with icy, Teutonic cool.

'I have got the brakes on,' squealed Irv in a voice that bubbled with panic.

We were on our way to Dawson for the start of our camping trip – or at least we were supposed to be. At this point we'd travelled no further than Muktuk's driveway.

We had with us three visitors from Monaco – Alain, Natalie, and Natalie's brother Philippe – and their French friend Paul. I would be driving a fifth dog team, while Stefan and Sebastian would travel by skidoo, hauling supplies. Sebastian, Philippe, Paul, a second driver and fifteen dogs were in the dog truck, leading the way up the hill. The remainder of our human contingent was in the pick-up behind, with twenty dogs ensconced in the attached dog trailer. But we hadn't progressed even halfway up that snowy, winding road when the pick-up had skidded, the wheels had spun, and we'd started to slide slowly backwards. I felt suddenly, fiercely sick. If it came to it, we could hop out and run – but the dogs were locked in.

Irv, who Anne had hired to drive us, was a round character. Rings of brown curls framed his moon-shaped face above a well-padded torso. Now he became rounder still. His eyes, previously spherical brown marbles, grew in size to bulge like plump figs while his face took on the look of a giant apple, red and shiny with perspiration. His mouth stretched in a horrified, silent yowl like a gaping bite into the fruit's flesh.

'Oh well,' said Stefan, with admirable Aryan sang-froid. 'The road flattens out soon anyway.'

The seconds dilated in synchronicity with Irv's face, which appeared to inflate like a pumped-up rubber mask. His tight curls appeared somehow to shake and simmer, like a brown chocolate fondue soon to overboil. And then the trailer rolled into the ditch and we ground to a well-entrenched halt.

We climbed out of the truck and walked anxiously round to the back. The dogs' eager faces peered out through the mesh of the trailer's doors. They were delighted as always to see us, but even they appeared to realize that sliding backwards into the ditch quite so early in the proceedings had not been quite the right thing to do. Their expressions took on a faintly quizzical gaze as if to say, 'Oh dear, *now* what have you done?'

Stefan disconnected the trailer from the truck. Slowly, we heaved it from the ditch. We edged it step by weighty step back on to the driveway and nervously, employing all our strength to prevent the heavy contraption with its canine cargo from running out of our control, we eased it slowly down the hill towards flatter ground where it could come safely to a standstill. But before we reached the plateau, we heard the unwelcome thrum of a skidoo – and there behind us appeared Frank leading four day-trippers with dog teams.

I don't remember Frank's exact words. I can't remember whether he unleashed a torrent of profanities, or just let slip a strangled squeak of despair as he drew his skidoo to a halt and watched his precious dogs in a loose trailer inching down the hill. His horrified expression, however, is for ever etched on my mind. His mouth fell slightly ajar, his eyes became intense, and he stared at us with a terrible blend of outrage and fear.

It took us around an hour to right the trailer and reconnect it to the truck's tow bar. Almost immediately, Irv spun the wheels again and, eyes wide with dread, he ground to a halt. In despair, Stefan accepted that he would not have the restful journey he had hoped for and took over the wheel for the next three or four hours while Irv's eyeballs gradually regained conventional proportions from the passenger seat.

It was eight o'clock by the time we arrived in Dawson. We'd had to stop in Pelly to drop the dogs and to leave a cache of supplies at the RCMP cabin. When we arrived back here by dogsled in several days' time, we'd be able to replenish our sleds and toboggans and continue along the trail as far as the snow allowed. Irv had driven the last section of road from Pelly but he'd limped along at a terrified trundle, and when we arrived at the Bonanza Gold Motel the proprietress was already in her pyjamas. We fed the dogs, then ordered pizza for ourselves and turned in for the night.

Things started well the following morning: one of the dogs cocked his leg and peed down my trousers. To be urinated upon by a dog is a sign that the animal loves you – or so seasoned mushers say – and should have been a wonderful portent for the days ahead.

In the dim, early-morning light, we fed the dogs and then ourselves, loaded the animals into the truck and trailer, and drove the short distance to the start of the trail.

The trail ran alongside Bonanza Creek. Just a few hundred metres from where we now staked out, harnessed and bootied the dogs, George Carmack, Skookum Jim and Tagish Charlie had unearthed their stupendous find. It was right here that, around 110 years ago, the hordes of hungry miners had surged to stake out the best claims. Right here, on this remote patch of land, the air would have echoed with the clamour of shovels digging, logs being sawn, and the voices of tough, mine-hardened men calling across their claims.

Now, though, Bonanza Creek was deserted. The white, feathery silence was punctured only by the excited barking of our own dogs. We packed our supplies – tents, sleeping bags and mats, stoves, fuel, horsemeat, kibbles, frozen pork, fish and chicken skins, and our own food, which we had precooked and frozen into slabs in ziplock bags – into the sleds and on to the toboggans that Stefan and Sebastian would tow behind their skidoos. Then finally, at ten or eleven o'clock, we waved goodbye to our drivers, unleashed our feverishly excited teams, and trotted away from the road and civilization.

I had six dogs in my team. (There should have been seven but Sprocket came into heat during the journey and was sent home with the drivers.) In the lead were Sonar and Pelly. Sonar was a black female with white chin whiskers and chest hair. She was fervently keen to please. Had she been a six-year-old child, she'd have been the one desperately stretching her hand high in the air to answer every question the teacher asked. She knew the rules and, calmly and diligently, she stuck by them. Neither laggardly nor excessively excitable, she trotted along at a perfectly even pace. When other dogs messed around in the harness, Sonar sometimes growled at them and told them to behave.

Next to her was Pelly, who had been in Saul's Quest team. Pelly was docile and biddable, a beautiful svelte black and cream coloured dog. He liked to eat. Next back were Val and Terror. Val was little, lithe and eager to run. She'd been in Saul's Quest team, too. Every time we stopped, Val leapt into the nearby bushes and chewed on the twigs and branches of any shrub she could find. When the team was at a standstill and there were no bushes to gnaw, she had an irritating habit of chewing through the lines instead. It was as if she wanted to make her point that she didn't much like waiting around: she wanted to pull. Terror had soulful brown eyes and longed to be loved. He had an aversion to his footwear, and each time the sled stopped he would bite at his booties, pulling them off with his teeth when he could. But when I went to refit them, he'd proffer his big, furry foot and gaze at me in a way that commanded instant forgiveness.

At wheel, nearest to the sled, I had Alex and Log. Log was a workaholic. Wildly enthusiastic, his legs pumped with an unfathomable energy. He seemed not to have figured out that the food and snacks would arrive regardless of how many times his paws touched the snow. And lastly Alex was perfectly even-tempered. He was large, affectionate and huggable with a tufty brown and cream coat.

We followed the path that, just a few weeks ago, the Quest teams had trodden. The markers indicated the way to us as it had to them. During the race, I'd seen the dogs and mushers only at the checkpoints. I'd had no idea about the pristine world they'd traversed once they'd left Dawson, trotted down the ice of the Yukon River, and then turned towards Bonanza Creek. It was wonderful to see it now.

After a short while, we passed Dredge Number Four. This great hulk of gold-mining machinery is deemed a historical monument. The dredges arrived in the Klondike after the majority of individual miners had left: the gold that could be profitably extracted by a man and his shovel was soon exhausted and, within a few years, the men with their sluice boxes had either moved on to goldfields new, or given up on their dreams and gone home. There was still wealth to be extracted from the Klondike, though. It just needed to be mined by more efficient means.

Dredge Number Four belonged to Joe Boyle's enterprise, the Canadian Klondyke Mining Company. Boyle was one of the big characters of the gold rush days. He was one of the first prospectors to arrive in Dawson: having heard rumours of gold during a visit to Victoria, he was already at the foot of the White Pass when news of the Klondike strike broke in San Francisco and Seattle. But Boyle had grander ambitions than most. He didn't want a single claim. He wanted more.

Within two months of arriving in the Klondike, Boyle turned on his heels and headed out again, against the flow of the incoming stampede. He was off to Ottawa where he lobbied politicians to grant him an eight-mile concession exclusively for hydraulic operations.

Boyle won his concession, which dredged up Yukoners' fury as well as gold from the creeks, in November 1900. Soon afterwards his rival Arthur Treadgold also secured a controversial concession for his Yukon Gold Company. But the battle was worth it. Boyle's first dredge cost two hundred thousand dollars to build and had paid for itself by the end of its first two months of operation. Dredges number two, three and four soon followed.

Boyle was a restless character, however, and in due course he tired of his lucre. Hungry for new challenges, he assembled a machine-gun unit consisting of fifty Yukoners and, leaving his mining operations under the management of his son, he marched them off to the First World War. On each lapel, he wore a maple leaf moulded from his own Klondike gold. He subsequently embarked on wild adventures in Eastern Europe, succeeded in the audacious rescue of a group of important Romanians who were being held hostage by the Bolsheviks, and fell in love with the Romanian queen.

Even when he was far away, though, Boyle's dredges continued to chew their way through the creeks of the Klondike, munching up the gravel, extracting the gold, and spewing out the muck to form the great mounds of tailings that still lie across the land today. Dredge Number Four was the last to close. It continued to operate until the late 1950s. Then it slowly sank into the mire until it was hauled out by the army and preserved. It looked to me to be an extraordinary creation. A strange mixture between a hulking boat and a several-storey building, this dawn-blue wooden contraption was dotted with square windows over five or six levels that lay not in orderly lines but as though they'd been spattered there by a spray gun. At the front and back, a welter of pulleys, cables and hefty, rusting chains held the moving parts like enormous metal drawbridges.

We stopped to stare at it for a few minutes, then continued on our way. The serpentine tailings were covered in snow now so that they appeared not as the brown scar tissue of money-minded ventures, but rather like the squeezed-out trail of a giant tube of toothpaste.

Then the terrain started to rise into the foothills of King Solomon Dome and the snow became deeper. Many gold prospectors were long convinced that this hill contained the mother lode, though geologists insist that such a treasure trove doesn't exist in this region. Fresh powder had fallen since the Quest, and nobody much had come this way in recent weeks. Following in the tracks of Stefan's skidoo, the dogs leapt and bounded with apparent delight through the downy whiteness as the sled plunged and pulled through the furrows. As we rose higher we drove into a veil of fine speckled snow and the view across the spruce-laden hills became soft in its mist. And then we met a snowplough.

We were travelling on road up here but the route was little used and we had never expected it to be freshly ploughed. The naked gravel surface would be horribly tough on both the dogs' feet and the sleds' runners. It seemed perverse that, after so many weeks in Whitehorse with sparse snowfall, we had come north where the ground lay covered like a duvet display in a bedding store – and almost immediately found ourselves in the path of a snowplough that had shovelled it all away.

'We've ploughed it down to the gravel,' one of the two snowploughing men told Stefan apologetically as we braked the sleds. The dogs stood tall and alert and barked in frustration at this annoying duo who had spoiled their fun. Maybe it was their anguished expressions that convinced them, for the generous snowploughers immediately offered to help: they'd turn round, they said, and try to spread a little of the snow back over the path. Stefan and Sebastian would follow on their skidoos, attempting to flatten the hard shards of broken-up snow into a passable trail. And lastly, we'd follow with our five teams of dogs.

It was a battle, none the less, to keep the dogs on the thin ribbon of snow that was left to us. It was chunky and churned up, and again and again they veered off towards the flatter gravel. Luckily, though, the snowfall continued and soon it had provided just enough covering to soften the abrasion to their paws.

We reached the summit and began to head downhill. We stopped at the side of the road for a late lunch – semi-frozen sandwiches that our coolbox had kept only vaguely warm, sticks of salami, and cups of hot soup. We packed up, hooked up our teams, fitted booties on the feet of those dogs who'd chewed theirs off, and the first four teams set off. I was waiting till last as I was travelling at the back of the pack, but, just as I was ready to pull out my snow hook and unleash my team, Stefan came up with a worried expression.

'I can't start my skidoo,' he said.

The skidoos failed to start on a regular basis; both Stefan and Sebastian were used to having to tease them to life. But I'd never heard either of them sound so quickly defeated. It appeared that this problem was more serious than usual.

'You go ahead,' he said. 'We'll try to fix it and then we'll catch up.'

A while later he reappeared on Sebastian's skidoo but the news was not good. They hadn't been able to repair the problem. We should wait where we were, he said. He'd go back to Sebastian and they'd keep on trying.

We were on a wide, snow-packed road. On either side, spruce forests stretched to the horizon. We tethered the sleds to trees; the dogs barked and whined for a while, upset that their entertainment had been curtailed, then curled up and slept in the snow. I sat for a while and chatted to them, then joined the others in a huddle by the side of the road. Time was dragging now. This was the first day of our great expedition and, as the minutes turned to an hour then more, the truth became clear: we were starting disappointingly badly. Two hours had passed and dusk had fallen before at last we heard the distant thrum of a skidoo and a headlight appeared in the distance.

But there was only one headlight, not two. As the beam drew closer it became obvious that Stefan had come alone.

'We still can't mend the skidoo,' he told us tersely. 'Perhaps we will never be able to mend it.'

He was looking visibly stressed. I'd never seen him looking anxious before – not all those weeks ago when he'd taken me with Fraser on that early incident-prone day trip down the Takhini River and Toby had broken his foot; not even yesterday when Irv's driving skills had seen us sliding backwards down a snowy hill and depositing a trailer full of dogs in the ditch. The fact that he looked worried now boded badly.

It was already seven thirty, so we were going to camp a short distance from where we now stood, Stefan said. There was a clearing in the trees a little way back, just after a creek, where we could stake out the dogs and set up our tents. It wasn't perfect but it would do. He would go on ahead and start to prepare the camp. We should turn our teams round and meet him there. Then, while he supervised the others in setting up the camp, I was to take the working skidoo and rescue Sebastian who was still stranded on the hillside. Sebastian and I would tow the broken skidoo to the campsite. What to do with it then was an issue for later.

Stefan roared off into the distance once more and we began to rearrange our lines and hook up the dogs: we'd moved some of them from their two-abreast running formation and staked the lines to trees as the dogs had more space and were more secure that way. Then we started to try to turn the teams round.

It took a while. To manoeuvre a dog team through a U-turn is rarely simple for inexperienced mushers. The dogs' natural inclination is not to swoop round in a wide, tidy curve, but to take the opportunity to double back and chat to the dogs behind, which leads the lines into not a neat turn but a nasty tangle. I was just trying to help Paul with his team when Stefan reappeared. Probably half an hour had passed since we'd last seen him, and still we hadn't moved. He was looking even more tense than he had before.

'What's the matter?' he hissed quietly to me. 'You go first. Just get on your sled!'

He grabbed my leaders and turned them round in a few seconds flat. I started off towards the campsite. Stefan turned the other teams round, then hurtled past to overtake me. He stopped the skidoo on the packed snow of the road, then led us left into the imperfect campsite. The snow was deep here. It came to the dogs' shoulders.

'Come on, Sonar,' Stefan called to my leader. Sonar was one of Stefan's favourite dogs and the affection seemed to be mutual. He grabbed the neckline that joined Sonar and Pelly and plunged through the snow with them. The dogs enthusiastically dived through the depths behind him. From the back, I stumbled about trying to balance and push the sled through the deep snow. Yet again, it occurred to me that these were wonderful creatures. Even now, when things had gone awry, they saw life as a great adventure. As long as they had food and love, they stayed happy.

'Right, I will take care of your team,' said Stefan. 'You take the skidoo and go and get Sebastian – he's been on his own up there for too long now.'

'How does the skidoo work?' I asked. I had never driven one before.

'The throttle is on the right, like this.' Stefan wiggled his thumb.

'And the brake?'

'On the left.'

'Are there gears? Is there a clutch? Can I stall it?'

'No. It's easy. Just go.'

My exit was delayed by a run-in with Natalie who had managed to tangle her team round the parked skidoo as she had tried to turn left into the clearing.

'It is a bad place to leave it!' she pronounced huffily. Realistically, though, the skidoo was the only obstacle in a wide, clear road. Had I been in a kind frame of mind, I'd have appreciated that we were all tired, that it was the end of a difficult day, and that she was inexperienced at driving dogs. But I was not in a kind frame of mind so I privately dismissed her as a blithering idiot who needed to learn to steer.

Finally I reached Sebastian, who had resorted to doing press-ups on the snow to keep warm. It was eight o'clock now, dark, and in his imagination, he said, he'd started to hear the howling of wolves. But this was Sebastian, the man possessed of perhaps the sunniest temperament on earth, and he was still smiling.

It was not a wonderful evening. We still had hours of work to set up the camp: heating water for both the dogs and ourselves; chopping wood for a fire; shovelling away the hip-deep snow in order to pitch the tent; and finally cooking our dinner. It was eleven o'clock before our pasta and sauce were ready and by then Alain was so exhausted that he'd gone to bed hungry.

Stefan, Sebastian and I were supposed to sleep in a separate, smaller tent but the idea of shovelling yet more snow didn't appeal. There were a few cabins scattered through the clearing. Obviously there was a small community here in summer, but in winter there was nobody and the cabins were empty. We pushed open the door of one of them – to lock one's cabin door and deny refuge to strangers would be to break the code of the north – and saw that most of the small room was taken up with a billiard table, neatly protected by a brown plastic cover. The walls were lined with well-thumbed paperback novels – Sidney Sheldon, Judith Krantz and the like – while one corner was occupied by a stereo. The floor and surfaces were littered with countless empty beer cans and cigarette butts. It was a bizarre little base in the middle of the wilderness but we had little energy to contemplate who might own the cabin and when they might last have been here. We laid our mats and sleeping bags on the floor.

'I think you'll need to wear your hat,' said Stefan as

I took mine off. He was right. From that point forward, my hat wouldn't leave my head day or night. Just seconds passed, and Sebastian's breathing betrayed the fact that he'd fallen into an instantaneous, deep sleep. I felt envious, briefly, then drifted into my own chilly slumber.

A man appeared with a tow truck the following morning. Sebastian had called Frank on the satellite phone the previous night to tell him of our predicament and, after some discussion, Frank had rung a Dawson mechanic and asked him to come out to us. Fortunately, we were still on a road that was navigable by motor vehicles. The new plan was this: having waved goodbye to the mechanic and the skidoo we'd continue along the trail that day, with Stefan and Sebastian riding on a single machine. The next morning Stefan would carry on with the four clients, but he would drive my dog team. Sebastian and I would drive the working skidoo back to this first campsite to meet the mechanic, who would – we prayed – deliver to us the mended machine. Sebastian and I would then each drive a skidoo to catch up with the others by nightfall. I was sorry, of course, to be leaving the dogs for a day but there was no doubt that this was the best solution. And, in any case, I hadn't driven a skidoo at all until the previous evening so I was in part looking forward to the new challenge of driving one through the upcoming hilly sections of the trail.

We continued along the road, past the point where we'd waited yesterday, and veered right into the Indian River valley. Now the track was narrow and bumpy, and perfectly covered with snow. Around us velvety white dunes rose and fell like the humps of a herd of albino camels. It was a bizarre but beautiful landscape, the result of many decades of mining activity.

An hour passed – or was it three? I was finding that my perception of time grew warped from my place on the back of the runners. I became so engrossed by the gentle rocking of the sled over the trail and the obstacles it presented – a slick lamina of pale turquoise ice where overflow had frozen; a violent camber; a rut or ramp that caused the sled to jump – that I'd look at my watch and be astonished by the hours that had passed.

Our camping spot that night was infinitely better than that of the evening before. In daylight, we massaged cream into the dogs' paws. My principal task for the evening, while the others shovelled snow to create room for our tents and chopped wood for a fire, was to melt snow on our two methyl hydrate stoves. These were rough, cylindrical, metal contraptions comprising an outer shell and an inner bucket with a lid. I poured one cup of methyl hydrate into a moulded metal bowl in the bottom of the outer shell, then lit the fuel so that it flared up in dramatic blue and orange stalks. Then I slotted the bucket, filled with snow, into the outer cylinder, put its lid on, and left it to reduce. By the time I'd filled the second bucket with snow and lit the other stove, the first stove would need attention again. The melting snow would by now have shrunk in volume and so I'd add more. Every twenty minutes or so, the methyl hydrate needed replenishing. As each bucket of water grew hot, I poured it into big yellow-plastic jerry cans. Kept in the cool boxes, this water would stay liquid until morning and could be used for the dogs' breakfast while we melted more snow for their lunch. When the jerry cans were full, I prepared more water for ourselves. We needed to refill our Thermoses, to cook the pasta for our own dinner, and to do the washing up afterwards. In all, to melt enough snow for thirty-four dogs and seven humans took two hours. And in the morning, we'd do it all again.

We had no idea how cold it was. Our thermometer recorded temperatures to minus thirty, but when we crawled shivering from our sleeping bags the following morning we found that the mercury had slithered down into its bulb as though it, like us, was trying to conserve every last droplet of heat.

Chivalrously, Stefan and Sebastian had given me the warmer, middle berth in the small unheated tent that we three shared, but during the night I'd been shatteringly cold none the less. As day dawned, we woke up with skull caps of snowy, white ice encircling the tops of our heads so that we lay like a trio of congealed pontiffs.

Inside my sleeping bag I'd kept on the clothes I'd worn during the day except for my parka and snow pants: merino wool long johns, fleece trousers, a polypro undershirt, a merino wool sweater, a thin fleece, a thick fleece and my hat; on subsequent nights I'd add a third fleece, a balaclava and a second pair of long johns. Additionally, I'd been wearing the felt liners from my boots to prevent the perspiration in their fabric from turning into foot-shaped ice blocks overnight. I'd spread my parka over the top of me. In my fleece trouser pockets I'd kept everything that I wanted to keep from freezing: compact digital camera, spare batteries, contact lenses and a small bottle of solution.

My snow pants, which I hadn't worn during the night, were frozen so that they almost stood up by themselves.

My sleeping bag was solid with ice where I'd breathed moisture on it. Veterans of winter camping insist you must never breathe on your sleeping bag. You should pull the bag's head tight around your own so that just a small circle around your nose and mouth stays open to the elements. But it was so cold I couldn't bring myself to heed this advice and I'd spent the night hunkered deep inside the warm down. The icy lumps my breath left wouldn't thaw during the day, of course. The temperatures would stay well below zero. The sleeping bag would keep its frozen patches till we reached the cabin at Scroggie Creek with its roaring wood stove.

My boot liners, which I'd kept on my feet inside my sleeping bag, were warm but the boots themselves were frozen so that, when I put them on, the cold cut through the liners and my feet soon became chilled and numb. I thawed them too quickly by the fire; then the pain was searing so that I had to walk up and down screwing up my face and biting my tongue to stop myself shouting in agony.

We emerged from our tent at seven thirty but by nine o'clock my body still was not functioning. My main assignment of that hour and a half had been to roll up the sleeping bags and mats in the tent that Stefan, Sebastian and I shared. In normal temperatures, it would have been a ten-minute task. As it was, the air that needed to be squeezed from the bags was perishing, and my hands became so intensely sore when I pressed them into the down that I spent more time doubled over warming my digits in my trousers than actually packing up the bags. In the end, this simple job took me half an hour or more.

In those conditions, the tiniest tasks became

complicated. I had to plan for an hour or two in advance if I wanted to brush my teeth: I needed to put the toothpaste in my pocket, next to my skin, where it would thaw just enough to allow me to squeeze a small quantity on to my brush. Other ablutionary matters were easier than expected. My contact lenses froze in their solution a couple of times, but once thawed seemed none the worse for their experience. As for going to the loo, it wasn't something one loitered over, but briefly exposing one's buttocks to the sub-zero elements was never especially uncomfortable. Washing my face was more troublesome by far: the cleansing wipes I had brought turned out to be useless as they had immediately frozen into a solid papery block. My moisturizer, on the other hand, had truly triumphed. From its frozen block I was able to chip tiny bits which melted as I massaged them into my face. I didn't even conceive of washing below the neck.

Finally that morning we made sufficient headway in our battles against the cold to feed the dogs, to melt snow, and to eat our breakfast: eggs that had been beaten then mixed with chopped onion and bacon before being ladled into ziplock bags and frozen in slabs. Blasted for a couple of minutes in the frying pan they made a deliciously tasty hot eggy mess.

Still, it was eleven thirty by the time Sebastian and I left for our campsite of the day before. It was only a 45-minute journey by skidoo, but in this remote land of no mobile phones we had no firm rendezvous time with the mechanic. We had a satellite phone, but communication depended on a signal and the batteries had a painfully brief life at these temperatures. The satellite phone couldn't be kept on permanent standby to receive unexpected calls; it had to be saved for summoning help in an emergency. And so we arrived at the designated point on the road and waited. We drank cups of hot water (we'd remembered the Thermoses but forgotten the tea bags) and ate some oatmeal. Sebastian gave another fine demonstration of his extraordinary ability for sleep by dropping off into a deep after-lunch snooze sitting upright on the skidoo while I marched up and down trying to keep warm. When finally after three and a half hours the mechanic arrived, I could have kissed him.

'This skidoo is done for,' he told us. 'I didn't think I'd ever fix it. I rang Frank last night and told him – he was pretty upset. In the end, I managed to get it going by using the parts from one of my own machines.'

We thanked him effusively. And then, in a final flourish of generosity that must surely guarantee this man a place in heaven whatever heinous sins he commits over the course of his life, he said, 'Anyway, I brought you some beers.' And he reached into the back of the truck and pulled out a twelve-pack.

Sebastian gave me a basic primer in driving snow machines before we set off to catch the dog teams.

'We're going to go at a nice, slow pace,' he said. 'But when you're going uphill, you have to go fast, otherwise you'll never make it. And when you're going across overflow, you have to go really fast, otherwise you might break through. And when you're going downhill, try not to use the brakes.'

We reached our camp of the night before at five thirty and collected the toboggans and supplies that Stefan had left for us to transport. Then we began to climb higher, into the Black Hills. Now the path became narrow, only fractionally wider than the runners of the skidoo. The way was clearly marked by the five dog teams that had passed earlier but on either side of their tracks the thin, packed trail dropped off deeply into snowy gorges. In an instant, my skidoo veered marginally from the path and the machine tumbled into the mire. I yelled an expletive, looked up – and there was Sebastian, a few metres ahead, pulling his own skidoo from the drifts. Strangely, we'd both dropped our skidoos at exactly the same moment.

Sebastian hauled my snow machine back on to the path – it was too heavy for me to handle alone – and we drove high into the hills. As the sun dipped beneath the horizon, the sky turned a blowsy pink. We rolled along a ridge, chugging up and dipping down with the hills' contours. The sky darkened to a more sultry shade while the snow that covered the distant peaks shifted between pastel pinks and purples.

And then, as we bowled over one more velvety knoll, we were greeted by the barking of dogs. Stefan and the others had stopped just ahead of us. They'd hoped to get to the cabin at Scroggie Creek that night so that we could have an evening by the warmth of a stove, but Stefan didn't know how much further that lay. Given that night was already falling, he'd decided it would be wise to camp where we were.

We made our preparations for the evening. Then, just as we were about to crawl into the tent for supper, Stefan noticed movement in the sky above.

'Look,' he said, pointing behind the tent's chimney from which puffy white smoke cheerfully chugged. 'The northern lights.'

They were barely discernible. In muted colours that suggested even this northern phenomenon felt unsure about revealing itself on a night of such homicidal cold, the milky spires crept timidly through the black. We watched them for a few moments, then dived into the warmth.

17

The dogs bounded through the deep snow, following the sunken footprints of a lone wolf. The wolf was the only creature to have passed this way since the last snowfall and it had left a meandering track of dark wells that pocked the still whiteness.

Then the wolf's prints curved away from the trail and into the bush, and the snow stretched unsullied before us. There was no point in trying to follow a skidoo across this terrain: the narrow trail was submerged and its route was invisible to our eyes. Within seconds, a skidoo driven by a mere human would tumble from the path and sink into the gulf.

The dogs alone could lead the way; only their noses could detect where fellow canines had trotted before. And so they leapt valiantly through the powder, following the route that we humans couldn't see. Every now and then, though, they'd miss their footing and drop down into the depths. The leaders – and sometimes the whole team – would vanish altogether for a moment. Then Sonar's head would burst up through the white, her black fur encased in snow so that just her dark eyes danced through until, a second later, she vigorously shook her coat and returned to her normal self. The dogs seemed to delight in the chaos, wagging their tails and turning back to look at me with a laughing expression that asked, 'What happened there?'

Then I'd have to walk to the front of my team, find the firm ground, haul the leaders back on to the trail and disentangle the lines before we could continue. I was at the front of the group of dog teams now. Breaking trail required energy not only from the dogs but also from the musher. In these conditions, one couldn't ride on the runners. The added weight of a person on the sled would make the job of pulling through deep snow too arduous for the dogs. I had to run behind the sled steering and pushing as it tipped and plunged through the churned-up snow.

The temperatures shot higher now and the sky gushed brilliant blue. The nights may have been cold, but during the day this bitter world was a dazzling heaven. The dogs seemed almost to bounce with joy through the starkly beautiful land and their pleasure was infectious. As I clumped behind the sled in my cumbersome boots and heavy winter gear, the endorphins whirled through my veins. It was wonderful to travel with these animals, to watch as they vaulted like gymnasts through the powder, their ears bobbing, their tongues lolling, and their entire bodies lit with the excitement of this big adventure.

As we came down out of the hills through a series of switchbacks, the trail became firmer. I jumped back on the runners and the dogs settled to a steady trot. Stefan went ahead on his skidoo, while Sebastian took up the rear.

I was travelling well ahead of the others now: each time we stopped to regroup it took them ten or twenty minutes to catch up. And so, with Stefan out of sight to the front and the others far behind, I enjoyed a magnificent solitude. The glorious quietness of the woodland we now drove through was broken just by the light creaking of the sled over the snow and the rhythm of the dogs' feet. Every now and then the dogs' heads would pivot to right or left and they'd spurt with speed – they'd scented a rabbit or a ptarmigan, perhaps – and I'd have to touch the brake to keep them at a safe, constant pace.

My mind slipped back to that conversation I'd had with Wendell and Gary when, during the Quest, we'd driven out to Pelly Farm.

'Not all bears sleep through the whole winter,' Wendell had said. 'Sometimes the older bears can't put on enough weight to last them through.'

It was March now; I wondered how many grumpy old grizzlies were stomping hungrily through these woods. The younger bears would have tripled their body fat in late summer by gorging themselves on berries. As much as a third of their pre-winter weight would comprise fat reserves. Their elders might not have waddled quite so plump to their dens.

Even if the bears were all sleeping, the moose most certainly weren't. A moose could charge a dog team, wreaking havoc. As Anne had explained weeks earlier, its legs whirl chaotically when it runs and if it careers head-on into a group of dogs it can cause injury and even death. During the Yukon Quest, if mushers encounter an aggressive moose on the trail, they are permitted to kill it in defence of life or property – but race rules require drivers then to salvage the meat for human use. The musher must gut the animal so that the meat doesn't spoil, then proceed along the trail and report the incident at the next checkpoint so that Quest officials can go out and collect the carcass.

Perhaps the most famous woman in the dogsledding world, Susan Butcher, once had a terrifying encounter with a moose. Butcher won the Iditarod four times in five years from 1986 to 1990, and the year she didn't win she came second. Her hopes of success in the 1985 race were dashed, however, by a starving, demented moose that ran at her team, killing two of her dogs and injuring another thirteen (Iditarod mushers start the race with sixteen dogs as opposed to the Quest's fourteen). Butcher managed to hold the animal off with her axe and by waving her parka in its face until another musher came by and shot it. Butcher's race was over; instead of proceeding along the trail she spent the next few weeks in the veterinary hospital.

I was just wondering whether any ethically-minded soul ate the crazed moose when Stefan reappeared on the skidoo, interrupting my thoughts.

'What should I do if I meet a moose?' I asked him.

'Get a gun,' he said.

We were nearly at the Scroggie Creek cabin now. Stefan had gone as far as Stewart River on his skidoo: the trail met the river in just a couple of kilometres, he said. Then we'd turn right and travel for a further seven kilometres along the river itself before our stop for the night. Stefan was going to go ahead to the cabin so that he could start to prepare the camp. I should wait where I was until the others caught up, then tell Sebastian that, once we were out on the river, he should overtake us and go on to help.

A few minutes later the rest of the group arrived and drew to a halt behind me, creating a line of stationary sleds and energetically barking dogs that snaked round the bend and out of sight. Over the din, I passed back Stefan's message and we wound through the woodland until, finally, we reached the river. We'd thought we'd be here twenty-four hours ago, but the difficulty of breaking trail across the hills combined with our slowness at dismantling our camp every morning had hampered our progress. That morning, due to the cold and the time it took our less experienced companions to bootie and harness their dog teams, it had been two o'clock by the time we'd set out on the trail.

There was a short but sharp drop down the river bank on to the ice. I steered the turn wrongly; my dogs took a short cut through the shrubs to the side of the trail. The sled tipped over the lip of the hill, caught a bush, and crashed over on to its side, knocking me off the runners.

'Oh, hell, now I'm in for a bruising.' The thought flashed through my mind as I clung to the handlebar of the upturned sled so as not to lose the team, at the same time shouting, 'Whoa! Whoa!'

But then, to my astonishment, the dogs stopped in their tracks. They looked round at me with what seemed to be patient but amused expressions.

'Oh dear,' they seemed to say. 'She's gone and fallen off. But she's the one who hands out the snacks and gives us foot massage, so maybe we'd better not leave her behind.'

I righted the sled, hopped back on the runners and whistled the dogs to go. In harmony, they trotted sedately on to the river.

We travelled across the river's surface, along the trail freshly broken between the reflective Quest markers by Stefan's skidoo. I wondered whether a month ago, or even a few days ago, the dogs would have stopped when I'd fallen. Their instinct is to run, not to wait. Back on that first full day's trip along the Takhini River, they'd dragged me along on my knees while I'd squawked incoherently from behind. But there was something about being out here on the trail with the dogs, something about our mutual dependence day after day, that forged a bond which seemed to work two ways. I was beginning to know each animal's ticks and quirks: Log regularly turned his nose up at his pork snacks so I tried to give him fish. Sonar was running well in the harness but at night she grew cold and miserable and had to be coaxed to eat. As I came to know each of their personalities, it became a pleasure despite the cold to sit with them each evening as I rubbed paw cream into those warm, furry feet that had hauled me along the trail all day.

Night fell as we pattered along the river. We hadn't meant to be out after dark: we'd intended to be at the cabin hours ago. For once, though, I was happy that our progress had been slow. There was a full moon that night and the sky gleamed like a faultless ream of pearl-grey silk that stretched to infinity. The plump moon cast a silvery light over the snow-covered hummocks that rose and fell where, many months before, the pockets of freezing river ice had jammed one against another. The other dog teams were far behind me again now; the skidoos had gone on ahead. And so I journeyed alone with my dogs through that austere but blissful world.

At last, I understood. For the first time, as I glided along the ice of the Stewart River to the sound of bootied paws on snow, I realized why a person would enter the Yukon Quest. Until now, I'd considered long-distance dogsledding to be a slightly mad, excessively extreme ordeal. I could see that the mushers relished the opportunity to be alone on the trail with their dogs, but I'd thought that this must be because they were slight loners, eccentrics perhaps, people who preferred the company of their dogs and the natural wonders of the trail to the hurly-burly of human interactions.

Before this point I'd seen some of the training and preparation that went into running the Quest; I'd understood the great financial outlay needed. But of the race itself I'd only seen the checkpoints. I'd watched the exhausted men and women who stumbled into them, their eyes bloodshot, their hair matted, their con-versation nil. I had strong, emotional memories of that dreadful time at Central when we'd waited for Saul and the others to come in off the mountain. I remembered Thomas sitting for a whole night on a bale of straw, dressed in Frank's cast-off neon-green parka, never giving up hope that, any minute, Saul and the dogs might arrive. I recalled Frank's anguish the next day as the rescue effort was coordinated, and the intense disappointment Saul had to endure seeing all his efforts come to so little. The Quest had seemed to me to be a romantic but half-crazy endeavour performed by misfits from the conventional world. But now, creaking alone along the river by the light of the full moon, at last I saw why. Out here, on that trail with a team of dogs, I felt I'd found a bitter heaven.

And then, with no warning, the dogs started to gallop. Jerked out of my reverie, I stumbled to lower the brake mat that would slow them. We rounded a bend in the river and there, in the distance, a thin plume of smoke stretched taut into the sky.

There was a steep slope up to the cabin. The dogs knew that supper, foot massage and sleep were a few bounds away. Wildly excited, they bolted up the incline. I lost my balance and fell into a heap in the snow while the dogs charged driverless up the hill and round the corner.

'Stefan! Catch the dogs!' I bawled as I picked myself up from the ground.

But the dogs had stopped of their own accord. Tails wagging, they turned to grin at me as I jogged, panting, round the bend. Some of them had been here before. They were veterans of the Quest trail and their laughing mouths shouted loud and clear that, despite my dreaming, I still had a very long way to go.

18

Scroggie Creek is a truly remote spot. It lies nearly a hundred kilometres from the nearest road. The only way of getting there in the winter is by dogsled, snow machine or – during the Quest when the cabin is designated as a dog drop and a landing strip is created – by the bush plane which ferries tired and injured animals back to the comfort of their dog trucks.

The trail that runs from Stewart River past the door of the tiny cabin and along the creek has been in use since the 1920s. Miners used to ferry their supplies down the waterway during the summer and store them at the cabin; then, as the winter months progressed, they'd travel with their dogs along the trail to collect the food and tools that they needed. Now the cabin is used by the Quest, and by trappers and others who, for whatever obscure reason, find themselves passing through this sublime but isolated spot.

'Harvey. The river trail is good. You may find two or three wolf snares, but nothing that should give you trouble. Rob,' said a note scribbled on a piece of cardboard and pinned to the door.

The cabin was minuscule. It seemed to me that it

would be impossible for seven of us to sleep in it but, when I suggested to Stefan and Sebastian that we'd need to erect a tent for the overflow bodies outside, they looked at me as if I was quite insane. In the cabin there was a stove. We were all sleeping in there whether we fitted or not. What's more, they said, all our gear was coming in too: our damp, frozen gloves, our parkas and snow pants, the dogs' booties. All would be slung from the beams on which vets from Quests past had signed their names in marker pen, and hung on the nails that poked from the walls. The next day, both drivers and dogs would start with dry kit.

I staked out my dogs, took off their harnesses and booties, and retreated inside to roast myself. With its rickety wooden walls and rough benches, the little shack was hardly a hall of high refinement. But to me, at that moment, no palace could have seemed more magnificent. There was even just enough melted snow in the pot to make a tepid and slightly brackish cup of cocoa.

The others had arrived by now and we set about our preparations for the evening. We melted more snow, fed the dogs, and applied their paw cream. We made long chains of their booties, attaching one to the next by their Velcro straps, and draped them above the stove to dry.

We'd lost a lot of booties along the trail – Alain, Natalie and the others had not used them on their two previous dogsledding holidays, when the weather had been warmer, and they were having trouble wrapping the Velcro tightly enough round the dogs' wrists. As a result, not only were some of the dogs' feet becoming sore where booties had fallen off and they hadn't stopped to replace them, but we were fast running out of dry footwear to shoe them with each morning. We'd chained up the used ones every evening and hung them in the tent with the stove but, exasperatingly, of the three nights we'd spent on the trail so far, those sleeping in the theoretically heated tent had only managed to keep the stove alight for one.

It wasn't just the dogs' booties that weren't thawing and drying – our own gloves were now thick with ice as well. On the trail itself, during the day, we wore thick, waterproof mitts, but for shovelling snow, feeding the dogs and so on, we needed freer use of our hands. To put on icy gloves each morning only added to our discomfort. Worse still, Stefan had put his foot through some ice on the first evening when he'd been collecting water from a creek and his boot's liner had been soaked. He'd optimistically placed it by the stove each night but, as the stove had gone out, it hadn't dried. Wet feet are one of the musher's worst nightmares – if one wears boots with wet felt liners, the liner can freeze to the foot and cause serious frostbite. Fortunately for Stefan his foot was holding out well, but it was cold and uncomfortable none the less.

It was midnight by the time we'd completed our chores and our dinner of rather mushy stew was finally ready to eat. And then we took our spots – two people lying foot to foot along the longer of the narrow benches that flanked two walls of the cabin, one person wedged on the shorter bench, and the remaining four of us packed tightly on the tiny floor. Within seconds, we were asleep.

Frank had reckoned that the stretch from Dawson to Pelly should take us four days, or five if the going was slow. Stefan had packed supplies for six. But when we woke warm and dry in the Scroggie Creek cabin, we greeted our fifth morning – and we were still at least two days' journey from our supplies at Pelly.

We'd used all our spare runners (replaceable plastic which slides along the sled's bottommost rail) following our rough passage over the gravel on our first day, and the dogs' booties were also in short supply. Most seriously, though, we were running out of food. We had rations for the dogs to last for a couple more days. But we only had one supper left for ourselves, although we did have a large block of frozen cheddar, a good supply of crispbreads, and a few other congealed and unappetizing morsels. This meant that by tomorrow night we had to get to Pelly, either to collect fresh supplies or to meet pick-up vehicles and return to Muktuk, or we'd be gnawing on iced cheese for supper.

Despite our problems, it was another incredible day. As the sun's rays began to filter through the raw dawn air, the sky turned electric blue. We all felt better after our night in the cabin. Even Sonar seemed revived. Last night, she hadn't wanted even to stand so that I could take off her harness and she'd left her kibbles untouched. But that morning she leapt up full of enthusiasm and went from strength to strength as the day progressed.

We travelled alongside the creek on the trail that miners and their dogs had used nearly a hundred years ago. In places we crossed wide plateaus of frozen overflow that shone in myriad shades of green. The dogs slipped and slid as they traversed the mirrored surface. Log, industrious as always, pumped his legs harder than ever. Once he lost his footing and rolled on to his back but even then his legs continued to spin energetically, wildly bicycling in the air until he righted himself.

One section of ice was ugly and broken, and the dogs' feet plunged into the freezing water as they crossed. They paused and turned round to look at me, their faces horrified and questioning. But at one whistle from the back of the sled, they jumped to attention and continued to run through the desperately cold water to firm ground on the other side. It was amazing what these dogs would do. It was astonishing, and emotionally touching, that they responded to so much that was asked, that even when they were cold and uncomfortable their trust was such that they deemed my decision to keep going the right one.

In warmer weather, it would have been worse, of course. Then the surface of the overflow ice would have cracked much more easily. The dogs would have been more frequently immersed, and our own feet might have taken a soaking, too. When running the Quest one year, Frank soaked his feet in overflow not far from where we were now. He had another ten or so hours on the sled before he reached Dawson, and by that time his boot liners had frozen fast to his feet. His boots had to be cut away from his leg; he said he howled with pain. Somehow, he escaped frostbite, but since that day he's only worn rubber bunny boots. If they fill with water, he can tip them out, change his socks, and his feet are dry.

That evening seemed to be colder than ever. After the relative comfort of the previous night, none of us was delighted to be camping in these frigid temperatures once again. We were all exhausted by now, and the cold was not only sapping our physical strength but had eaten into our social skills as well. As we set up the camp, a small spat broke out. Stefan asked Alain, Philippe and Paul to saw some firewood; this was a burn area and dry wood was plentiful. He showed them which timber to cut but, for some reason, they chopped green wood instead.

'What's that for?' Stefan asked, a little tersely, when he saw the green logs neatly stacked.

'For the fire,' Alain said.

'That wood is green,' said Stefan. 'It won't burn.'

'Philippe says it will burn,' Alain insisted.

There was little point in arguing.

'OK, we will see,' said Stefan.

We ate our dinner in the heated tent in virtual silence. It was curious really, how none of us was interested in conversation. Our bodies seemed to be channelling every last drop of energy into keeping warm and allowing nothing to be wasted in the superfluous acts of chatting and smiling. After I'd eaten I went immediately to the smaller tent to try to sleep. My boots were frozen solid, as usual, and so rigid that I had difficulty pulling the liners out of them so that I could wear them in my sleeping bag overnight. In the end, I lost my temper. I sat in the entrance of the tent, hauled on the felt with every iota of my strength and swore noisily at my boots.

Then I noticed that two pairs of feet had appeared in front of me. It was Stefan and Sebastian.

'Are you all right?' Stefan asked.

The next morning we were up at seven thirty but I was incapable of the smallest tasks. The stove, predictably enough, had gone out in the so-called heated tent the moment they tried to fuel it with green wood. My gloves were frozen, and my fingers in that desperately cold dawn air were seared with pain. Stefan asked me to help him fold a tarpaulin. It should have been easy enough. We folded it in half once, and then in half again. And then I said, 'No, I'm sorry, I can't,' and went to sit in a huddle by the fire that Stefan had built outside the tents.

'Don't try to be comfortable,' Stefan told me a few minutes later, having finished the folding of the tarp on his own. 'If you're actually in pain, it's OK to go and sit by the fire, but forget about feeling comfortable. You can't be comfortable when it's this cold.'

I whimpered that I was actually in pain and felt only the tiniest pang of self-loathing.

Stefan was exhausted and frozen too, of course, but he was experienced in such suffering and was dealing with it with greater stoicism. A couple of winters previously he'd trekked seven hundred kilometres across the length of Siberia's Lake Baikal. Baikal is the largest freshwater lake on earth and holds a staggering 20 per cent of the surface fresh water on our planet. The trek took Stefan and his companion five weeks.

'There were a few minutes every evening, when we were in our sleeping bags and had a hot drink, when we were comfortable. And for a few minutes in the morning before we got out of our bags it wasn't too bad. But that was almost the only time that was nice. The other twenty-three and a half hours were generally horrible,' he told me.

Philippe emerged from the larger tent. He too was desperately cold, and was furiously swearing in French. He'd had little sleep; he seemed to prefer not to dwell on the fact that, had the stove been alight, he'd have been a lot more comfortable.

But half an hour later the sun edged over the horizon and the air started to warm. I went into the small tent to roll up our sleeping bags and mats. They were agonizingly cold, again, but I was more relaxed now. I thought back to the way I'd felt earlier, to that utterly drained deadness that had consumed me. I wondered, if I'd been on my own, if I'd needed to pull myself together in order to survive, would I have behaved with greater strength? And I concluded that, no, I would not. I had been so entirely empty of energy, I had succumbed so totally to the cold in my mind, that I would have just crawled back into my sleeping bag to die. And most strangely of all, I would have been perfectly happy about it.

I wouldn't have died, of course. Not there. Within a short time, the sun would have risen and with it the temperature in the tent. I would have snoozed off for about half an hour; then I'd have woken up feeling quite warm and hungry for my breakfast. But it was interesting, if not very pleasant, to experience the feeling of such absolute defeat.

We were all struggling. Over breakfast, we agreed that we'd end our expedition at Pelly that evening. The cold was exceptional. It seemed wise to head home. Stefan called Anne on the satellite phone and asked her to send transport to collect us. But first, we had to get to the road.

We harnessed our teams and pressed onwards, climbing up and up. We'd hoped that one of the hills we'd climbed the evening before had been Valhalla, the highest peak on this part of the trail, but now we rose ever higher. As we climbed I had to help the dogs either by running behind the sled or by pedalling one foot against the snow while the other rested on the runner, and the ascent was a long one. Soon I became so warm that I had to stop to take off my parka and tie it to the top of the sled. A short while later, I halted the team again: I was still wearing two pairs of long woollen underwear – the morning had been so cold that I hadn't taken the second pair off after the night – and now I was working up such a sweat that I needed to remove the upper layer. It was strange after that perishing morning now to be so hot.

'Whatever you do, don't sweat,' Frank told his clients again and again. I was certainly breaking the rules today.

Finally, I arrived at the top where Stefan was waiting with his skidoo.

'I take it that was the hill,' I said to him.

'I really *hope* that was the hill,' he said.

The tail end of our group was far behind, though. They'd asked to be taken on a demanding trail when they'd booked their trip, but some of them weren't fit enough to help their dogs up the inclines.

'We've only done twenty kilometres in two and a half hours.' Stefan winced as we waited for them. 'We're far too slow.'

But the terrain was wonderful once more. Mushing through this land was tremendously exhilarating. We travelled now through swathes of woodland that had been decimated by fire. The charred trunks of spruce soared upwards, sparse, black and strangely beautiful. It was worth every moment of the night-time discomfort for this.

From the back of the sled, time fell away. I was astonished to find that it was four o'clock when we stopped to eat and I looked for the first time at my watch. Stefan mixed the horsemeat with warm water that we were carrying in the coolbox and I fed my dogs. The others hadn't caught up yet.

'There's a road to Pelly Farm, right?' Stefan asked as we sat on the skidoo and munched on cold, hard cheese and crispbreads. He'd never been out there but he knew that I'd gone during the Quest with Wendell and Gary to mark the revised trail. Pelly Farm lay some distance before Pelly itself; while it now seemed we'd have difficulty reaching the tiny town that night, we should be able to make it to the farm quite easily, and wait there while our pick-up drove out on the snowy back road to collect us.

What we couldn't fathom was how the folk at Pelly Farm would react to our appearing out of the blue with thirty-four dogs and asking if we could stake them out in their yard for several hours. We realized Frank must know the Bradleys, who lived there and whom I'd met during the Quest, as he'd lived and worked in Pelly Crossing for years and it's not a large community. What we didn't know was whether they had been friends. Would the Bradleys welcome us on to their property with open arms and beaming smiles – or, as Sebastian wondered out loud when he joined us, would they just shoot?

Stefan phoned Anne. Pelly Farm shouldn't be a problem, she said. The issue was that she was having trouble finding drivers to come out at all at this short notice. And then the batteries on the sat phone died.

Just before we arrived at the farm, this wonderland granted us one last, incredible view. As I came round a bend with my team, a wide snow-covered valley un-furled beneath us. The sun had just set and the full, round moon was hanging low in the deep-lilac sky, glowing like a shiny Christmas bauble.

The dogs weren't interested in the view, though. Some of them knew where they were again and so, near the end of the trail, they started to run faster.

Our teams were close together now. We arrived at Pelly Farm at seven thirty and the Bradleys, well versed in the code of the north that demands hospitality to strangers in need however annoying they may be, didn't shoot. Instead, they brought out straw for the dogs and warm water to mix with their kibbles. They invited us into the house and brewed a large pot of coffee.

The armchair in the Bradleys' living room seemed to me to be the most comfortable piece of furniture in the world. It was as if the cushions were swallowing me up, soft and luxurious like a fat person's hug. I drank one cup of coffee, then another. And then, after about half an hour, fine needles of pain started to tingle through my body. As the warmth of the room filtered through my flesh, the tips of my fingers started to feel sore and sensitive from frostnip; for the first time, the joints in my hands became swollen and creaky.

Harvey was there too – the man for whom the note had been left on the door of the Scroggie Creek cabin. We'd assumed that Harvey and Rob must both be trappers but Harvey, it turned out, was on a recreational mushing journey of his own and, coincidentally, he was staying with his dogs at the Bradleys' farm that night. He was travelling all the way to Old Crow, far to the north, and expected to arrive there by the end of April. He made a long journey such as this every year, he told us. He kept his supplies in his truck which, every now and then, he went back to collect, leapfrogging it ahead of his dog team as he progressed along his route. He'd tried other systems. In the past, he'd asked people to ferry the supplies for him, but they'd turned out not to be reliable. Once a trapper had disappeared altogether with his cache so he'd had no dog food for a section of the trail. He'd been forced to feed his team with his own rations and go hungry himself.

Stefan called Anne on the Bradleys' radio phone. Frank and Saul were driving up in the two trucks, she said. They'd left at six thirty. It was three hours' drive to Pelly, then another hour and a half to Pelly Farm. They'd be with us at about eleven.

I was surprised it would take them so long to drive the Pelly Farm road.

'When I came out here during the Quest, it only took an hour,' I said.

'Yes, but you were with Wendell,' said Dale.

The Bradley uncles brought out a photograph album containing snaps of the farm in years gone by. The farm had been founded not by their family but by another at the turn of the century. The Bradleys had bought it in the fifties. One photo showed one of the uncles in younger years standing with the carcass of a vast black wolf. The stretched-out animal stood taller than the man who had shot it.

'It's been pretty cold these last few days,' I commented. 'Our thermometer only goes to minus thirty, and the temperatures were too low for it to register.'

'When I'm on the trail, I don't carry a thermometer,' Harvey said. 'I leave it behind on purpose. It just makes things worse if you know how cold it is. If you see it's minus forty you think, "Minus forty! I might die out here!" and then you get in a panic. It's better not to know.'

'Yeah,' said Dale. 'And this morning it was minus forty-two.'

19

I slept like a bear in winter – and a young, fat, berry-gorged bear at that. For several days after our return to Muktuk, my body shrieked each time I went outdoors. The skin started to peel from my chin, which felt curiously sensitive to cold air. The joints in my hands were stiff and sore, while my fingertips were tender with frostnip until the skin hardened and sloughed off. The second morning after our return, I developed a sudden, severe back pain that lasted a few hours and then disappeared. I'd noticed none of these ailments while we'd been on the trail. My body hadn't bothered to communicate problems that weren't immediately relevant to my survival while I'd been out in the cold. But now that I was warm and dry, it howled.

I felt able to do little other than eat, drink and sleep. Stefan and Sebastian weren't much better. We intended to cut the hair on the dogs' feet on the Tuesday, then Wednesday, then Thursday. But managing anything much beyond the basics of clearing up after the camping trip, feeding and watering the dogs, cleaning the yard, and lounging on the sofa drinking cocoa and chatting to the ever-cheerful Rocky seemed beyond the strength of any of us. On the Friday of that week, Marty left. His seasonal contract had come to an end and, on the Thursday night, we drove to a local pub, the Kopper King, to have a few drinks to send him on his way. We'd been back for three days already but, still, Stefan, Sebastian and I nearly fell asleep in our beer.

The dogs we'd taken camping were on reduced duties, too. Despite the fact that we'd been feeding them snacks of fish, pork and chicken skins every hour or so on the trail, they'd lost weight in the cold. Now they needed to rest, eat and recuperate.

The camping trip had been worth the exhaustion, though. The memories were incredible. We'd only been really uncomfortable for a few hours each day and the cold had in itself been an interesting, if challenging, experience. But the rest of our journey had been truly magnificent. The sense of working together with the dogs as we pushed up hills and skidded over ice; the glorious views from the ridges; the endorphin highs created by running to the peaks; the joy of watching the dogs leap through the soft snow; the beauty of riding the sled along the river beneath the still grey light of the full moon; the intense pleasure of simple rewards: a roaring fire, a hot cup of tea, a dazzling panorama – all these easily outweighed the discomfort that we'd suffered through the cold.

By the following Monday, though, I felt I'd more or less recovered from that expedition. I drank one last cup of cocoa and then boarded a flight back to Dawson, where I'd arranged to spend a couple of days with John Overell.

*　　*　　*

I caught a lift from the tiny, one-room airport into town with a man known as the Buffalo. The Buffalo was the airport's all-in-one human resource. He was check-in man, baggage handler, courier service and taxi driver all neatly bundled into one large – though not terribly bovine – package.

We drove from the airport to the 5th Avenue B & B, where I'd again booked a room. As he drove, the Buffalo was almost entirely silent.

'What?' Tracey exclaimed the next morning when I commented on his taciturn manner. 'He didn't talk? But Buff never *stops* talking. He's the most talkative man I know. He must be sick or something.'

Maybe it was my fault, for I'd been lost in my own thoughts. As we passed the Bonanza Gold Motel where we'd stayed that night nearly two weeks ago my mind slipped back to that awful incident with Irv and Frank's look of horror when he'd come round the corner on his skidoo to find his dog trailer loose from the truck. With a pang of nostalgia, I gazed at the turn-off to Bonanza Creek Road, where we'd started our dogsledding journey the following morning. Suddenly, I really wanted to go back twelve days in time and to do the whole trip again. It had been a tough week but the good moments, for me, had far outweighed the bad. If anyone had given me a dog team and a laden sled right then, I'd have leapt on to the runners and jogged joyfully with the dogs up every one of those hills.

Had I done so, the snow on the trail would have been very different from that which we had mushed through, for in Dawson it was the first day of spring. After a couple of weeks of temperatures of forty below, today the mercury had bounded up the thermometers and, for the first time in six months, edged above zero to show a sappy plus six. The streets echoed to the dripping of melting snow.

The shops and people, too, were eagerly throwing off their winter restraints. The Riverwest Restaurant and Coffee Shop on Front Street, which had been closed when I'd been in Dawson a month ago, had now flung open its doors to the encroaching sunshine and was serving its appropriately labelled tuna melts, burgers, muffins, sandwiches and coffee to a crowd starved of its produce for months.

'It's melting!' I heard teenagers exclaim to each other as they installed themselves in one of the restaurant's booths with steaming cups of tea.

'Enjoy the first day of spring!' trilled the woman in the bookstore as I paid for my purchases and left.

The following morning, Dawson was not just dripping. Water cascaded from the buildings' pitched roofs. The town's soggy wooden boardwalks became precarious – if you weren't deluged by an icy shower flowing from above, you stood a good chance of being knocked sideways by one of the great chunks of snow that frequently crashed from the rooftops.

'You've got to be careful at this time of year,' smiled the woman in the Dancing Moose gift shop.

It was too hot now to walk around in hat and gloves. It was liberating, at last, to bare my head and hands to the elements, yet it was also curiously unnerving. I had become so used to the cold that I found it difficult to leave the sanctuary of the B & B without taking precautions against the weather. As a result my pockets bulged perpetually with surplus woollens.

Other people seemed to have similar problems. The sudden arrival of spring appeared to have left half the town with a wardrobe conundrum, and there was no general consensus over what to wear. Some walked around in full winter gear and must surely have been too hot, while one brave soul had taken to the streets in just jeans and a T-shirt and, presumably, caught a chill. I settled for two fleeces fewer than usual (I now wore a mere three layers of wool and fleece over my T-shirt) and was rather too warm.

I went to a concert that evening featuring Toronto-based jazz musician Laila Biali. Dawson now, as a century ago, prides itself on its thriving arts scene. As I walked to the venue, I was astonished to find that the town's roads had been dug up. I had never before realized that Dawson's winter roads consisted of several feet of snow on top of their gravel base. I now discovered that, rather than clearing the roads with each snowfall, the town's authorities merely packed the snow down and spread fresh gravel on top. The boardwalks, rather than lying roughly level with the road as I had assumed, were actually raised considerably above it.

The snow now lay in broken slabs streaked with brown dirt where the gravel had been layered as the winter progressed. These jagged shards formed high embankments down the centre of each road. The ramparts came to chest height, making it impossible to cross the road except at intersections where the way was left clear.

'They pile it all into dump trucks and take it out of town,' Tracey explained as I ate my breakfast the next day. 'If the thaw comes quickly, we have problems with flooding. On this corner here, outside the house' – she pointed through the window – 'we always have huge puddles. It's because the underground sewerage drains haven't thawed so the water has nowhere to go.'

Dawson was, in any case, built on naturally boggy ground. It had always suffered from a surfeit of mud.

'The main street was nothing but mud, and the pack-horses and mules were always getting stuck in it,' Arthur Walden wrote of the town in the early days of the gold rush. More than a hundred years later, the horses and mules were gone but the springtime mire remained.

'For about the next month, the condition of the roads will slowly deteriorate,' Ron from the internet café told me later that day. 'They're just dirt roads and the water has to go somewhere, so we end up with lots of potholes.' The authorities attempted to maintain the roads through the spring, he went on, but while the thaw lasted they fought a losing battle. Once everything had dried out in a few weeks' time, though, the roads would be good once more.

At the concert, I sat next to a man called Grant. He asked me what I was doing in the Yukon. I told him I was trying to learn about sled dogs.

'I used to run dogs,' he said. 'I raced a little bit, but mostly I used my dogs to work my trapline.' He was a gentle, grey-haired man with small circular glasses. He looked as if he ought to be an academic, not a bush-man.

'I sold my trapline a few years ago, though,' he went on. 'I just got tired of killing things. I don't have any-thing against anyone else trapping. It just isn't for me any more.'

Now, he ran a market garden. In the springtime, he germinated his seeds. He then sold his crops into

Dawson's grocery stores and restaurants through the summer.

'I used to want to travel,' he told me. 'I'm fascinated by the world. I love looking at maps of places like London, at all those tiny streets whose names are familiar from Charles Dickens novels. But I'd hate to go there. The maps are good enough for me.'

He paused and took a long sip from his Alexander Keith's. 'The last time I went south, I flew back into Whitehorse and I thought, "Maybe I'll just stay here from now on. I never want to leave the Yukon again."'

20

When John Overell was nine-years-old, he was taken to the Natural History Museum in London. There he saw on display a turtle that was labelled as extinct.

'But I'd just been to a scientific lecture about that very same species of turtle,' John told me over lunch of fat, tasty burgers in Dawson's Downtown Hotel. 'I knew it wasn't extinct.' So this precocious Canadian child earnestly informed the Natural History Museum's curator that his information was wrong. The curator went to look the turtle up – and found that somebody had inadvertently switched the labels of the museum's displays.

Now, decades later and with rather greyer, wispier hair, John is Dawson City's only vet. In fact, he's the only vet in the whole of the northern part of the Yukon Territory. His practice stretches from McCabe Creek, just south of Pelly Crossing, all the way up to Tuktoyaktuk on the Beaufort Sea and takes in pretty much every community in between: Inuvik, Aklavik and Old Crow. With his calls and clinics, John covers an area the size of the whole of the British Isles, but without the convenience of motorways.

'Sometimes I get flown into places that aren't accessible by road,' he told me. 'Sometimes I go out to the gold mines and such.' There were still plenty of individuals working placer mines around Dawson, and making a living from it.

'Why do miners keep dogs?' I asked him. 'Is it just for companionship?'

'For companionship, and also to keep away the bears.' John paused, then went on to explain. 'A good bear dog is one that makes a lot of noise, and chases the bear just a little bit. You don't want a dog to chase the bear too far, though. If the dog goes too far, it just ends up annoying the bear. Then the bear can turn round, and now you've got the bear chasing the dog. And when a dog gets scared, it runs straight home.'

He went on to tell me the story of a miner he'd known. The miner was sitting with some companions in his cabin one evening when his dog gave chase to a bear. Nobody paid much attention until, a short while later, the dog bolted into the cabin, cowered under the table – and an angry bear charged through the doorway in furious pursuit. The bear wasn't interested in the people, John said, but it was hell-bent on getting that dog. Still, even though the bear showed no direct desire to eat him personally, the poor miner could hardly ignore its presence in his kitchen and so he was forced to shoot it. He was pretty browned off, apparently: shooting a bear in one's cabin creates an awful mess.

When he ran clinics further afield in Inuvik and Tuk, John travelled by plane, packing his veterinary equipment into five large plastic boxes. His dream, he told me, was to run effective mobile clinics throughout the remote communities of the north. It was with this intention that he'd come to Dawson and set up his practice in 1998. Until then the town had had no vet. To begin with, he'd worked out of the back of his truck. His first surgery was performed on an outdoor table; his then-wife had held an IV sack above the patient while tourists snapped photos from the sidelines.

Funding the dream was a perpetual nightmare, however. To fly to Inuvik with all his gear and an assistant to help with operations cost him around four thousand dollars. His assistants always told him that he behaved differently when he was up there, he said. He was more tense and less chatty. Then, after about five days, he would suddenly relax.

'You broke even, didn't you?' they'd ask him.

The problem was that many people this far north, where work was often seasonal and the cost of living was high, didn't have a lot of money to spare for veterinary care. Sometimes they paid with fish or caribou or fur. But sometimes they simply couldn't.

'It's a living creature. I can't just say, "Come back next month when you've got the money."' John shrugged hopelessly. As for the euthanizing of elderly animals, 'How can I bill someone for killing their nineteen-year-old dog?

'I am an awful book-keeper and a dreadful businessman,' he told me with resignation. One year, John was nominated for a prize awarded to small businesses. 'I actually talked to someone from the Chamber of Commerce. I told them, "I *cannot* win. Because if I win, you guys are going to look really stupid."'

And so John did without a lot of the equipment that vets in high-tech urban centres take for granted. Walk-on scales for dogs would have cost two thousand dollars;

John used bathroom scales which he stood on himself while holding the dog in his arms. Then he deducted his own weight.

Once during the Yukon Quest, for which John worked as a volunteer vet, an injured dog was brought in by a musher. The veterinary team had no X-ray equipment and the other vets couldn't tell what was wrong. John said that he palpated the dog's foot, then told the others, 'He's got a broken toe.'

'How on earth can you tell that just from palpation?' the other vets demanded. But John was right. He'd been working for years with no X-ray machine and his palpation skills had become finely honed. Still, now, he has no X-ray. If he needs to X-ray an animal, he has to send it by plane to Calgary.

'One of the Quest vets once was complaining about his on-call hours,' John went on. 'He was whinging because he was on call every other weekend. I didn't say anything. I just smiled. But Kathleen, the head vet, saw me smile and she asked, "So how long have you been on call for, John?" I told her, "Seven years."'

After lunch, I joined John on his house calls. A thirteen-year-old dog called Fifty Bucks (because that's how much the owners paid the adoption shelter when they took him) had a tumour on his bottom. Another dog had lice. Veterinary textbooks apparently claim that lice can't live in cold climates; they say that only fleas and ticks can be found this far north. But in the Yukon, John explained, these tiny creatures didn't obey the text-book writers' rules. Here, there were no fleas or ticks but the dogs and cats did provide hospitality to this one particularly hardy strain of louse. It was the same with tapeworms. South of

60, John said, if tapeworms freeze they die. But not up here. Here, tapeworms had adapted to the cold.

'So, is your work mostly with dogs?' I asked him as we left the lousy animal, jumped back into the truck and drove to the house of a dachshund called Dieter who was due a vaccination. John was now carrying a film canister full of dog hair and lice: he'd expressed an interest in learning more about the critters so the dog's owner had presented him with some specimens.

'It's about seventy per cent dogs,' said John. 'About twenty per cent of my work is with cats, a little bit is horses, and the remainder of the work is with exotic animals – iguanas, tarantulas and other things people keep as pets.' He also did wildlife work – mostly eagles, ravens and other birds – but for that he didn't charge.

He was busiest in the summer when people had a few tourist dollars in their pockets. The problem with Dawson, as I'd seen before, was that the short summer season forced people to make almost all their year's income in about four months.

'I have a friend who throws a party each May,' John said. 'He calls it his "See you in September" party. And it's no joke. Until then, nobody will have the time to go out.'

The summer, too, brought the porcupines out and the job of extracting their quills from the faces of over-inquisitive canines provided a lot of John's work. If left, the quills can infect, and even work their way through the body to emerge in a different part. One dog – not a patient of John's – once dropped dead for no apparent reason. The vet performed a necropsy and found that a porcupine quill had needled its way into the dog's heart.

Dieter duly jabbed, we climbed back in the truck. We drove past a paddock where two horses stood.

'You see they just have that lean-to over there.' John pointed to the far side of the paddock. 'That's all the shelter they need. With that, they can stay out here in minus forty and they're absolutely fine. They just grow a thicker coat. Horses should never be kept in barns – the ventilation is too poor and they stand all day with their feet in faeces, urine and dust. In eight years working up here with horses kept outdoors all year round, I've never yet come across a respiratory problem. But in the south, where they keep them in barns, horses are always having problems with respiratory issues and with their feet.'

We were back on Front Street now, and we stopped at the Riverwest café for a coffee. John's stories moved on to the dogsledding world. He didn't just work for the Quest. He was also the head vet for the Percy de Wolfe and had worked for other races too. At one pre-race vet check, an inexperienced musher had brought in a dog that John saw clearly shouldn't compete.

'I just took one look at this dog and, without even touching her, I said, "You can't run that dog."'

'Why not?' said the musher. 'I mean, I know she's rather fat, but she runs really well.'

'You can't run her,' said John, 'because you'll be dis-qualified.'

'But why?'

'Because you'll end up with too many dogs.'

The next morning, the dog gave birth to a litter of nine puppies.

* * *

John picked me up at eight o'clock the next morning and we drove out to his clinic six kilometres from Dawson. He'd only been based at these premises since the previous summer and the renovations had been problematic. Some of the windows had no glass. John had erected a temporary plastic wall to divide the building in two in an attempt to keep the heat in but still the winter fuel bills had been astronomical.

A dog called Hank arrived with his owner. Poor Hank had an issue with aggression. He should have calmed down when he was told to: now he was going to be castrated.

I was slightly nervous about watching the operation, which John performed with the help of his assistant, Chris. I'd only seen an animal being castrated once before – that was a calf in Argentina and, embarrassingly, I'd almost fainted. But this procedure was all very clean and tidy. The dog was anaesthetized, there was not much blood and the little balls popped out easily enough, like lychees from their skins. A short while later, Hank came round. He seemed inappropriately cheerful.

There should have been a second dog to be fixed that morning but the owner, who was driving with the animal from Inuvik, called to say she couldn't make it. The Dempster Highway was closed. Even had it been open, she'd have had to drive twelve to fourteen hours on a solitary gravel road. It was a long way to go for an appointment with the vet.

21

Buffalo still wasn't talking on the return journey to the airport. It must have been me.

Back at Muktuk, spring had hit even more soggily than it had in Dawson. Here in the north, I was discovering, springtime was not a season of blue skies and yellow daffodils; it was a time of brown, sloppy mud.

The dog yard, once white with packed snow, was now mired in puddles. The dogs themselves were filthy. They wore long brown socks of matted fur, and the humans too had smears and splodges over their clothing where the dogs had jumped up to say hello.

Scooping poop now was a mucky affair. The poop was soft and partially diluted. It stuck and drooped from the shovel in a way that the frozen waste of winter had never done. Its smell was more potent, too.

'I hate this time of year,' Frank grumbled, standing at the door of the garage before which a veritable lake had formed. 'It's so ugly. It makes me depressed.'

'How long does it take to dry out?' I asked him.

'Well, some years it's just a week or so. But I don't think it's going to be just a week this year.'

The water around Ichabod's house was particularly

plentiful. It formed a wide, flooded moat around the dog, who perched on the one dry spot like a damp canine king taking refuge behind his watery defences. Sebastian laid down a couple of wooden pallets for him to stand on and for a couple of hours he trotted happily between them. He'd hop up on to one wooden platform, look rather pleased with his new raised perspective on the world, turn round, and then skip self-importantly over to the other.

'Hey, look at me, everyone,' he seemed to gloat to the others. 'I'm the king of the castle.' But within a day or two, half the yard had shallow wooden platforms from which to air their canine views over the swampy land that surrounded them.

The old dogs that roamed free seemed affected by springtime, too.

'I think Minto's coming into heat,' Sebastian told Frank one morning as they stood in the kitchen. Frank looked out of the window over the dog yard to Minto's house.

'Minto's not coming into heat,' he said after one glimpse at her posture. 'She's in heat already – *oh shit!*'

Before he had pronounced the final 't' of that expletive, Sebastian was already halfway down the stairs into the garage, grabbing his boots and sprinting across the yard to see if he could haul Bozo away from her. Once two dogs have locked in place, there's nothing you can do to separate them. But Bozo was a poor old man and he hadn't quite managed it. His lust unsatisfied, he was sent hobbling on his way and Minto was escorted to the isolation block. There would be no puppies this time.

* * *

And then, it snowed. On the Sunday morning, I woke up to find several inches of thick, fluffy powder covering the ground, and it kept snowing for most of the day. It seemed incredible after the thaw, but the snow that now fell was probably the deepest I'd seen in Whitehorse all winter.

The following day I drove out with Sebastian to Fish Lake. Frank was taking some clients on a camping trip and needed Sebastian to man one of the trucks. I went along for the ride. It was a long, narrow back road and I sensed that Sebastian would be glad of the company in these fresh, snowy conditions – though realistically I would have been of little use had the truck digressed into the ditch.

I helped harness and hook up the teams. It was a chaotic start. At the head of the lake the dogs could not be staked to conveniently spaced posts as they could in the yard and now, at the end of the season, they were becoming tetchy. Mischief and Pelly started to fight. Frank dived to the ground, punching Mischief on the hard bone of his head and losing his glasses as he went. To shock a dog in this way is often the only effective means of breaking up a dog fight but still, despite Frank's force, Mischief scarcely noticed. It was interesting to see the dogs in what Frank called their primitive mode. They were different creatures indeed.

This was my last week in the Yukon. On Friday morning, I'd be heading home to London. But before then, Stefan was going for two nights to Fish Lake with two Parisians, Davey and Charlene, who were going to work at Muktuk for a couple of weeks in return for this trip. A friend of Stefan's from Germany, Fabian, was coming too and I was invited to join them. On the first day, we'd make our way to a cabin along the trail (Frank's group was on a longer trip and a day ahead of us, so they'd be gone by then). The second day we'd embark on a simple day trip from there, so that we could spend the second night at the same cabin before making our way home the way we'd come.

'Holy smokes!' exclaimed Stefan as he veered off the road into the fresh, piled-up snow of the verge. We were climbing Muktuk's drive in the truck with the dog trailer behind and, for a fraction of a second, we were gripped by a horrible sense of déjà vu. But Stefan was able to right the truck before the dog trailer left the road and he drove easily out of the snow bank.

'That's the first time I've ever done that,' he said rue-fully as we continued more carefully up the slope.

We drove for about an hour, along the Alaska Highway and then up the meandering back road that led to the lake. We unloaded and staked out the dogs, and packed the sleds and toboggan with our supplies. Stefan would drive the skidoo on the first day; after that, Fabian and I would take turns.

Our departure from Fish Lake was not an impressive one. Given that Frank's hook-up and departure yesterday hadn't gone smoothly, Stefan decided that we'd try a different approach. We'd start by hooking up the first three teams: Fabian's, Davey's and lastly Charlene's. When they were ready to go, Stefan would set off over the lake on his skidoo and they would follow. I would wait until last. To minimize the chaos of having too many over-excited dog teams all hooked up and raring to go at once, and to release an extra pair of hands to help Davey and Charlene who had never driven a dog team before, I'd leave my dogs safely

291

staked out alongside the truck until the others were out on the ice. Then Sebastian (who was not coming camping but would drive the truck and trailer back to Muktuk) would help me very quickly to hook up my team, we'd gather the cables from the truck so that we'd have them to stake out the dogs at night and, stuffing the cables swiftly in my sled, I'd be neatly on my way.

Fabian set off efficiently enough. Davey did not. There was a steep decline on to the lake; Davey lost his balance and fell off his sled. As Sebastian sprinted over the ice to hold his leaders Charlene, for some unfathomable reason, decided this might be a good time to pull the rope that anchored her own team to the truck and thus release her dogs. To compound this confused thinking, she failed to lower and stand on her brake mat before starting. She shot down the hill, wildly out of control, her frenzied dogs galloping fast towards Davey's team. I managed to jump on her runner as she went and pull her brake down just before her dogs entangled themselves with the team in front.

But my moment of triumph was short-lived. Running back to hook up my own dogs, I overlooked the fact that I hadn't tied my sled to the truck at all. Sebastian and I were just hooking up my leaders when I realized – there was nothing to hold them. Sebastian quickly tied the rope – and just then, Stefan roared back on his skidoo. He had left his camera in the truck.

Unfortunately, in the seconds during which Stefan had driven back across the ice, Davey's team had sniffed an opportunity for trouble. They'd tried to follow Stefan as he'd U-turned across the ice, had tangled themselves in their lines, and now they were starting to fight. Fabian planted his snow hook and left his sled to help Davey

– but his team broke free and set off across the snow on their own. And no sooner had Stefan charged back across the lake to sort out that lot than my team made a bid for freedom themselves. As Sebastian and I grabbed the cables from round the back of the truck, their barking fell eerily silent. We rushed to the front just in time to see them loping out across the snow to join the others. Sebastian's knot had slipped.

'They've gone!' I exclaimed in horror to Sebastian.

Sebastian just shrugged. 'Oh well, Stefan will catch them,' he said. There was nothing we could do, after all. We stood no chance of outrunning them.

Our orderly formation at last assumed, we made our way out across the ice. I had six dogs: Sonar, the placid black female who had led my camping team on the Quest trail, was joined in the lead this time by Dawson, a charming, friendly, thick-haired white male. Then came Trooper and Sue. Trooper was an affectionate female with a black face and white blobby eyebrows, and I'd held a soft spot for Sue since the day she'd been so obliging in helping me cut the hair on her feet.

At wheel I had Vanek and Marley. Marley was behaving like a five-year-old with a sugar rush. For the first half-hour, he kept jumping over the central gangline, barging into Vanek, and generally making a nuisance of himself. But Vanek didn't seem to care. Even in the weeks since I'd known him, this beautiful blond had matured from a nervous, shy creature to a strong, confident dog. In the harness, he pulled consistently, even when Marley was leaping about like a jack-in-the-box. Vanek was only thirteen months old, but he had the tolerance of a middle-aged veteran.

The snow was fresh and the weather was outstanding. It had stopped snowing now and the skies were blue, with the occasional fluffy cloud that reflected the powder upon the lake.

We made our way across the flat, white expanse. In the distance, the hills around the lake rose soft and voluptuous. After a while, we left the lake and continued along a narrow trail flanked by shrubs and bushes whose feeble skeletons slouched beneath the heavy new snow. Then we began to climb through rich panoramas. I was at the back of the group, and I purposely left some distance between my own team and the sleds in front. Now I watched them weave along the ridges that lay before me – tiny, perfect silhouettes against the sparkling snow.

There was a cabin at Mud Lake, where we were to spend the night, but when we arrived there we found that someone else had beaten us to this idyllic spot. Felix was a gentle, mild-mannered man. He'd worked all winter as a mushing guide for Sebastian Schnuelle, who had competed in the Quest and ran a tourism operation from his base, Blue Kennels. Now the clients had gone home and Felix had come on a solitary, end-of-season expedition with ten dogs. He'd no doubt been dreaming for weeks of the peace and privacy that he'd enjoy on this trip. And then we'd turned up, five noisy humans and twenty-four barking, howling dogs.

He seemed relaxed about his fate. We protested that he must stay in the cabin, but he preferred to go out and pitch his tent by his dogs. Slightly embarrassed, we melted our snow, fed our dogs with kibbles and ourselves with steak and potatoes, and then settled down for an easy, cosy night.

Stefan and Fabian opted to sleep outside: the night was mild and the cabin was cramped. At two thirty in the morning I woke to find the stove had gone out. After my griping on our previous camping trip about the clients who wouldn't keep the stove alight, I didn't have much choice but to get up and fix it.

'Even if I have to sit up all night coaxing it,' I thought to myself stubbornly, 'this fire is going to be alight and the cabin warm in the morning.'

It was a temperamental contraption. If I closed the vents, the flames expired. If I opened them a fraction, the fire roared terrifyingly, the metal of the stove glowed angry and red, and I worried that the whole cabin would burst into a raging conflagration. The fire settled in the end but I was quietly relieved when, the following night, the temperatures dropped and Stefan and Fabian chose to sleep in the cabin too. Somebody else, then, could take responsibility for the stove.

On our second day it snowed and we lost the trail. Stefan drove my team now and I rode in the sled bag. It was pleasant just to watch the world go by from this low vantage point, to see the dogs' feet pattering and their tails waving as they ran. The trail had to run to the right, Stefan said, and marched out on foot across rough land, calling to the dogs while I rode on the runners. But we never found the way, and after lunch we decided we'd abandon our outing and return instead to the cabin for a cup of tea. It seemed luxurious, now, to enjoy this effortless expedition into the snowy woods, to come home early to a warm stove, and to spend the afternoon with a hot drink, chatting and gently snoozing.

And so my final day's dogsledding dawned. Fabian drove the skidoo in the morning and I took his team:

Jeta and Cooder, Belle and Log, and Alex and Casper. It was a hot, sunny spring day. The skies were deep, swimming-pool blue. Every now and then, the dogs' heads pivoted in unison to one side or the other, alerting us dozy humans to the white-feathered ptarmigans that perched to the edge of the trail, or flitted low between the bushes.

At lunchtime, I gave the team back to Fabian and I drove the skidoo. I accelerated well ahead of the dog teams, and chugged along the winding trail surrounded by spruce trees whose branches were so laden with snow that their twigs and needles slouched like rows of misshapen Christmas-tree angels.

I came out of the woods and drove on to the surface of the lake. Then I stopped and waited. Fresh snow had covered our tracks of two days before. This seemed like virgin territory now. It was a clean, unsullied, soundless world.

Tomorrow, I'd be returning to the concrete and crowds of London. It wasn't a prospect that filled me with joy. Eleven weeks ago, I'd been nervous about coming here to the far north. I'd worried that its cold would be debilitating and its inhabitants terrifyingly tough. But as the weeks had passed I'd grown to love the Yukon. The people who lived here were passionate about their unspoiled land. They took perpetual delight in the tracks of a fox in the snow, or the distant sighting of a herd of caribou. Even after decades of living in the dark sub-Arctic, Yukoners still exclaimed over the northern lights with undiminished joy. I'd been infected by their enthusiasm. At that moment, as I sat alone engulfed by silence, I could happily have torn up my air ticket and stayed with them in their remote paradise.

The creak of a sled and the patter of paws on snow cut into my thoughts. The teams came round the trail's final bend and emerged on to the lake. Sonar and Dawson appeared first with Trooper and Sue, Vanek and Marley and Stefan riding behind. Then came Jeta, Cooder, Belle, Log, Alex, Casper and Fabian. I watched the dogs trot towards me one last time, their movements almost balletic as they danced rhythmically through the deep, fresh powder. Their tails pointed up with enthusiasm, their ears were pricked and alert. They were joyful, beautiful, mischievous creatures, these sled dogs. I sat still and watched until they passed me. And then I fired up my skidoo, and reluctantly I followed them through the blissful white wilderness towards home.

Bibliography

Extracts from *Barrow's Boys* by Fergus Fleming copyright © 1998 by Fergus Fleming, reprinted by permission of Aitken Alexander Associates Ltd. Extract from *The Travels of Marco Polo*, translated with an introduction by Ronald Latham, copyright © Ronald Latham 1958, reprinted by permission of Penguin Books Ltd. Extracts from *Ploughman of the Moon* by Robert Service, copyright © Robert Service 1945 and 'The Spell of the Yukon' by Robert Service, copyright © Robert Service 1907 reprinted by permission of M. William Krasilovsky. Extracts from *My Father, My Teacher*, written and directed by Dennis Allen, copyright © 2005 BRB Father Productions Inc. the National Film Board of Canada, reprinted by permission of Dennis Allen. Extracts from Dr Giesbrecht's video for Discovery Channel Canada reprinted by permission of Dr Giesbrecht. Extracts from *On Blue Ice* by Jane Stoneman-McNichol, copyright © 1993 Town of Inuvik, reprinted by permission of the Council of the Town of Inuvik.

ON A HOOF AND A PRAYER
Around Argentina at a Gallop
by Polly Evans

At the age of thirty-four, Polly Evans decides to fulfil
a childhood dream – to learn how to ride a horse.
But rather than do so conveniently close to home, she
goes to Argentina and saddles up among the gauchos.
Overcoming battered limbs, a steed hell-bent on
bolting, and an encounter with the teeth of one very
savage dog, Polly canters through Andean vineyards
and gallops beneath snow-capped Patagonian peaks.
She also survives a hair-raising game of polo and a
back-breaking day herding cattle.

Taking a break from riding, Polly delves into
Argentina's tumultuous history: the Europeans' first
terrifying acquaintances with the native 'giants'; the
sanguinary demise of the early missionaries; and the
gruesome drama of Evita's wandering corpse.

On a Hoof and a Prayer is the stampeding story of
Polly's journey from timorous equestrian novice
to wildly whooping cowgirl. It's a tale of ponies,
painkillers and peregrinations – not just around
present-day Argentina, but also into the
country's glorious and turbulent past.

9780553816792

BANTAM BOOKS

FRIED EGGS WITH CHOPSTICKS
Around China by Any Means Possible
by Polly Evans

When she learnt that the Chinese had built enough
new roads to circle the equator sixteen times, Polly
Evans decided to go and witness for herself the way
this vast nation was hurtling into the technological age.
But on arriving in China she found the building work
wasn't quite finished.

Squeezed up against Buddhist monks, squawking
chickens and on one happy occasion a soldier named
Hero, Polly clattered along pot-holed tracks from
the snow-capped mountains of Shangri-La to the
bear-infested jungles of the south. She braved
encounters with a sadistic masseur, a ridiculously
flexible kung-fu teacher, and a terrified child
who screamed at the sight of her.

In quieter moments, Polly contemplated China's long
and colourful history – the seven-foot-tall eunuch
commander who sailed the globe in search of treasure;
the empress that chopped off her rival's hands and
feet and boiled them to make soup – and pondered
the bizarre traits of the modern mandarins. And, as
she travelled, she attempted to solve the ultimate
gastronomic conundrum: just how does one
eat a soft-fried egg with chopsticks?

9780553816785

BANTAM BOOKS

KIWIS MIGHT FLY
Around New Zealand on Two Wheels
by Polly Evans

When Polly Evans read a survey claiming that the
last bastion of masculinity, the real Kiwi bloke, was
about to breathe his last, she was seized by a sense of
foreboding. Abandoning the London winter she took
off on a motorbike for the windswept beaches and
golden plains of New Zealand, hoping to root out some
examples of this endangered species for posterity.
But her challenges didn't stop at the men.

Just weeks after passing her bike test, Polly rode from
Auckland's glitzy Viaduct Basin to the vineyards
of Hawkes Bay and on to the Southern Alps. She
found wild kiwis in the dead of night, kayaked among
dolphins at dawn, and spent an evening on a remote
hillside with a sheep-shearing gang. As she travelled,
Polly reflected on the Maori warriors who carved their
enemies' bones into cutlery, the pioneer family who
lived in a tree, and the flamboyant gold miners who lit
their pipes with five-pound notes, and wondered how
their descendents could have become pathologically
obsessed with helpfulness and *Coronation Street*.

The author of the highly acclaimed *It's not about the
Tapas* reaches some unexpected conclusions about the
new New Zealand man – and finds that evolution
has taken an unlikely twist.

9780553815573

BANTAM BOOKS

IT'S NOT ABOUT THE TAPAS
Around Spain on Two Wheels
by Polly Evans

After working for four years at a London book publishers, Polly Evans moved to Hong Kong where she spent many happy hours as a senior editor on the city's biggest entertainment weekly. But fighting deadlines from a twizzly office chair and free use of the coffee machine seemed just too easy. So Polly exchanged the shiny red cabs of Hong Kong for a more demanding form of transport – a bicycle – and set off on a voyage of discovery around Spain.

From the thigh-burning ascents of the Pyrenees to the relentless olive groves of Andalusia, Polly found more adventures than she had bargained for. She survived a nail-biting encounter with a sprightly pig, escaped over-zealous suitors, had her morality questioned by the locals, encountered some dubious aficionados on the road and indulged her love of regional cooking. While she pedalled, Polly pondered some of the more lurid details of Spanish history – the king who collected pickled heads, the queen who toured the country with her husband's mouldering corpse, and the unfortunate duchess who lost her feet. And wherever she cycled, she ate and ate – and yet still she shrank out of her trousers.

It's not about the Tapas is funny, irreverent and inspiring. It established Polly Evans as one of the most exciting new voices in female travel writing.

'A hilarious account of her epic adventure around bike-mad Spain'
Daily Express (Book of the Week)

'This true triumphant tale of her travels will appeal to anyone who's eager for adventure'
OK!

9780553815566

BANTAM BOOKS

Polly Evans is very cowardly and not at all fond of danger. She does, however, have an unfortunate tendency to seek out discomfort and sometimes even downright pain. It was this ugly trait that led her six years ago to throw in her comfortable office job – complete with its twizzly chair and free use of the coffee machine – and to take off on a leg-battering bicycle tour of Spain.

The result of her endeavours was one very sore set of limbs and her first book, *It's Not About the Tapas*, which was short-listed for the WHSmith People's Choice Travel Writing award. She indulged in further escapades the following year, this time swapping pedal-power for a motorbike to travel around New Zealand and to write her second book, *Kiwis Might Fly*. Polly's third book, *Fried Eggs with Chopsticks*, tells the story of her sometimes-desperate battle to tour China by public transport while *On a Hoof and a Prayer* sees her learning to ride horses in Argentina.

Polly is also an award-winning journalist. When she's not on the road, Polly lives in London.

Visit Polly's website for photos of her trip
www.pollyevans.com

Acclaim for

On a Hoof and a Prayer
'Full of colourful anecdotes . . . a jolly romp of a read'
Sunday Telegraph

Fried Eggs with Chopsticks
'Funny and astute, this is an engrossing portrayal of
one of the world's most fascinating countries'
Wanderlust

Kiwis Might Fly
'The perfect read for those seeking thrills,
spills and the über-male'
Glamour

It's Not About the Tapas
'A hilarious account of her epic adventure
around bike-mad Spain'
Daily Express (*Book of the Week*)

Also by Polly Evans

IT'S NOT ABOUT THE TAPAS

KIWIS MIGHT FLY

FRIED EGGS WITH CHOPSTICKS

ON A HOOF AND A PRAYER

and published by Bantam Books